AARDMAN: AN EPIC JOURNEY

AARDMAN: AN EPIC JOURNEY

Taken One Frame at a Time

AN AUTOBIOGRAPHY

PETER LORD & DAVID SPROXTON

WITH DAVID GRITTEN

FOREWORD BY MATT GROENING

INTRODUCTION BY NICK PARK

**SIMON &
SCHUSTER**

London · New York · Sydney · Toronto · New Delhi

A CBS COMPANY

First published in Great Britain by Simon & Schuster UK Ltd, 2018
A CBS COMPANY

1 3 5 7 9 10 8 6 4 2

Simon & Schuster UK Ltd
1st Floor
222 Gray's Inn Road
London WC1X 8HB

www.simonandschuster.co.uk
www.simonandschuster.com.au
www.simonandschuster.co.in

Simon & Schuster Australia, Sydney
Simon & Schuster India, New Delhi

A CIP catalogue record for this book
is available from the British Library.

Hardback ISBN: 978-1-4711-6474-3
Trade Paperback ISBN: 978-1-4711-6475-0
eBook ISBN: 978-1-4711-6476-7

Typeset in Palatino by M Rules
Printed and bound by CPI Group (UK) Ltd, Croydon, CR0 4YY

*The Aardman story isn't just about two blokes
called Dave and Pete. We dedicate it to all
the talented and dedicated people who have
worked at Aardman over the past four decades
and have made this adventure possible.*

CONTENTS

FOREWORD
BY MATT GROENING

I was hooked on Aardman's animations when I saw *The Wrong Trousers* for the first time in 1994. Sure, Wallace and Gromit are a couple of the sweetest animated characters ever created. Yes, the film as a whole is a brilliant display of ingenious stop-motion clay animation. The turbo trousers, museum heist and climactic toy-train chase are all virtuoso examples of the art of suspense, timing and jokes. But what got me, what made me crazy with delight, was that penguin! That sinister, silent, rubber-glove-on-his-head penguin. I have since learned the penguin's name is Feathers McGraw (another brilliant touch), but man! When the penguin first moves in as a boarder with Wallace and Gromit and suddenly jerks his head towards the slow-thinking but suspicious Gromit, it made me laugh out loud with the joy that comes from the unexpected but wholly delightful surprise. And the Hitchcockian scene when Gromit spies on the nefarious penguin from inside a Meatabix dog-food box sealed the deal for me: *The Wrong Trousers* is one of the greatest animated movies of all time.

So many things make Aardman animations splendid: the beautifully goofy character designs, the punchy stories, the unforeseen sight gags, the subtle but hilarious dialogue, the ingenious music and sound effects, and the perfectly imperfect charm of hand-sculptured Plasticine art (including the occasional thumbprint). I was able to visit Nick Park, Peter Lord, Steve Box, David Sproxton, David Alexander Riddett and Richard Starzak at the Aardman studio in 2002 and it was like getting a peek inside Santa's very busy toy workshop. (Apologies to the unnamed animators sick of being compared to elves, but you're all so cute and industrious!)

No doubt you agree that Aardman's animations are hilarious in their absurd believability (or believable absurdity). The short films, including all the Wallace and Gromit miniature masterpieces, the features (my favourites are *Chicken Run, The Pirates! In an Adventure with Scientists!* and *Wallace and Gromit: The Curse of the Were-Rabbit*) and all the rest of Aardman's prolific, decades-long output are unmatched in consistent brilliance. I think this is due to the shared vision of congenial collaboration, in which you can see clay characters actually think – something that is very difficult in animation. Aardman creatures have humanity, heart and soul, and I want to visit and revisit them often. They are so real I dream they're having other adventures when I'm not watching.

I have a pack of very young kids these days, and they're not quite old and immature enough to view my own subversive animated shows. Then again, I'm not ready to watch the slick, peppy, limited animation that is aimed at their tender brains. So bless Aardman and the glorious *Shaun the*

Sheep TV series, a show I enjoy as much as my kids do (even if they tell me I laugh too loud). As they get older, I will take great pleasure in showing them the more sophisticated Aardman productions. I can't wait until they're ready for Feathers McGraw.

INTRODUCTION

BY NICK PARK

I first became aware of Aardman in my teenage years. Obsessed with animation and making my own 8 mm films at home, I would draw my inspiration largely from the TV. There was an innovative show on the BBC in the early 1970s aimed at hearing-impaired children – it was called *Vision On*. It was a visually creative show packed with surreal and funny animation in various techniques. These animated spots grabbed my attention, particularly the ones done with clay animation. I was even more excited when Morph came on the scene as the programme evolved into *Take Hart*. I was eager to know who was behind all this animated magic, but back then there was no internet, and so I was thrilled when the BBC's *Blue Peter* went behind the scenes in Bristol to meet Morph and his friend Chas, and the guys responsible for giving them life – I was ecstatic. That's the first time I 'met' Peter Lord and David Sproxton. And, strangely enough, they did uncannily resemble Morph and Chas, at least in mannerisms. Little did I know then that I would join them a few years later and they would become such lifelong mentors and friends. Pete and Dave, that is, not Morph and Chas.

A year or two later, while doing my communication arts degree at Sheffield Polytechnic, my dad phoned me: 'You've got to see this thing on TV called *Animated Conversations*, it's right up your street.' Renowned animators had contributed to this remarkable BBC series, but my dad perceptively described one short, *Down and Out*, and how the clay characters were so expressive, subtle and well observed. It was so human; funny but sad. There was great empathy and pathos coming through the Plasticine. Aardman were now not just creating loveable children's characters, but, as filmmakers, were able to reach adult audiences, too.

I longed to meet these guys, and once, as a student, I ventured to chat to Pete at the London Film Festival, but I don't think he recalls the encounter. I was just another student fascinated with Aardman. I would've loved to have asked him and Dave to come and speak at the National Film and Television School, where I was studying animation, but somehow reverence and shyness got the better of me. Then, a few months later, my opportunity came. At the NFTS we had a fund to invite lecturers of our choice to visit, and I discovered that a fellow student knew Pete and Dave from way back, and she described how nice and approachable they were. This gave me the confidence to write and ask them if they would come and give a talk – and, to my surprise, they immediately said yes!

Pete and Dave's visit was a highlight of the student year, and admiration from the students abounded. There weren't many stop-motion animators around back then, never mind 'clay' animators, so Pete and Dave felt to me like kindred spirits and, as a film student, I liked the way they were thinking as filmmakers, too. On their visit, they also happened to see a little project I was beavering away on called *A Grand Day Out*, and, at that time, I'd only shot some tests and early footage of Wallace and Gromit. I was more than chuffed when they showed eagerness to see my work, and I was beside myself when they called a month later and asked me come and work for them in Bristol.

Pete and Dave were expanding Aardman and taking on new projects and commissions, and they needed more animators. In the mid-1980s, Britain was leading the way in TV commercials; ad agencies were adventurous, looking for new graphic styles and techniques, and Aardman were gaining a profile as a very unique company to go to. It wasn't a difficult decision for me when asked to work for Aardman, the one place in the animation world I admired the most. They were inspiring and creatively interesting – and I was thrilled to become a part of that journey.

It seems a lifetime ago now since I joined Aardman, and a lot of water (and Plasticine) has gone under the bridge. I'm personally grateful for all the opportunities that I have been given, and for the way Pete and Dave recognised talent in me early on and gave endless support, guidance and opportunities not just to myself, but to many other directors and creatives, nurturing them and giving them chances to develop. This continues to be the Aardman way today, and there are many talented men and women in all the various departments who contribute to this environment. Many people see a name and think it's all down to an individual's talent or 'genius', but no one knows the weeks and months and years of development; the round after round of feedback, comment and rigorous criticism (and thankfully encouragement) that go into each production – and Pete and Dave, along with our development teams, never pull any punches. Aardman has become this unique environment, a creative pressure cooker for talent and ideas, and I'm very grateful for it, as are countless others, even if, on occasions, there is need to let off steam.

When I walk in the studio today, some thirty-plus years on, and see Aardman, this industrious, diverse hive of creativity – stop-motion, as well as digital and CGI projects, simmering away, boiling away or even under extreme pressure – there's a buzz that few visitors can resist commenting on. It's evident that people love what they do.

I often wonder how Pete and Dave feel about what they started when they emerged from the clay back in the early 1970s. This is Pete and Dave's story about how they created this wonderful and unique animation company, and, hopefully it's just the first chapter in Aardman's amazing story so far.

PROLOGUE

LET'S PUT ON A SHOW . . .

As kitchen tables go, it wasn't memorable, fashionable or even pleasing to the eye. A big, solid, heavy piece of Victoriana with thick turned legs, it had served its purpose by the 1960s for David Sproxton's parents, who relegated it to their garden shed, out of sight.

In 1970, however, David and his best friend Peter Lord, both sixteen years old at the time, found themselves in need of such a table – for their own creative purposes. The two boys lived in a leafy, sedate part of suburban Surrey, which felt far removed from the ground-breaking shifts in the outside world. Popular culture was subversive and youth-driven, from the protest marches and revolutionary fervour on student campuses in Paris, London and the US, including radical films such as *Easy Rider* and underground magazines like *Oz* and *International Times*, all happening to the soundtrack of blistering, rebellious music by artists like the Stones, Bob Dylan and Jimi Hendrix. There was definitely 'Something in the Air', in the words of a hit record of the time – but there was no fighting in the streets anywhere

1

near their quiet neighbourhood. Yet Peter and David, both articulate and artistic, were aware of this turbulence, and were even making their small contribution in keeping with the spirit of the age.

The previous year, Peter and David had started up a magazine with school friends – a somewhat subversive publication named *A Tasty Straight*. They printed the cover on David's brother's printing press, and circulated copies confidentially, away from the prying eyes of teachers, to a couple of dozen classmates.

Their tendencies towards creativity and self-expression were inherited. Peter's mother Woody was a talented artist, while his father (also Peter) worked on the sales side of the BBC, where he had been a radio producer. David's mother Margaret had been to art school where she learnt the craft of silversmithing, carrying it on into later life; his father Vernon, a minister and a BBC religious programmes producer, was also a keen amateur photographer who shot home movies and had even converted a small pantry in his house into a darkroom.

Peter and David regularly hung out at each other's homes. One rainy afternoon, they were at the Sproxtons' house in suburban Walton-on-Thames, somewhat at a loss for what to do, when David dug out his father's camera from the depths of a cupboard. He pulled it out so they could take a better look. It was a spring-wound 16 mm Bolex with a reliable single-frame shooting capability, and Vernon Sproxton used it on his short documentary films. (The boys didn't know it then, but this particular model was also widely favoured by filmmakers working in animation.) It seemed to be both an opportunity for a new hobby, and perhaps even a professional tool. More importantly, it seemed to invite David's question: 'Why don't we make a film?'

That question would change the entire direction of these two boys' lives. From the movie world, perhaps the nearest equivalent is the teenage Mickey Rooney defiantly cajoling his young friends in the film *Babes in Arms*: 'Let's put on a show ... right here in this barn!' Quite unwittingly, David and Peter had stumbled across their destiny.

After examining the camera and finding a roll of film, they decided to make an animated movie. But how, they asked themselves, would they actually shoot their film? Where would they place the camera? Vernon Sproxton helped them set it up.

Their first thought was to commandeer an obvious surface – the kitchen table, which they duly cleared, setting up the Bolex camera on a photographic copy stand of Vernon's on the table top. As Peter likes to observe, a kitchen table is part and parcel of 'the great tradition of British amateurism', a place where inventors, would-be scientists, even fledgling animators, could start from scratch and test out their ideas in secrecy, without outside supervision or intervention. They then drenched the room with light, using a couple of Photoflood bulbs, closed the curtains and set to work.

They only had a sketchy idea of how animation created movement from a series of static images, but, by chance, the two boys were already in possession of certain skills that usefully complemented each other. Peter had a range of artistic talents: at school, he maintained a large-format journal he called *By Popular Demand*, for which he wrote little stories, created collages and drew comic strips. David, on the other hand, had been given a camera by his father when he was a child. He had a great interest in photography and had read a lot of books about the technical processes involved in filmmaking.

Nevertheless, 'basic' was still the right word to describe this first creative attempt, in which Peter would draw a character in chalk on a dark piece of art card placed under the camera and David would shoot a single frame. Peter would then erase part of the figure – its head or limbs – redraw it in a different position, and David would shoot another frame. And so the afternoon wore on. They were creating images that would move, but, in those pre-digital days, the actual result, the animation, remained locked away in the camera until the film was processed. They were doing the work, yet had no idea of what it would actually look like. And since they hadn't thought of anything even remotely resembling a story for the moving figures, they could simply continue drawing and erasing to their hearts' content.

Under these conditions, the two friends began work on their first short film. As it progressed, chalk figures were supplemented by 'cut-outs' – pictures of characters they found in the colour supplements of Sunday newspapers. Instead of having to go through the process of redrawing, they could simply separate the limbs of their subjects, move them between frames and make them seem to run and dance.

David acknowledges their major influence in this new

4

development: both he and Peter loved the animated short films Terry Gilliam created for the Monty Python troupe, which featured comical cut-outs of sepia-tinged Victorian photos.

Very soon, however, the boys faced a problem. So painstaking and time-consuming was this work, it was immediately clear that the Sproxtons' kitchen table could not meet their needs. It was used by the whole family, especially at mealtimes, so David and Peter could hardly monopolise it, and there was no way they could leave their equipment on the table overnight for successive days of work.

They needed a space of their own, they decided, and within a week a spare upstairs bedroom became their next port of call. Officially, it belonged to David's brother, but he was away at college at the time, so the boys commandeered it, placing the copy stand on a desk space. It was here, in this temporary 'mini-studio', that their first short was completed.

At the end of their labours they had a film that ran for some three minutes. They called it *Trash*, which they regarded as a knowing homage to Andy Warhol, who in 1968 had produced a film called *Flesh*. (Unbeknownst to the boys, Warhol had also produced a film called *Trash* two years later – beating them to the punch by a matter of months.)

In truth, *Trash* had no story or structure, it was just a series of moving images that were arresting or amusing. Still, the process of making it had proved stimulating enough for Peter and David to embark immediately on another short.

This second effort was largely more of the same, again

involving characters and cut-outs with chalk outlines. Sticking with their choice to give their early shorts a title already taken by well-known films, they called it *Godzilla* – though it in no way resembled any aspect of the legendary Japanese monster movies bearing that name.

Peter and David were aware that they were making steady progress in their experiments with animation. They now had two short films under their belt, and the ever-helpful Vernon Sproxton, through his contacts at the BBC, sent the films to be developed. David and Peter were delighted with the results, and felt the films were good enough to show to their supportive parents. They gathered in the Sproxtons' living room for their first premier. The hours of work that the boys had put in flashed by in barely a couple of minutes. There was no narrative to follow, and the quality of the animation was inevitably poor. But, even so, there was something there – the magic of animation, which as Peter says 'never gets old'. For those few minutes, they could watch things moving on screen and know that they had given them life.

The assembled audience did what all loving parents would and bestowed praise on their sons' novice efforts. Peter and David were encouraged by their reaction, but didn't allow themselves to get carried away. As Peter puts it: 'For us it was an experiment, a bit of fun. We had no sense then that we might be taking the first steps on a career. When we sat down to watch our first amateur efforts, we never even dreamed it would lead on to great things.'

* * *

Still, the boys had caught the animation bug, and were keen to continue making their short films.

The only snag was that, while there was space inside the Sproxton home, Peter and David were setting up temporary studios for each job, but there was no single area in the house they could call their own. And now they really needed a table on which they could set up a rostrum. Within the garden shed they uncovered that big, solid Victorian kitchen table. It hadn't occurred to them before now, but suddenly the table became part of the solution.

As David remembers, it was a cumbersome object, with drawers – desperately outdated in the eyes of two teenagers back then. 'We hauled it out of the shed, took the drawers out and painted it gloss black.' That immediately made it look a little bit cool; in 1971, the boys might well have called it 'groovy'.

'First of all we bolted a copying stand,' says David. 'Then my father helped me build a rudimentary rostrum which became the "stage" for our early drawn animation efforts. And that big old table was the perfect base for this construction.'

Meanwhile, Vernon Sproxton, impressed by Peter's drawing ability and pleased that David was collaborating with him on creative pursuits, was doing his best to promote the boys' animation talents.

In this spirit, he and Margaret invited Patrick Dowling, a BBC colleague of Vernon's, to dinner with them and the two boys. Dowling was the producer of *Vision On*, a strikingly visual programme aimed at an audience of children with impaired hearing; it could easily be followed with the sound off. Presented by a host who also signed for deaf viewers, every show featured a single theme and included upbeat sketches and live demonstrations of art, along with short animated films in different styles.

Vernon Sproxton soon steered the conversation towards the boys' animated projects. They gave their guest *Trash* and *Godzilla* to watch at his leisure, but did not expect much to come of it. A week later, however, Dowling phoned Vernon and asked him to put David on the line.

What Dowling had to say was astonishing: he'd seen the potential in their films, felt David and Peter might be able to contribute to *Vision On*, and asked them to create something over the summer. He sent them a full list of themes for the following season and said that, if he liked what they came up with, then perhaps – just perhaps – he might include it in one of his programmes. He promised to pay for any processing costs, and arranged to send them a 100 ft roll of film.

It was a wonderful, unexpected opportunity, but what Peter and David did with it would change their lives – and ultimately stake their place in film history.

* * *

The boys were both avid fans of *Vision On* – not only because it was a smart, hugely entertaining show, but also because it showcased a wide variety of animation, some experimental, some traditional, but all, it must be said, cheap. BBC budgets in those days were never lavish, and Dowling was a master at acquiring animated films from unlikely and economical sources. Two schoolboys fitted the bill nicely. But how best to impress him? David and Peter decided to spread their bets and offer him work that showcased several techniques and styles.

At their school, they tried their hand at pixilation – a classic technique where human beings take the place of animated puppets. They positioned their camera at the library window, directly overlooking the playground. They shot a frame every few seconds, which made it look as if everyone in the playground was desperately rushing around to no purpose – except for a handful of pals they had ordered to stay virtually still. It just about worked, but they knew the results didn't reach the level of expertise *Vision On* would expect.

They took half a dozen school friends down to the local park and got them to jump in the air repeatedly, taking a frame every time everyone's feet had left the ground, to create the illusion of flying. But the other boys swiftly lost interest. As David puts it: 'In reality, it is very wearing jumping up and down twenty-five times for just one second of film.'

Then they remembered a clip from a remarkable black-and-white film they had seen on TV a year or two previously. Though they didn't know the name of the film or the director, they could immediately recognise the material used. The animation was stop-frame and the moving figures were very obviously modelling clay or Plasticine. Only years later did they discover that the film was called *Clay, or The Origin of Species* and had been made in 1965 at Harvard University by a man named Eliot Noyes.

Even now, it is an astonishing piece of work to watch. Everything on screen is clay, which transforms itself endlessly into various shapes against a blank backdrop. Eyes become a face, then hair grows over it; a worm inches across the screen, chased by a bigger one, and turns into a hoop. A dinosaur is formed, then a bigger one, who devours the first. A jaunty score by a jazz quartet gives it an almost relentless quality. The clay seems to mould itself into a horse, a bird, a whale, a stag, an alligator and a mermaid in dizzying succession; little wonder, then, that it inspired and encouraged two young would-be animators.

In those distant days, before home video-recording, it was almost impossible to see the film again, so, while they couldn't recall the detail, Peter and David were left with the memorable impression of Plasticine, brought to life by an artist's invisible hands. Inspired, they decided to add clay animation to their repertoire of experiments designed to impress Patrick Dowling.

David called Peter to discuss an idea that linked to one of Patrick's themes – to shoot down on to a low-relief Plasticine scene. David placed a board under the camera on which Peter sculpted a pretty thatched-roof cottage, which gradually metamorphosed to become an elephant. 'Not the world's greatest storyline,' as Peter admits.

Ironically, it wasn't the boys' ambitious excursion into Plasticine that engaged Patrick Dowling's attention, nor was he bowled over by their attempts at pixilation or time-lapse animation. Instead, what caught his eye was a conventional piece of 2D cel animation in classic cartoon style.

Peter and David had never tried anything like this before – but had read a lot of books and had a lot of ideas. David enterprisingly called a London animation studio called Halas and Batchelor and asked if someone could show them around and explain how 2D cartoons were made. A friendly, helpful producer named Dick Arnall agreed, and spent a whole afternoon showing them each stage of the process and answering all their questions.

The boys returned home enthused, bought a few necessary supplies suggested by the producer, and set about preparing.

'In reality, this was the next step in what we were doing at the time,' David reflects. 'We were moving from chalk drawings and cut-outs to something more controlled and thought-through: 2D animation.'

He built a light box which would serve as Peter's drawing desk, and he and Vernon modified a wooden camera stand, which they secured to the top of the old Victorian table.

Peter did the drawings while David traced and painted. They devised a short, simple comic sequence, lasting only about twenty-five seconds. In profile, a less-than-athletic superhero character in a cape strolls towards what appears to be a hole in the ground; he pauses, tests his footing, decides that it's solid and walks right over it. But, one step later, he falls into an invisible hole. After a pause, his arm emerges from the ground, finds the first hole, which he pulls over his body, then climbs out and continues walking.

Peter had already sketched this hapless character in his notebooks and journals. He'd even given him a name. Most superheroes – Batman, Superman, Spider-Man – have names

11

with that common ending, and there seemed no reason to depart from custom: his creation had to be a 'man' of some sort. Peter had always relished the word 'aardvark' and he simply took the first syllable and attached it to the 'man' suffix. The fact that the character had none of the attributes of the animal – he wasn't South African and he didn't live in a burrow or eat ants – didn't really matter.

His name, then, would be Aardman. So it was that the old kitchen table played its part in Aardman's origin story. It was effectively the cradle of a business venture that has gone from strength to strength continually for more than forty years.

That 25-second animated short starring Aardman was Peter and David's first commercial success – if only a modest one. Patrick Dowling received the work they had done on the 100 ft roll of film he had given them. All their short films combined added up to no more than three minutes in length, but *Aardman and the Hole* was the one he liked, and the boys received a call from a *Vision On* director asking if they could reshoot it; there was too much flare on the original, and David had to adjust the lights to reduce it. Second time lucky, the BBC approved of the adjustments and agreed to pay £25 for it.

But who would be the beneficiaries of their cheque? Peter and David decided it was time to give themselves a name, and spent a few hours deciding on one. 'Superanimation?' A little pretentious. 'Dave and Pete Productions?' Possibly not. 'Lord Sproxton Productions?' Faintly misleading. Finally, the boys settled on calling themselves Aardman Animations; it was a tribute to the little superhero who had brought them their first income. The boys calculated, too, that with the double 'A', it would at least come first in any alphabetical listings. They swiftly opened a bank account and registered Aardman Animations at Companies House.

* * *

Viewed from today's perspective, the success story of Aardman seems delightful – if wildly unpredictable. In the first instance, Peter and David had no master plan. Returning to that notion of kitchen-table amateurism, they made their careers up as they went along, especially in their teenage years.

Back then, it would have been hard to envisage them as the major British success story they and their company became. Did these two boys seem destined for great things? Probably not. True, they were clever and well-read. They were always likely to get into university – and duly did so. They had a strong sense of British culture and a sharp awareness of the often tumultuous times in which they were growing up. And they were fun to be around; both of them possessed a quick, intelligent wit. But that was equally true of several thousand British kids navigating their way through adolescence in the late '60s and early '70s.

Back in 1971, David and Peter didn't appear to be boys destined for influence and fame. They were a little scruffy, their hair was getting long (even for the times) and they were already disdainful about a career in 'the professions'. They didn't have the chiselled good looks of future movie stars or pop idols, or the sculpted physique of professional sportsmen in the making. They lacked the self-assurance of young men from affluent families, destined to ease into roles as captains of industry; though, in a sense, that was precisely what Peter and David were to become.

They had advantages, too, even if they weren't as immediately obvious. For one, they both benefited from parents who were ethical, left-leaning in outlook and viewed life through a prism of creativity and artistic endeavour. These same parents were loving and supportive of their sons and encouraged them to follow their passions and dreams; Peter and David were never shoe-horned into 'respectable', well-paid work that would have bored them.

Significantly, both their fathers had connections with the BBC, and on occasion were able to strategically introduce the boys to colleagues who might further their dreams; but that was the extent of their privilege. Both families broadly regarded money as a means to house, feed and clothe themselves; it was never important in its own right.

Above all, Peter and David had each other. They were a match made in heaven, sharing both a friendship and a set of values, but with contrasting skills and temperaments that neatly complemented each other: Peter the more extrovert and talkative, a man blessed with great drawing ability; David the quieter, more considered of the pair. As well as being more pragmatic (a quality that would enable Peter to realise his ideas), David was the one who was interested in technology and technique, which would solve many of their problems. They both came up with ideas, but Peter would be the one typically to flesh them out. In film industry terms, if Peter is a writer-director, then David is a born producer.

As it turned out, David and Peter took many of their families' values with them into their professional careers, running Aardman as a company that favours creativity above all and actively seeks to be a place where artistic endeavour can flourish. Both men often say of their work at Aardman: 'It's not about the money.' And it's not, yet their company has been wildly successful for the majority of its forty-plus years of life, all the while breaking new ground in ways that few other British film companies have even approached.

David and Peter have remained at the helm for more than four decades and look back with pride on Aardman's astonishing growth from its humble beginnings.

Could they have guessed at such a future, back when they were sixteen-year-old school friends, hunched over that old Victorian table in the garden shed as they tried their hand at animation?

They didn't have the faintest idea.

1

TEENAGE KICKS

'We were thrown together in a schoolroom,' David Sproxton says of his original introduction to Peter Lord. He was twelve years old at the time and had just started his second year at Woking County Grammar School for Boys. A new pupil had been ushered into the room and was directed by the teacher to the only remaining empty desk – the one beside David. They exchanged names, and David immediately noticed that this small newcomer had a twangy drawl to his voice, quite unlike the clipped tones of his English classmates. American? Australian? At first, he wasn't quite sure.

In fact, Peter Lord had spent the previous three years with his family in Australia; his father had accepted a job offer from the corporation, selling TV programming from an office in Sydney.

Peter had loved his three years Down Under, a period bracketed by magical voyages there and back. It was the very end of the period when a six-week sea voyage around the world was a practical choice rather than an absurd luxury, and the family travelled aboard the SS *Chusan* – one of the last P&O liners. From Tilbury docks they crossed the world, docking on the way in such exotic places as Aden, Bombay and Singapore.

He found Australia largely agreeable, too, though the school he first attended was far too hearty and sports-oriented for Peter's bookish tastes. It was simply the wrong place for a boy with an artistic temperament, and, thankfully, he was soon hand-picked for the smaller Woollahra Demonstration School, an eccentric and experimental place that catered specifically for pupils with an artistic or creative bent. Under a charismatic teacher, Ken Imison, he spent two happy years immersed in books, drawing, writing short stories, visiting local museums and generally expanding his outlook. It was during these years, and strictly outside school-time, that he also discovered American comic books – both superheroes like Spider-Man and the anarchy of *Mad Magazine*. It was a wonderfully low art form, guaranteed to be disapproved of by adults.

On graduating from Woollahra, he found himself at Vaucluse High, a much more alien establishment, with its enthusiasms for science, sport and corporal punishment. He wasn't sorry when his parents plucked him out of it to return to England, though it was still a shock to leave the glories of a house on Sydney Harbour for London's commuter belt. The family lived temporarily in a succession of houses bordering south-west London, before putting down roots in a semi-detached house in Walton-on-Thames – an affluent riverside market town, some 10 miles from Peter's new school in Woking.

As it turned out, the Sproxton family also lived in Walton-on-Thames, so Peter and David would travel to and from school together on the train. All the conditions were set for a blossoming friendship.

It helped that each of the boys was discreetly impressed by the other. On that very first day, when Peter entered the classroom as a new boy, he had sat down, pulled out a notebook and casually started sketching in it. 'I suppose I recognised Pete's artistic ability and his quirkiness immediately,' David remembers. In addition to his nonchalant manner, he was even using a Biro. These were frowned upon by the school's headmaster, an old-fashioned stickler for discipline named John Goode.

In the context of Woking's rather inflexible regime, Peter seemed an individualist – possibly a rebel – but that admiration cut both ways. David and Peter quickly became pals, and Peter was soon invited to the Sproxton family home. The experience astonished him – he had never before encountered a family so busy and creative; the whole house felt abuzz with activity. 'They made an enormous impression on me,' he recalls now.

David's father Vernon was keen on photography, and had his own darkroom in the house. Margaret, David's mother, an art school graduate, had trained in a variety of arts and crafts and continued with her silverwork until later in life. As for David's siblings, both older than him, his brother Andy was interested in typography and design, and ran his own printing press from the attic, while his sister Ruth was already showing talent as a textile and clothes designer. The

Sproxtons were a family of creative, practical, can-do hobbyists, and their home was a stimulating place to be.

They were an intriguing bunch. A man who defied conventional expectations, Vernon Sproxton was a man of many parts and, though a minister, was a Congregationalist: 'That's the church of the people, not High Church and all the authority that goes with that,' David observes. 'Dad was pretty left-wing. We were one of the very few Labour-voting houses in our street in leafy Surrey. And in terms of values, my parents would always say: "Do what interests you, what you have a passion for." They never said: "Get yourself a job, make yourselves a lot of money." And we were always told we should treat other people fairly. That was my parents' expectation.'

The Sproxton children were encouraged to pursue their creativity; Andy and Ruth were both talented artists, Andy played guitar, and all three of them took piano lessons.

Peter was rather dazzled by the Sproxtons, yet in truth his own family were hardly conventional. 'I suppose we were a fairly conventional middle-class family,' he observes, 'but definitely at the creative end of the spectrum. Both parents were immersed in arts and the media.'

His mother, known as Woody, was an art teacher who left her job for a time to raise her children, but returned to teaching at a local comprehensive. She loved to draw and paint, producing delicate pencil drawings of Peter and his siblings, and her children were always encouraged to follow suit. Even today, Peter's drawing style owes much to her example, light sketchy pencil strokes that gradually resolve themselves into a firm line. 'The table was always covered in pencils and paper, and the cry was always, 'Mum! What shall I draw now?' Peter remembers.

And then there was Plasticine, the ubiquitous plaything of British children at the time. 'As early as four I can clearly remember sitting in the basement kitchen with my mother, playing with the stuff. She would make figures and animals, and I would try to copy her,' he adds. 'I can picture a dog sled we made between us, though, in retrospect, I think she did all the work. There was always Plasticine at home, near to hand – as there is today.'

His father (also named Peter) had been enterprising enough to jump at the offer to take himself and his family off to Australia for a spell, at a point when he found living any longer in suburban Bristol an uninspiring prospect. 'I can see now he was having a mid-life crisis,' Peter reflects, 'quite a successful one in his case.'

Peter credits his father with instilling in him the idea that work should be fun: 'As a sports reporter, he was mostly on the radio, though I saw him on TV once or twice. On a Saturday, I'd sometimes go into Broadcasting House with him and watch him work. Not that it seemed particularly like work. I remember cheerfulness and laughter and a clubby informal atmosphere, which has stayed with me. Everyone seemed to be having a good time; they were doing creative work and clearly enjoying themselves. After work, or as soon as the sun was over the yard-arm, they'd go to the BBC club bar and carry on the conviviality there. Though this was my only experience of the world of work, I knew instinctively that this was special, and I was always trying to recapture that mixture of creativity and informality at Aardman.'

* * *

The boys' taste for animation continued to flourish, though even in the late '60s they had still not quite realised that it might lead to a sustainable career for them both.

They shared a similar sense of humour – one which was rooted in the wealth of eccentric British comedy that enjoyed a kind of golden age in the 1960s and '70s. 'We both watched Spike Milligan, *Monty Python's Flying Circus*, especially Terry Gilliam's cartoons. And then there were Peter Cook and Dudley Moore, all that stuff on TV,' David recalls. 'I also loved Michael Bentine, who was truly eccentric.' (Notably, Bentine, a founding member of the Goons, devised and hosted two TV shows with puppets: *The Bumblies* and *Potty Time*.)

'And on the radio you could hear shows like *The Navy Lark*, *The Men from the Ministry*, *Round the Horne*,' David adds. 'You could still hear episodes of *The Goon Show*, too. And in all these shows there was an element of sending up authority. Many of them were made by people who had seen active service in World War Two, and, looking back, the anti-authority attitude probably stems from those years. In the case of Spike Milligan, in retrospect he seemed to be working out his own trauma from the wartime years through the vehicle of his comedy. Still, we found all those shows really funny.'

Inevitably, both boys were influenced by the upheavals

sweeping the Western world in the late '60s and early '70s. 'It was a big thing, the idea that youth could turn the world around,' David recalls. 'There was a feeling in 1967, 1968 – in Prague, Paris, London, San Francisco – that this was the youth of the world, many of them students, wanting to change that world, and not accepting the way things were. We all felt very much part of it. We were a little younger than that – but not much. We were definitely thinking: *You can change the world. That's what our job is.* We sort of got caught up in all that, and it did influence the way you thought.'

He remembers attending the first free rock concert in Hyde Park in 1968, as well as seeing Jimi Hendrix play live: 'I was wearing my Oxfam striped blazer from some girls' school somewhere – and my loons,' he says, smiling at the memory.

The two boys differed in their musical tastes: David liked jazz and blues, and played bass in a band, while Peter was (and still is) a lover of British folk music, though back then he also favoured progressive rock and 'psychedelic' bands.

At the age of eight, David discovered the joys of film. His parents took him to see the majestic *Lawrence of Arabia* and the young boy was enthralled by the wide-screen spectacle with its astonishing desert vistas. Its director, David Lean, immediately became his firm favourite. Because cameras and photography were part of his home life, it was the stunning images on screen that most intrigued him. How would one go about creating them, he wondered?

'At this stage, Freddie Young the cinematographer was my inspiration,' he recalls. 'It was what I saw on screen rather than the writing and storytelling that impressed me. I was too young to understand the subtleties of David Lean's direction, but I really appreciated the way Freddie used the big canvas of the cinema screen to create amazing images.' Young had written a book about his craft, and David devoured it, eager for all the information he could get.

For his part, Peter's tastes were eclectic ranging from the fantasy spectaculars of Ray Harryhausen to the latest and most obscure French New Wave films. At arts cinemas, he discovered great international cinema through directors like Kurosawa and Fellini. But Peter especially loved comic books, both American and British, and pored over them endlessly. There was fun and inspiration to be found everywhere, from Frank Hampson's lantern-jawed hero Dan Dare, to the anarchy of the *Beano* in its golden age, to the superb creations of Will Elder and Mort Drucker in *Mad Magazine*. By the time he started at Woking Grammar School, Peter had absorbed these and many more, and was already writing and drawing his own stories in the notebooks he always carried around with him. It was yet another form of self-expression – and one that certainly would not have found approval with the strict regime imposed by headmaster Goode.

As the '60s progressed, a new subversive comic culture appeared, and Peter grew to love the work of such 'underground' cartoonists as Robert Crumb, creator of *Mister Natural*, and Gilbert Shelton, who invented the permanently stoned Fabulous Furry Freak Brothers. The two teenagers also earnestly worked their way through hippie-generation underground magazines like *Oz* and *International Times*, which fiercely opposed the establishment on any number of counts – the Vietnam War, legalisation of drugs and workers' rights – and presented their editorial content in swirling, psychedelic designs.

It wasn't long before the two boys, along with friends from school, got around to producing their own underground magazine. It came to be called *A Tasty Straight*, which one of their number insisted was slang for a joint. Neither of them had even tried marijuana but that did not deter them; it seemed like a workable title.

They ran off a couple of dozen copies and circulated them to a select band of school friends.

Peter's talent for drawing strip cartoons was the main selling point of *A Tasty Straight*, while his girlfriend Karen provided some artwork. Various members of this small collective contributed their own stories. The publication only lasted for two issues, but the experience of creative collaboration with others had been a useful one.

Around this time, Peter had met Karen at a local folk club – *The Star* in Guildford – where she insists 'he fell over my feet'. Clearly no great harm was done, except possibly to his dignity, and they remain together as man and wife to this day. Shortly after that, David met his lifelong partner, Sue. Both girls were pupils at the temptingly close Woking County Grammar School for Girls.

Peter maintained his drawing and writing in a large-format journal, which he hopefully titled *By Popular Demand*. It was a collection of skits, cartoons and photo-collage much influenced by the writings of Spike Milligan and the drawings of Ronald Searle. It wasn't quite as confrontational as

25

A Tasty Straight, more a means to amuse and interest his pals, though it confirmed him as someone who already had a knack for telling stories – and entertaining others.

Then came that fateful rainy afternoon at the Sproxton home when David sought out his father's old cine-camera and said: 'Why don't we make a film?' Intrigued by the idea, he and Peter made several, and when the BBC paid £25 (£1 a second!) for their short *Aardman and the Hole*, they finally realised that there might be a career in this.

Registering their enterprise under the name Aardman Animations somehow made their ambitions feel that much more realistic. Meanwhile, they faced the prospect of sitting their A-levels the following summer. While they had their minds set on university, they also knew they wanted to take a year out after their exams – hopefully to think of various ways they might pursue a future together in animation.

* * *

Still, for these seventeen-year-old boys, fame and fortune – or even a steady job – seemed an awfully long way off. At that point, it even seemed possible that their success with *Aardman and the Hole* might be a fluke, marking the high point of their prospects as would-be animators. Peter reflects: '*Aardman and the Hole* was really very primitive in every way, but it had a good story – or at least a decent one. If it hadn't had that story, I often wonder whether our career would've ended before it began.'

As it was, Peter and David had been invited by Patrick

Dowling to the BBC Television Centre for the *Vision On* end-of-season reception and drinks party – a heady experience. There they met the show's host, the legendary Tony Hart, his co-host Pat Keysell and director Clive Doig. Everyone was friendly and welcoming, treating the two teens as equals and fellow professionals. That much was flattering, but would things go any further?

As the evening drew on, it became clear that they would. Patrick and Clive told the boys they were in their plans for the following season of *Vision On* and asked them to produce thirteen more Aardman short films over the coming year – one for each episode of the show.

At a stroke, that neatly took care of their plans for a large portion of their pre-university gap year. Peter and David had no need to think twice about the offer – they planned to spend the next few months making their Aardman sequences.

David had already done some work experience, arranged by Vernon, which involved spending time in a Soho film cutting-room with an editor named Arthur Solomon. This had little to do with animation technique, but still, watching the principles of editing being applied was all useful background knowledge. David had attended dubbing sessions, too, where he witnessed the craft of sound mixing, along with visiting TV studios and a location shoot with his father.

Back at Woking County Grammar School, their peers were intrigued that the boys would be making a whole season's worth of Aardman short films for *Vision On*. The gossip about their plans spread around the school and swiftly reached the ears of headmaster Goode, who was predictably less than pleased.

Goode summoned David to his office and told him to buckle down and find a steady job, assuring him that the media offered no reliable long-term work prospects. David, whose father had carved out a career in the media that was both successful and interesting, had the presence of mind to stay calm and tell the head that he was aware of the pitfalls, but would take his chances anyway.

Through all this, Peter and David's friendship never wavered, though it was already clear that they had very distinct personalities: Peter, the extrovert, freed up to express himself through animation; while David, the enabler of the pair, took on board all the technical aspects, production issues, liaising with the *Vision On* office and trying to ensure their work stayed on schedule.

'There was always that yin and yang thing with us,' David explains. 'In our last year at school, we were both involved in a summer-school production of *The Royal Hunt of the Sun*. Peter was on stage, playing a demented Spanish priest, and I was somewhere hidden away on the balcony, in charge of sound – says it all really!'

The boys duly sat their A-levels and pondered their options: where would they spend their gap year creating their Aardman sequences? They both ruled out the option of staying at their parents' homes in Walton-on-Thames; for one thing, most of their friends from school were moving away to various universities, and, like most boys in their late teens, Peter and David were enthused by the idea of living independently away from home – somewhere Sue and Karen could stay with them for spells.

But where to go? They had almost no money of their own, and it wasn't as if the BBC would be paying them any retainer in advance. As for London and the Home Counties, even the most modest rental properties were far too expensive.

In the end, David's older brother Andy came to the rescue. He now lived in York, where he ran a small photographic gallery, and offered to find the boys some accommodation nearby – a family intervention that would make both sets of parents feel more at ease.

Andy found a small three-storey terraced house in the market town of Malton, east of the city of York. The rent was a mere £3.50 a week – unthinkably cheap in leafy, affluent Surrey – and yet still at the very limit of their budget.

By this point, David had wheels. He had amassed £100, enough to buy himself a yellow Morris 1000 van, formerly the property of the Post Office. It wasn't exactly pleasing to look at, but it could hold several people and a lot of stuff, which made it ideal for the task at hand. He also did some door-to-door selling for Betterware, another source of income to fund the move north.

Of course, the faithful old Victorian table had to go with them; it still served as their camera rostrum. The boys elected to work on the top floor of the house, but it was impossible to get the heavy, cumbersome table up the narrow stairs without shortening its legs.

As a working studio, the house was just about usable. As a living space, however, it turned out to be a disastrous choice – especially in the winter months. The boys had no money to speak of and ate in every night. When Sue stayed with them, she cooked, and they mostly ate vegetarian food: 'A masterclass in eating well on a tiny budget,' as Peter puts it.

Then there was Malton itself – charming in its way, but unlike anywhere David and Peter were used to. It was a typical, traditional market town, full of farmers and Land Rovers on cattle market day. The boys felt like strangers in a strange land – the first and quite possibly last animators in the town. Relief came at weekends when they would scrape together the petrol money and drive into York to see Andy and his partner Val at his gallery; their artsy friends were stimulating company, and David and Peter felt much more at home around them.

Still, there was always the work – creating thirteen short 2D films (each lasting one minute or less) featuring Aardman. But this, too, was challenging – to put it mildly. 'It was trial and error,' Peter says. 'We were still total novices at our craft, and we made every sort of mistake in animation and in storytelling. We'd send films off to the BBC, believing they were complete, but, if they really weren't working, Patrick and Clive would require changes. It might be an extra close-up, or a longer character-reaction – and it could take days or even weeks to put right.'

David recalls: 'Our lack of storytelling skills and gag writing was clearly evident, which is why Patrick offered a little later to help us develop Morph.'

Yet both Peter and David had a bloody-minded,

determined streak – and they ploughed on, fulfilling the thirteen-film task required of them, even though they had fallen out of love with the process. Drawn animation was proving to be difficult and rather mechanical, and the Aardman character had severe limitations. Even the BBC started to voice reservations about him. 'He just wasn't very compelling or interesting,' says Peter. 'To be honest, he wasn't really a character at all. I couldn't describe him to you now. And it was always just him, he didn't have another character to play off. By the end of our time in Maldon, we were ready to kill him off, and I think the people at *Vision On* felt the same way.' So they did just that – and never again used Aardman in any of their future films. Had they been told then that this little character's name would one day be known all over the world, they would never have believed it.

After six wintry months in Malton, it was time for Peter and David to go their own ways – to different universities. Despite all the hardship and frustrations, their friendship had survived, and they correctly assumed they would have a working partnership once again.

* * *

The boys rarely saw each other during term time, largely because they were 100 miles apart. Peter started his student days at York, while David went to Durham, where he quickly gravitated towards other students who shared his interests. One group were enthusiasts for Durham University theatre, for which they constructed sets and rigged lighting. David, who had long been interested in lighting and photography, eagerly joined up, using his lighting design skills in Durham's Assembly Rooms Theatre, running the technical aspects of its shows from the lighting box at the rear of the auditorium. 'I was in my element,' he recalls happily.

He was good at it, too, and requests for his lighting design skills came his way from other student groups staging revues, light opera and sketch shows destined for the Edinburgh Fringe Festival. In his second year, David became technical director, though he had to pull back a little for his final year to concentrate on his Geography degree.

For his part, Peter discovered that while he enjoyed university life, he wasn't a perfect fit for academia. An inveterate reader, he had chosen to study English literature, but was somewhat taken aback when he realised that there was more to the course than simple appreciation. Peter simply loved books and had anticipated he would mainly be talking about them and their pros and cons with his fellow students, rather than venturing into the field of literary criticism demanded by his tutors. It was harder work than he had expected.

York itself was a constant delight, an intriguing, picturesque city with a rich medieval history, high city walls, cobbled streets and excellent pubs. His girlfriend, Karen, who was studying art history at the University of Essex, joined him as often as possible; York was an attractive setting for young lovers.

In her absence, rather than wearing himself out with reading literary criticism, Peter drew cartoons and comic strips for various student publications and helped to run an 'alternative' kitchen named Gumbo in the student union bar, which opened up once a week. He helped prepare the food and also booked local musicians to play. Peter had loved his time in York, but he had the sense that he was waiting for his real life – which meant animation – to kick into gear.

Despite having expressed a few doubts about the Aardman character, the BBC's *Vision On* team were keen to retain Peter and David's services over a second season, and offered them a new contract: £50 per sequence for all thirteen shows. Because Peter and David would both be occupied at their respective universities, they would need to do the work over the summer and complete it before the second season was broadcast. It was the equivalent of offering the boys a summer job, and, apart from anything, the boys could use the money.

However, when Peter and David cast their minds back to the previous winter in Malton, they realised what an uphill task it represented. They had struggled long and hard with 2D animation – and whenever the *Vision On* team had requested changes, their task became unbearably frustrating and time-consuming. It was clear to them that they could not provide thirteen more Aardman sequences in the space of just ten or so weeks. And, actually, that suited them just fine, as they were feeling increasingly that their futures did not lie in 2D animation. 'It became really tedious, 2D work,' David recalls. 'Once you've storyboarded it, the fun stops, basically.'

Instead, they started reminiscing about the time they had tried to break into *Vision On*, and mulled over the various styles and techniques with which they had experimented when they were assembling a 'show reel' for Patrick, in the hope that something might catch his eye.

In retrospect, they realised, what had really intrigued Peter was clay animation, exemplified by Eliot Noyes and his brilliant film *Clay, or The Origin of Species*. Peter especially was hugely fond of Plasticine as a medium; it took him back to his early childhood at home, when he and his mother had sat at their kitchen table and moulded it into various intriguing shapes.

Peter and David remembered how much they had truly enjoyed working with clay, and thought maybe, just maybe, it could be the answer to the dilemma they were now facing.

They had to be guided by the themes for each episode of *Vision On*, one of which was food, so they retrieved their old stocks of clay and devised another 'metamorphosis' story. This one started with a table covered by a gingham table-cloth, with cutlery laid out and a meal of sausages, potatoes and peas on a plate. The food begins to move – slowly at first, then faster and faster – whirling around the plate and grad-ually changing form to become a small animal, somewhat like a bear, which finally staggers onto its feet and stomps off, biting an animated human hand as it departs.

In itself, it wasn't much – any more than *Aardman and the Hole* had been much. But, like that earlier little experiment in 2D animation, Peter and David's first proper venture into working with clay was a hugely important milestone in their subsequent careers.

In the short term, it enabled them to satisfy themselves that clay was the ideal medium with which to fulfil their animation contract for the next season of *Vision On*. 'It began our second career in animation,' Peter reflects.

Working with clay, he and David felt a sense of relief – of liberation, almost. This was a medium in which they could suddenly experiment. It enabled them to feel almost like pioneers, testing the possibilities and boundaries of new techniques and approaches. Even the short film featuring a meal on a table felt ground-breaking: the Plasticine did not lie flat – it stood up of its own accord, effectively giving it another dimension. Peter and David had stumbled on something. Their work at this point may have been a little primitive but, as far as they knew, and as far as the team at *Vision On* was concerned, nobody else in the world was producing animation that looked like this. As Peter says: 'Instead of being very tiny fish in a huge pond, we looked around and found that we were the *only* fish in a pond of our own making.'

It also gave them a huge psychological boost. Whereas the 2D animation on which they had worked in Malton would always feel like hard work, their foray into clay felt spontaneous and exhilarating.

This wasn't to say it was easy. Animation is seldom easy. They were still limited by modest budgets and the tiny 'sets' on which they worked at David's house, not to mention the themes laid down for each episode by the *Vision On* producers, which had to be followed. Nevertheless, the switch to clay meant they could approach their work with something like relish.

For the first season in this new medium, every short film

they made had a different setting and different characters. Mountain climbers, tramps, and cops and robbers all made brief appearances; but, in their third year of *Vision On*, they landed on new, repeatable characters for the show, who were worth returning to more than once. 'The Gleebies' – four little clay creatures in primary colours, just over 2 inches tall, with tiny arms and long, pointed noses – were there primarily to make a mess of Tony Hart's desk, spilling pots of paint, knocking over jars of pencils behind his back, and generally getting in the way. 'They were like a foil to Tony, effectively,' David notes. 'He'd come back, see the havoc they'd caused, and of course it would get a reaction from him.'

The Gleebies only appeared in five *Vision On* sequences, but working on them gave a tremendous boost to Peter and David's confidence. Although still hobbyists, they had gained valuable experience of animation in its varied forms and had even earned some decent pocket money.

They considered their options and decided they would sit their finals in the summer of 1976, and give animation a go as a career at least for a few months. It was time for both of them to leave home, and they settled on Bristol as the place to relocate.

There were good reasons for this choice. Clearly, it would be cheaper than London. Peter remembered it fondly from his childhood days before he and his family moved to Australia, and Sue was already there, reading History at Bristol University. The city also had a small but active creative community – both the BBC and ITV (in the form of its regional station HTV) had bases there. There was a clinching factor: it was where *Vision On* was recorded, so Peter and David would be close by for filming. And there were vague hints from the BBC that there might be more work for them out west. So Bristol it was.

2

META-MORPH-OSIS

Their summer plans were thrown into confusion in April 1976, when Peter and David received a letter from *Vision On* producer Patrick Dowling informing them that the show was being cancelled; its current season would be its last.

Without question, it was a disaster: *Vision On* was their one regular source of income, their only commission – and at that point their only entrée into the world of television. A huge void opened up in front of them. In his letter, Patrick alluded to a future spin-off series, also featuring Tony Hart; but there were no guarantees for Peter and David that their work could be found a place within the new format.

The phrase 'go west, young man' suddenly sounded less promising. But Peter and David chose not to be crushed by this new development, and – with a degree of resilience and bloody-mindedness – decided to move to Bristol anyhow and take their chances that the new show would want animated sequences from them.

There was an important item of personal business for Peter

first, however: he and Karen had decided to get married, almost the first of their contemporaries to do so. The strength of the links between the Lord and Sproxton families was evident from the ceremony: David was Peter's best man; Vernon Sproxton conducted the service; while David's brother Andy was the wedding photographer, his photos faithfully recording the shocking state of gentlemen's fashion in 1976.

After a short honeymoon in Paris, Peter and Karen headed west and joined up with David and Sue – 'quite something when you think about it,' Peter muses now: 'All four of us were twenty-two years old. David and I had gone to the same school in Woking, as had Karen and Sue. That year we all graduated, Karen and I got married, we all moved to Bristol and declared we were in business as Aardman Animations. Quite a year for us all, 1976.'

Like any start-up, they had little work initially. They all signed on, which allowed them to pay the rent and eat, and Karen found a job with an insurance company. The hot summer of 1976 meant there were no heating bills needing to be paid. They found small flats to live in and started to build their network of contacts to help them find work and a bigger space to work in. But the prospects for a career in animation looked pretty bleak.

Peter and David chose to stick to what they knew best: coming up with ideas for a series they hoped might interest the BBC. Peter was intrigued by the idea of adapting *The Magic Pudding*, the classic Australian children's novel by Norman Lindsay. It had a host of animal characters that seemed to lend themselves to animation, but the publishers in Sydney were far from encouraging, memorably saying that proposals to adapt the book into animation came along 'as regularly as the garbage man'.

The big problem for the new company was that they were still outsiders in broadcasting. They had met people from the BBC, and even knew the names of producers, but they had little idea of how to pitch a well-crafted proposal for a stan-dalone series. And this was emphatically a buyers' market. So dominant was the BBC in animation programming at that time that it could pick and choose from experienced programme-makers without the need to take a risk on two young novices.

Then Patrick Dowling called them. The vague reference in his April letter to plans for 'a sort of spin-off programme' with Tony Hart for the following year had come good. The corporation had green-lit Patrick's projected idea for the new show and, best of all, there was room for animation in his plans.

Dowling even suggested David and Peter come in to see him for a meeting, to talk over any ideas they might have for a new animated character who could function as a foil for Tony Hart. He specifically mentioned that the Gleebies Peter and David had created for *Vision On* had been well received.

This was everything David and Peter could have wanted to hear. There was no firm promise of regular work, but it was an ideal chance for them to pitch their ideas to someone who already knew and admired their work. At the very least it was a toehold.

As more details emerged about what was needed from

Peter and David for the new show – *Take Hart*, as it was to be called – the prospect seemed more and more promising.

What Patrick was looking for was some comic relief. Tony Hart would go on to become a beloved, hugely popular figure in children's television. He was a gifted artist who had also designed the legendary *Blue Peter* badge. He prepared all his pieces, and carried them out superbly and quickly – an essential requirement for television – but he hadn't been trained as either an actor or presenter. For all his easy, avuncular manner, he couldn't help coming across as rather serious. In short, he needed a comic foil.

To some extent, this had briefly been the function of the Gleebies, created by Peter and David for *Vision On*.

'The Gleebies were ancestors to Morph in a way,' says David. 'They were a foil to Tony, but they were a start for us, and we were lucky to get that break. It was the Gleebies that put us in a strong position to come up with a single character who was somewhat similar.'

The new show to replace *Vision On* was *Take Hart* – a programme that encouraged children to believe that everyone could be an artist. In the first episode, Tony is seen earnestly producing a piece of stencilled artwork. Suddenly, a ball of Plasticine rolls onto his table and starts getting in his way. Initially just a blob, it transforms through various shapes before becoming a little man – 13 cm high, terracotta in colour, and a troublemaker by instinct.

This was the first screen appearance of their new character. And they named him Morph.

41

* * *

By the time they began work on developing Morph, David and Peter had moved into a space in the upmarket Clifton area of Bristol. They had befriended Bill Mather, also a contributor on *Vision On*. Bill's creation was a character called The Digger who was discovered every episode down a hole on a building site. With his shovel, he would unearth a different, interesting object each week, with surreal and comic results.

Bill, who was in his thirties, had recently left the BBC graphics department to work on an animated film based on the life of Victor Hugo, and another experimental animated short about his son's audition to become a choirboy at St Mary Redcliffe Church in Bristol, which was constructed around the recorded real-life conversation between a boy and his choirmaster.

Bill had moved into a space above Bristol's Antiques Market and invited David and Peter to share it with him. They readily agreed, primarily because it gave them an alternative to the cramped room they used as a studio in the house in Cotham. The new space was itself quite small – only about 600 sqft – and they divided it in two, sharing it equally with Bill. Finally, they had room to stretch. They had a studio.

In the relative comfort of these new surroundings, David and Peter immediately set to work on their new creation. 'We came up with a character that was pure clay, with no armature [the framework or skeleton on which the clay is moulded]. He was very flexible and versatile,' recalls David. 'Morph was terracotta in colour, and funny and mischievous. It worked well. Peter was always a natural sculptor, and he just loved taking this clay, bringing a character to life and doing things with it.

'At that point, it was just the two of us, me and Pete, doing everything, including coming up with the stories. We decided to introduce a new character called Chas. He was originally called Kaolin, as in Kaolin and Morph(ine), but was quickly renamed Chas. He was almost like Morph's twin brother, but slightly paler in colour – cream, I suppose. He would behave badly, act as a foil to Morph, and made up half of a double act. We thought that with the two of them – and their occasional companion Nailbrush [who barked like a pet dog but literally was a nailbrush] – we might get a series out of them. So we worked up this idea, and Patrick helped us put it all together.'

Peter and David also agree that Morph marked a huge turning point in their careers, in the sense that creating the Morph episodes allowed them to get a lot of valuable work under their belts – even if they were just inserts into *Take Hart*.

'From 1976 to 1981, that was mostly what I did,' Peter recalls. 'The majority of our time was probably taken up with Morph – writing designing, building and shooting – and I animated him week in, week out over those five years. We both learnt an awful lot, especially in the first year. You can tell this by looking back at the first episodes we shot, which, I'm happy to say, look awful! I mean that in a good way, because you can see the rapid learning curve we were experiencing in model-making, lighting and shot composition. Well, you can see it in Morph himself. He looks quite different in the early stories; positively Neanderthal. He's got a small sloping forehead and enormous feet and a sort of slumping, lumbering walk. Over the years, he's defied time and become more youthful looking.

And then there was the storytelling. When you look at some of the early stories you think "what the hell were we thinking?" There were some extraordinary non-stories. In one episode, Morph must have got some grass seed from somewhere, and scatters it in his box. And then when he lifts the lid – wouldn't you know it? – it's full of turf. Which we dug up, incidentally – a small square of grass – from Clifton Downs. That was the punchline, supposedly. But ... not a very *good* punchline! There were some poor stories in the early days.

Still, I do think that period was really crucial to us. There was all that learning that came through doing it, creating dozens of stories, from thirty seconds to five minutes long. That's how you work out storytelling.

I always think the most important thing about Morph is that he's really expressive. And that may sound completely obvious. Surely animated characters are meant to be expressive, aren't they? But others of that period just aren't.

For instance, I was brought up on *The Magic Roundabout*, which was charming and delightful. But Eric Thompson, who wrote the script for the British version, never even listened to the original French version. He would just look at it mute and come up with a story. If you turned the sound off again, you wouldn't have any idea what was going on. And above all, you wouldn't know what any of the characters were *thinking* – except perhaps Dougal, the shaggy dog, who would sometimes frown, I recall. But because of the flexible material we were working with – Plasticine – we could convey much more of what Morph was feeling and thinking.

So, if Morph was bored, say – you knew it. The look on his face, the slump of his shoulders, the shape of his whole body conveyed boredom. I can't imagine how you'd know if any of the characters from *The Magic Roundabout* were bored without being told by the narrator.'

Very quickly, Morph and his adventures on *Take Hart* were being well received by the BBC and by the public. 'He was a character, and a mischievous one,' Peter says. 'He was irreverent and anarchic and people really warmed to him. When I think back now, it was extraordinary – that first season, which we started in 1976, was a bit dreamlike.'

Yet, as David points out, 'We didn't really know any other people who were doing what we were doing.' If there was a technical problem, David could turn to his growing network of contacts in the BBC and beyond, but there were not that many people that Peter go to with a specific stop-frame issue and ask, 'How would you go about solving this?'

'It made for rather a solitary existence,' Peter adds. This was far more true for him than for David; alongside Peter, he was doing the production work, book-keeping, operating the camera and liaising with the lab. But he also got to move around the city (mostly on his bike) meeting graphics people and editors, 'so there was a network of professionals around us'. David was also socialising with these new acquaintances, and was regularly in and out of BBC Bristol, dropping in film or collecting rushes: 'Pete had a young family at home and couldn't socialise like I could. He probably did feel isolated – but that wasn't true for me.'

Fortunately, the same year they started work on the one-minute Morph episodes, they fell in with a group of local animators, who provided them with the feedback and professional camaraderie they lacked.

Bill Mather's delightful five-minute film *Audition* was itself inspired by the pioneering work of American animators John and Faith Hubley in the '50s. Like them, Bill had taken a 'natural' unscripted audio conversation and used animation to illuminate and expand it. He knew the idea had more potential and he took it to Colin Thomas, a BBC television producer in Bristol who headed up an experimental programming unit. Together they devised a plan for a six-part series showcasing short animated films that featured characters lip-syncing to genuine recorded (but unrehearsed) speech.

Colin invited Peter and David as well as three other animators he had head-hunted – Andy Walker, Derek Hayes and Henry Lutman – to make films for the series, which would be called *Animated Conversations*. The Aardman duo, who were already interested in the idea of creating animation for adults as well as children, offered to make two films, with all the others contributing one apiece. 'The BBC was making the series on every kind of shoestring,' Peter recalls ruefully.

'I suppose Colin and Bill knew what we'd been doing with Morph and could see we were good animators, but the idea of making a character out of Plasticine and then making it talk [in lip-sync] was unheard of. It seemed unlikely.'

The group mulled over locations where intriguing conversations might be overheard and recorded. One of the suggestions was the nearby Salvation Army hostel. Colin secured the permission of the management and then Peter, David, Colin and a sound recordist turned up and placed mikes discreetly on the reception desk.

The crew retreated to a nearby corridor, out of sight, and waited patiently for a couple of hours, overhearing routine conversations at the desk – nothing that was remotely worth recording, or the basis for an interesting story on film. As Peter puts it, 'We could have sat there for four hours and never got anything of substance at all.'

Then, an elderly homeless man wandered in and explained his plight to the staff: he was hungry and wanted a meal. He has been to the Salvation Army building across the street, where meals were served, but they had sent him over to this one to get a voucher. The old man cannot see why there is a problem, and the receptionist, sounding faintly irritated by all this, is baffled too. Then a kindly Salvation Army captain arrives at the desk and gets involved.

They tell the homeless man to go back across the street, because he genuinely can get a meal. He is unsure and suspicious, as if a trick is being played on him. Finally, the captain agrees to take him himself, but in the end the poor man shuffles out of the lobby, looking lost and confused.

For the purposes of *Animated Conversations*, it seemed to work well: three characters, three voices, a touching exchange full of pathos between two authority figures and an old man down on his luck, clearly accustomed to rejection wherever he went. It would summon a range of responses from anyone watching the film – sympathy, sorrow, wry smiles.

'It was good luck and good timing that this guy came along with his confusing request – and it made good drama,' says Peter. 'So, fortunately, the film we made had some heft to it. It was *about* something. But we were still really lucky to get that conversation.'

Peter and David called the film *Down and Out*, succinctly summing up the homeless man's predicament.

'It was so new to us at that time,' Peter reflects. 'There was only conversation, really – no gags, nothing surreal, none of the things most people associate with animation. When we started on the project, we didn't know how it was going to work. That was the truth of the matter. Colin Thomas, our producer, was wise, because early on, the first go around, we thought we'd need some amusing animation – some magic, some transformations. We suggested a few half-assed ideas, and Colin said: "I think it's better simpler." It was good advice, and as a result we ended up shooting it quite straight. It's like it's almost documentary. Nothing outlandish or remarkable happens. It's just these people in a room, having a strange conversation. So why is that a good idea? We didn't *know* at the time it was a good idea. But I think now, with hindsight, there's a great magic in that idea – putting together the very real soundtrack with the very contrived images.

Everyone knows that in animation nothing's happened by chance. Any uninformed viewer knows there's no accident in any of this; it's contrived. And somehow between the two – super-naturalism and super-artificiality – the result was really interesting. That's all you can say.'

With their raw material successfully recorded, Peter and David returned to their office and started working out how they would create lip-sync animation using clay characters. They had never attempted such a thing before and there was one simple lesson they needed to learn: though the project was designed to be an exercise in lip-sync, getting the sounds to match the lips was much less important than the movement of eyes and eyebrows. 'Usually when we watch people talking, all our focus is on the eyes,' Peter says, 'We discovered that performance of the face – of glances, focus and eyebrow movement – was the truly expressive thing. That's what brings animation to life.'

Their second film for *Animated Conversations*, made in 1978, was called *Confessions of a Foyer Girl*, and featured recorded conversations between two young women who worked in a local cinema. While they talked about their humdrum daily lives, images relating to what they were discussing appeared on a cinema screen behind them. Peter and David agreed later it didn't quite work; the tiny budgets meant there was no effective means of illustrating the girls' lives, and the subject matter lacked the emotional weight of *Down and Out*.

Perhaps because there was no track record for adult-oriented animation, the BBC was clearly unsure about the *Animated Conversations* films, and sprinkled them (eventually) at different time slots across their schedules. *Down and Out* was finally broadcast on BBC Two, more than two years after it had been completed. At the time, it felt like a noble experiment that would go no further.

The *Animated Conversations* project was fascinating and they learnt a lot about animation and performance, but, at the time, it didn't feel as though it would help to define their career. It didn't break through to a large audience, nor was the money particularly good. It felt like an interesting excursion, a holiday between creating Morph episodes. They had no idea then how important it would prove to be.

So it was back to Morph.

'We'd started in 1976 when the first [sixty-second] Morph film was made,' David says. 'And then within just three years we'd got a commission to make a full series – twenty-six episodes of Morph, each of them five minutes long, which was pretty good going, and almost full-time work for us. It was a big deal, because fundamentally there was still just the two of us.'

David and Peter had pitched the idea for a series of five-minute Morph films to Patrick Dowling, who agreed to champion their idea within the BBC. He would even produce it, he said.

His offer met with a mixed reception. David, who concedes Patrick could be controlling and not always easy to get along with, thought it could only help to have such an experienced executive attached to the project. Peter, however, regarded Patrick, who was around sixty at this stage, as 'old school' and had found him irritating in their previous encounters.

'I remember us going to the BBC's Television Centre with this idea,' says Peter. 'Here we were, young and gaining experience as animators, but we didn't know much about storytelling in the longer form – so Patrick was our way into the BBC.'

The two young animators discreetly asked if they could make the new show with another producer, but they were turned down. 'There was an obvious *quid pro quo* here,' Peter reflects: 'You can do this series as long as Patrick is involved. We didn't ever really get on with him. I think we always felt slightly manipulated by him. Somewhere in my old sketch-books I have a funny little drawing, which was done at that time, with Dave and me in the background, dressed in pauper's rags, trying to get his attention, and Patrick, facing away from us, his head down over a piece of paper, mumbling and talking about something else. The drawing has some humour, because Patrick used to do that. He wouldn't address us. He had a habit of carrying on a separate monologue while you were trying to talk to him. We didn't love him, but there you are.'

David saw it another way: 'I think I knew perhaps more than Peter all that needed to be put into place to make a programme. We were incredibly green. Apart from writing and making the series, there were issues like contacts with editors, sound studios, labs, voice artists – and the need to get this sold abroad. We didn't have that knowledge and expertise, and Patrick was offering to help us up the ladder. Yes, he would take a fee and be part of the production, but without him we weren't going to be trusted by the BBC to bring the series in. I don't think Pete liked the idea of being told what to do. I was keen to learn!'

Looking back on all this now, Peter reflects: 'Without Patrick, would we ever have got the gig? Probably not. And then, in fairness, he wrote and produced the series, I animated it and Dave shot it – and it worked out very well.'

Up to a point, at least. Financially, the series was a disaster. It had a budget of just £2,000 an episode, which had to cover everything – the editor, sound people, lab work, Patrick's fees and Peter and David's wages. 'I think the editor made more money than anyone else from the series,' David says. 'We overran badly and settled on making just twenty-six episodes instead of the planned thirty. We just about survived financially.'

This 26-episode series was called *The Amazing Adventures of Morph* and was narrated by Tony Hart. In order to get the series made, Peter and David had undertaken another of their many relocations in Bristol. Their newest place was larger, with enough space to accommodate a model-making room and an office. It was in a white, triple-fronted Georgian house overlooking the river. The Stork House, as it was known, had been a pub in the nineteenth century and (according to local gossip) also a brothel at some stage in its history.

They rented two floors at one end of the building. 'On the downstairs level,' David recalls, 'we closed off all the windows and built a small set – which again was Tony Hart's "art studio".'

They set to work with relish. Each of the twenty-six episodes had a title and a definite theme – 'How It All Began',

'Morph's Birthday Party', 'Morph Plays Golf', 'The Day Nothing Happened'.

To flesh out each episode, they decided to create a 'family' around Morph – not only his friend Chas, but his formidable grandfather 'GrandMorph', who zoomed around on a skateboard. There was also a little girl named Folly and a big brute of a character named Gillespie, who towered over Morph and lumbered around the set.

Peter and David felt they were finally hitting their stride as animators: 'We started to think that the 5.55 p.m. slot – just before the early evening news on BBC One – would be our career!' David recalls.

There was also at this time a sense that word was finally getting out about these two promising young men, especially when *Blue Peter*, the flagship BBC children's programme, paid them a visit, coming down to Bristol to film them at work.

To mark the occasion, Sarah Greene, *Blue Peter's* vivacious host, presented Morph with a coveted Blue Peter badge, which he received graciously. The 'ceremony' was shot by Peter and David; to her amazement, it took two whole hours and required no fewer than 400 frames to be shot, between each of which Peter would move the clay figure of Morph ever so minutely.

Even allowing for a little hyperbole, this was a prodigious rate of animation, and Sarah probably didn't take into account the time when Morph was standing still and doing nothing! But it is true that, at around twenty seconds a day, the average rate of animation for Morph was extremely fast.

Before showing the film of the badge ceremony, she

warned her young viewers: 'Don't blink! It really does last only sixteen seconds.'

The *Blue Peter* segment about their work was excellent exposure, and the first time that they found themselves on the other end of a camera. Peter and David were finding that, just as their work had seemed more professional and sophisticated as they continued to animate the Morph episodes, the same was true of *The Amazing Adventures of Morph*.

David's particular favourite was screened in 1981, the twenty-fourth out of twenty-six. 'It was time-consuming and expensive to make,' David remembers, 'but *GrandMorph's Home Movies* is so much what Aardman's all about – character-led storytelling! And it's also a film within a film.'

In the episode, Morph joins his family to watch as his skateboarding grandfather, GrandMorph, plays them an old black-and-white home movie projected onto a screen. We learn that, as a young man, GrandMorph had ambitions to be an actor, but instead started making films – including some of his own family.

In his film, we see Morph as an infant, unsteady on his feet and often falling over. His family, seated around him at home watching the film, all giggle. Tony Hart's voiceover of the film, given to him by GrandMorph to read, comments on his every move: 'He was a very sweet and contented baby – quite unlike Morph as he is today.' After a while, Morph becomes enraged, starts haranguing his family, then approaches the screen, furious at the way he has been embarrassed. Finally, he steps into the screen and continues the squabble on film – he's a terracotta character in a black-and-white world.

There's a playful sophistication about the episode, and Peter and David's career looked promising. 'It was very steady work, and we were doing it every day,' Peter says. 'When we started *The Amazing Adventures of Morph*, we said we'd do thirty episodes by a given date. We missed four because of a deadline we couldn't reach. Still, twenty-six was considered pretty respectable.'

David recalls, 'We were behind schedule and Patrick may have recognised that our lack of experience had made us overambitious in terms of scheduling and budgeting.'

By this stage of creating Morph episodes, Patrick had made himself a more marginalised figure, doing less scriptwriting. Much of his time was now devoted to another show he was producing called *Why Don't You?*, which actually encouraged the children watching to spend less time in front of their TV screens and do something useful and creative.

As a result, he now left the scriptwriting to Peter and David – which of course delighted them. They ended up writing the final five episodes of *The Amazing Adventures of Morph*. As Peter acknowledges, being in charge of this entire process on their own 'taught us a lot about storytelling and thinking up ideas'. They also had to deal first-hand with the knotty problem of meeting that modest budget of £2,000 per episode without Patrick's help. But, again, it was invaluable experience.

Despite their success, Peter insists they had no grand vision. 'The only future we could clearly imagine was a career in kids' TV. Kind of like Peter Firmin and Oliver Postgate – the double act who had made wonderful children's series like *The Clangers* and *Noggin the Nog*. When we started doing Morph, if we imagined any future in the business, it was probably that.

At the time, we did think and hope that Morph might somehow make our fortunes. We looked at the Mr Men, the Wombles, maybe even Paddington Bear, and we saw the toys and the T-shirts associated with the characters and we thought, *Merchandising! That's the way to make money.'* We hoped that a lucrative business in Morph merchandise would follow. But sadly it never did.'

BBC Enterprises, as David notes, 'wasn't set up to promote a series like this. They advised us twenty-six episodes would be enough – which it wasn't if you wanted more overseas sales.'

Still, although the money failed to roll in, Morph would eventually prove to be a game-changer for the Aardman team – a fact that would only be recognised in later years. 'I often wonder what would have become of us if we hadn't created Morph,' Peter reflects. 'Nick Park was a big Morph fan when he was younger, so you wonder: without Morph, would Nick have ever done Plasticine stop-motion animation? And, similarly, if we'd never made *Down and Out*, then Nick probably wouldn't have done *Creature Comforts*.'

There were advantages in being associated with Morph in the late 1970s: 'That was pretty much a full-time job, the Morph series,' Peter recalls. 'It was almost our whole working week. Fortunately, we had a young accountant, not much older than us, who advised us to create a limited company. We had registered the name Aardman Animations years before, but that was just a trade name. Now we formed a small new company (with Patrick, who we later bought out) just to make the series, which we called Morph Ltd. And the practical side-effect of that was that, as an employee of Morph Ltd, I could claim a steady income and therefore qualify for a mortgage. David and I were both twenty-six or so, and our small income was hardly secure, yet in those days housing was relatively cheap. And the cost of the home Karen and I bought at that point was two and a half times my annual salary. Karen herself had no income then – she was bringing up the kids. But you could buy a home then in what is now a very fashionable area. You'd have to be earning £100,000 a year to buy that same house today!'

In 1980, David and Sue became homeowners too – her grandmother had died and left her a modest sum of money which they used as a down payment on a small house in the pleasant Montpelier district. It would be another decade before they bought anywhere bigger, but it was a good start.

There was one more notable event that helped Peter and David to realise how far they had come since arriving in Bristol less than four years previously. In June 1980, they were contacted by an official from the British Council with a posh, breezy voice who told them the Council had entered *Down and Out* in several animation festivals abroad, as part of its mission to promote British culture in other countries.

One of these was the Melbourne Film Festival, where it had already been short-listed for an award, and it had also been chosen for a screening at the upcoming Zagreb Animation Festival in Croatia.

Peter and David were thrilled – but even more so when the man from the British Council asked if they would like to travel to Zagreb as representatives of the UK. Everything, including flights, meals and hotel rooms, would be paid for – the festival sponsors covered all that.

What was not to like? The chance to spend five days watching films by other animators from across the world, to meet their counterparts from dozens of other countries, was an irresistible offer, and it turned out to be a revelation.

British animation was about to undergo an amazing change, but, in 1980, it was still underrepresented in international festivals. The *Animated Conversations* series, which hadn't made much impact at home, provided two UK entries in competition at the festival – *Down and Out* and Andy Walker's film *Filling Time*. Andy's film was based on dialogue recorded in a dentist's surgery. As Peter tells it, 'It was less dialogue than monologue, which is the dentist's preferred method of communication – naturally the patient isn't in a position to talk back.' Andy accompanied them to the festival, and it was his film that won a prize. They were pleased for him – and also, Peter adds, 'insanely jealous!'

Peter and David correctly guessed they would have a genuinely good time, with lots of food and drink, socialising, and any number of films from other countries to watch, learn from and appreciate. It would be a fine opportunity to take a break from their work schedule, let their hair down a little and enjoy themselves – all for free.

What they had not anticipated was that Zagreb would make them feel differently about their status as animators.

When they were labouring on the early one-minute Morph episodes, Peter in particular felt professionally isolated, knowing no one else who was doing exactly what they were doing in clay animation. In addition, almost all British animation was commercially driven and targeted at children or TV commercials; because David and Peter also wanted to make grown-up animation, it often felt to Peter that he was isolated from fellow professionals and working in a void.

Zagreb swept away those negative feelings at a stroke.

'We got there and what struck me was the immense respect accorded to the grey-bearded maestros of the animation world. Their work, which was so highly revered at a festival like Zagreb, was almost entirely unknown back in Britain. For the past thirty years and more, they'd been building reputations, especially in the Soviet states of eastern Europe – and I hadn't seen any of their stuff before. In Britain, animators were a more or less invisible breed – they certainly weren't the star guests at civic ceremonies or the subjects of television documentaries – but here they were treated as serious artists.

A lot of it was political, subversive, full of rebellion and anti-government themes. And there were pure art films, especially those from the National Film Board in Canada. The winner of the Grand Prix that year was a Russian film, *Tale of Tales* by Yuri Norstein, which is generally considered one of the truly great animated films. The whole experience was a world away from children's TV. We were suddenly experiencing a whole world of animation. And we were sort of part of it,' Peter recalls. 'We realised we were part of an international community of filmmakers. We had a place in it, albeit a tiny foothold. We discovered a warm, encouraging group of people – many of them also experimenting, defining a place in this exciting world. I felt very connected to them. In a sense, I felt I'd found my tribe.'

Only four years after they had started working – alone – on Morph, and unsure of their future and where they stood in the world of animation, they now had a jaunty, new-found confidence.

3

A New Decade

By the early '80s, Peter and David could look back on the progress they had made in the previous few years, having created in Morph a nationally beloved character, then overseeing a 26-episode series starring him and his family. By the end of the series they were writing, animating and shooting the five-minute episodes independently.

They certainly could not survive on Morph alone, yet their visit to the Zagreb festival had not only been wildly enjoyable, but had given them a new self-assurance – they felt they legitimately had a place in the international world of animation, and it was richly deserved – but with no funding in the UK for this type of work, their future still felt unsure.

'From around this point it seemed that things happened for us,' Peter recalls. 'They weren't accidental, but they weren't planned either. We weren't naïve, and I don't believe we drifted through life bumping into good opportunities. But generally there's no denying that our timing has been good. It was true in 1976, at the moment when the producer cancelled *Vision On*, our one gig, and suggested the new programme *Take Hart*. That was how Morph came into being. Yes, we grabbed that opportunity when it came – but it came at exactly the right moment. Had we stayed at *Vision On*, we would have been members of a team doing short, quirky, different films. The new opportunity gave us the chance to develop a character. So it was really good timing – and we had the right instincts to go with it.'

Proof of their good instincts in leaping at a chance had been finally confirmed when *The Amazing Adventures of Morph* was nominated for a BAFTA award in 1981. Not only that, but each episode was regularly attracting audiences of 13 million. Yet despite this success, the BBC were unwilling to commission a second series.

'Morph was a critical success but not a financial success,' David stresses. 'We got occasional repeat fees and the odd royalty, but certainly not enough to sustain us. In fact, to this day, Morph is in deficit – but we love the character.'

'I remember very well the strange lull after the Morph series,' Peter recalls. 'It had been a labour of love for two years – I animated all day, every day, But when we finished we were back to "one-offs", title sequences, short pilots for other people (Captain Beaky was one, Purple Monster was another) and inserts for documentaries, that sort of thing. Opportunities for longer projects were few and far between.'

Yet, as Peter mentions, among those opportunities were TV title sequences, which were becoming more sophisticated and sometimes employed special effects. No one in the BBC graphics department specialised in model or physical special effects, so Aardman received commissions from them at a higher level than they had experienced to date – 'not hundreds of pounds for a minute, but a few thousand for thirty seconds,' as David puts it. 'There wasn't a constant stream of these shoots – though there were enough to pay the bills, and I increased my skills and reputation as a cameraman.'

Aardman moved its premises again, this time occupying part of a building called the Production House in the Cotham area of Bristol. They used a windowless Victorian-era workshop as a studio, with an office upstairs. It was actually a little smaller than Stork House, but it had access to better-equipped editing rooms – and at least they were around other people in the same business.

Still, it wasn't quite the big breakthrough they were longing for, and there often wasn't a need for much animation in many of these shoots, so Peter was not as involved. The future felt unclear to him and, considering his options, Peter found himself on the verge of making a truly radical move.

* * *

While reading *American Cinematographer*, a magazine for film professionals, Peter's gaze fell upon an advert placed by a US animation company called Broadcast Arts; they had a vacancy for a 'clay animator'. Peter sat bolt upright; it felt as though the ad was addressing him personally: 'How many of us clay animators could there be?' he wondered.

It turned out that Broadcast Arts employed eight people, were based in Washington, DC, and had already made a feature-length stop-motion animated film, called *I Go Pogo*, adapted from a 1940s comic strip by former Disney animator Walt Kelly. It was about a friendly American possum who inhabits a swamp and decides to run for president.

I Go Pogo had opened in the United States in 1980, but was not released in any other territories, so Peter had never heard of it. Still, the fact that Broadcast Arts had 'made it' placed them ahead of Aardman and suggested that they at least had ambition. Somewhat intrigued, Peter replied to their ad. They promptly replied and invited him to the States to talk things over.

'The company wasn't going anywhere much,' he says now, 'so I went to Washington just to see if it might work out.'

He had never visited America before, and was fascinated by it. Brought up on American TV and movies, the city struck him as both familiar and astonishingly foreign. The fire hydrants, the policemen's uniforms and the big-rig trucks were familiar enough, but he was taken aback by how different the American people seemed to be from the British, even if they spoke the same language.

Peter spent two weeks with Broadcast Arts, even doing a little animation and storyboarding with them. As a company, they seemed ahead of the curve; they were already doing work for the newly launched MTV, the American all-music video TV channel that for a time became hugely influential.

Like Peter, BA's bosses, Steve Oakes and Peter Rosenthal, were both in their late twenties, which eased their transatlantic differences. They were friendly enough, the staff were young and enthusiastic, and they all seemed eager for Peter to join them.

It would have been a big wrench, however, and Peter found himself weighing up the pros and cons. Certainly, America would have been an exciting place to work, and Broadcast Arts gave the impression they were clearly going places in the animation world. Peter remembers his fortnight with them as enjoyable.

A couple of factors gave him pause for thought, however. While he fitted the Broadcast Arts profile in terms of age and experience, he felt something set him apart – something quite separate from his British background. He and Karen were now the parents of two young children; there was Tom, who was three, and little Helen, who had been born the previous Christmas. Only one of the Broadcast Arts team was a parent, whereas at Aardman a workplace would evolve that often took into account the demands of parenthood. Peter could not imagine the Broadcast Arts work ethic accommodating an employee's occasional need to take time out from the office at short notice to deal with child-related problems at home.

After he had spent his two weeks there, Steve Oakes and Peter Rosenthal warmly wished him well and expressed the hope they would see him again. Essentially, they had left a vacancy open for Peter, but they also seemed vague on the details of his employment – including whether or how they would go about securing a work visa for him.

On returning home and talking it over with Karen, the magnitude of the leap they had been considering suddenly seemed more than a little daunting, and they agreed to shelve any major decisions for a time. Peter decided there had to be lucrative and interesting work to be done in Britain; he and David would just have to find a way of unearthing it.

Weeks and months passed, and then came the clincher: Broadcast Arts made the decision to relocate to New York. Washington, DC, had struck Peter as a liveable city, but this new development, as he recalls, 'changed the pace a bit. I couldn't picture my two young children in Manhattan, and by then Karen was pregnant with our third child. If BA had been more pushy and proactive, sorted out housing, day care, offered me more money and taken care of our visas, I think I'd have gone. But I got this sense ... It was a young staff, hardly anyone else in the company had kids. I just chickened out, I think.' In June 1983, he committed to remaining in Britain.

This was a stressful period of uncertainty for David who had to contemplate where his own future would lie without Peter. He even considered going to the National Film and Television School (NFTS) to study cinematography. He did go to India as a camera assistant with Nigel Ashcroft, a producer who made documentaries and also ran his company from the Production House: 'I felt if we weren't going to continue in the animation business, I'd better get some decent camera work under my belt.'

In the end, Broadcast Arts did not survive too long (it changed its name to Curious Pictures in 1993), though it produced *The Pee-wee Herman Show* three years later.

In retrospect, Peter had clearly made the right decision to stay in Britain. It was a timely one, too, for as it turned out, the world of advertising was beckoning Aardman from London.

* * *

Two significant things happened in the UK media world in the 1980s – and, as it turned out, Peter and David were in a position to capitalise on both. One was the boom in advertising, a phenomenon in keeping with the times. After the gloom of the '70s, a decade marked by economic anxiety and industrial unrest, it felt as though Britain had turned a corner in the '80s, with the 'Big Bang' freeing up the nation's financial sector in the City of London, and a prime minister in Margaret Thatcher who often invoked Britain's imperial greatness – and went to war over the Falklands. Comedian Harry Enfield's abrasive character summed it all up later in the decade with one word: 'Loadsamoney'. The country felt buoyant and optimistic. People wanted to buy things again, and the advertising industry was poised to help them do just that. Aardman could play its part, too.

The change that came first, however – one they hadn't seen coming – was the arrival of Channel 4, the new TV channel that significantly altered the face of British broadcasting. It was touted as a channel on which independent, challenging programming would find a home, and part of its remit included serving the interests of minority groups. Its aim was to provide a contrast and an extra choice for viewers beyond the two licence-funded 'public service' channels – BBC One and BBC Two – and the commercial channel ITV.

Some thirty-five years on, Channel 4 is part of a familiar

TV landscape in Britain, but in its earliest days it seemed brave, innovative – even revolutionary. There was a headiness about its approach, a sense that it would experiment with new forms of programming for which the other three channels were unlikely to find a suitable pigeonhole.

'I always think Channel 4's thing was being different,' says Peter. 'It had a brief to commission films for what were then considered minority groups. Happily for us, adult animation seemed to fall into that category. Channel 4 sparked an explosion of animation in Britain, and we found ourselves in the middle of it, in amazing company: Joanna Quinn, the Brothers Quay, Erica Russell, great talents pouring out of the colleges and out of the woodwork.'

Peter and David joined a group of other animators at a reception for the soon-to-be-launched Channel 4 at the Cambridge Animation Festival in September 1981. It was a stylish event, held in the rose garden of a grand Georgian house in Cambridge owned by Clive Sinclair, the brilliant consumer electronics inventor who devised the first affordable pocket calculator and the eccentric Sinclair C5 'electric tricycle'.

They were an impressive group. There was Bob Godfrey, who had won an Oscar for his short animation film *Great* about Isambard Kingdom Brunel, and who in the '70s presented *The Do-It-Yourself Animation Show*, a major inspiration for a teenager in Preston named Nick Park.

Andy Walker, after beating Peter and David to win a prize in Zagreb, went on to enjoy a long, successful career, which included animating five series of *The Story of Tracy Beaker*.

Derek Hayes made short films, commercials and music videos for TV, and worked as a consultant for Aardman in later years.

Back in 1981, all these animators could see that Channel 4, still a year away from launching, could be a viable outlet for their skills. But how to make the connection? The channel's formidable chief executive, Jeremy Isaacs, a major TV producer and documentary-maker for Thames, Granada and the BBC, was wandering among the guests. Isaacs was suave and faintly daunting; it needed one of the group to take a deep breath, break the ice and approach him. David, who probably came across as the most businesslike of the animators, was persuaded by the others to introduce himself.

Isaacs had no idea who David was, and nor was he aware of Aardman's work to date, yet he responded to David's observation that it was difficult in Britain to raise funding for animation that, though not necessarily commercially driven, was serious-minded, took risks and was targeted at adult audiences. Much of his argument ticked boxes for Isaacs; part of his remit was to be an alternative to Britain's existing TV channels. He asked David to send Channel 4 some ideas along with a 'show reel' of the work Aardman had already done.

Three months later, David and Peter found themselves sitting in a London office opposite Paul Madden, the new channel's first commissioning editor of animation. As David recalls: 'Our conversation wasn't really going anywhere, and then Jeremy Isaacs put his head round the door. He said he'd just seen *Down and Out,* was very impressed, and could

Channel 4 have ten more short films in that vein by the time the channel launched? The problem was, that was only nine months away. I voiced my doubts about completing ten, so Jeremy said: "OK, five now and five of something else later."' Nothing more needed to be said: Channel 4 wanted to be in business with Aardman Animations.

Clearly, it was the authentic, social-realist tone of *Down and Out* that had captured Isaacs' attention. Now it was incumbent on David and Peter to think up new places and situations for their eavesdropping, again with real people doing the talking who were unaware they were being recorded.

David himself favoured putting a mike on a door-to-door salesman; as a student he had spent a summer break knocking on doors and trying to sell Betterware household products. He had been surprised by the number of people, often elderly and usually lonely, who were all too willing to find solace by chatting away to a complete stranger about their lives.

He and Peter drew up a list of venues where they might strike conversational gold. Apart from the door-to-door salesman, they considered a hostel for young men on probation; a well-appointed retirement home; the editorial office of a local magazine; and a theatrical agency in Weston-super-Mare. They set about their task with relish. In the end they recorded at eight or nine different locations.

'The whole feel of Channel 4 was so exciting to be around,' Peter recalls. 'Suddenly, here was a commission to make adult animation! And all these people – not only in animation but in other areas of the arts too – who had been in hiding, waiting in the wings, suddenly came out into the open. It was very exciting. The channel's thinking was radical, and so was some of their programming. Sure, some of it was terrible, but still ...'

The icing on the cake came in the form of another agreeable aspect of their relationship with Channel 4: 'Realistic budgets!' says Peter with a sly smile. 'Most unlike our experience with the BBC at the time! And, famously, with Channel 4, you had their injunction [when work was being commissioned]: "Don't forget to put in your profit margin." Before that, we'd never even dreamed of such a thing! So the idea that there was a reminder to put it in was music to our ears! And it was very smart of them as they wanted to ensure we had the necessary cash to develop the next project for them.'

Peter now reflects that their first commission with Channel 4 'was effectively "Son of *Down and Out*". Out of everything we had done that we sent them, that was the admired film. So in the new series, *Conversation Pieces*, our aim was to recapture some of its raw energy. And it turned out to be very difficult. Although our filmmaking skills were mightily improved, it seemed impossible to find a soundtrack as compelling as the one we used for *Down and Out*. We discovered the hard way how difficult it was simply to walk round a corner with recording equipment and stumble on an intriguing conversation.'

David adds: 'We knew it was a hit-or-miss thing with documentary recording like this, and that it often needed substantial audio editing to achieve any kind of coherence in a piece. What it did teach us was that most real conversation is dull, mundane and insignificant!'

Peter reflects: 'People would often say: "Oh, I heard this riveting conversation on the bus the other day. It was hilarious. It was fascinating." But, of course, you're never on that bus. And if you were, the sound quality would be terrible, the people would be suspicious of you hanging a microphone over their shoulders, and it probably wasn't that hilarious in the first place. So, for a hundred reasons, it just doesn't work. God knows, we tried.'

It was Peter who thought up the idea that a theatrical agent's office could be fun: 'I think we were imagining something like [Woody Allen's film comedy] *Broadway Danny Rose* or something. And maybe in the days of music hall, someone would have come in with a singing dog act. We went to see such an agent, but it was a very low-key business. The bloke did all his work on the phone. No one ever came in, except when an assistant brought him a cup of tea, so there was literally nothing to animate.'

This difficult time, he says now, taught him a lesson about the surreptitious recording of conversations: 'It's fatal to speculate beforehand on the material you're going to record. You *never* get what you hope you'll get.'

The secret is to work with what you've got, and find the stories you don't expect. A typical example from the new series is *Late Edition*. It was set in the office of a listings magazine, a small local version of *Time Out* called *Out West*. It doesn't make any social point – there's none of that heft behind it. It's just a wry, dry observation of the way people work.

We recorded for a whole morning in that office, using only two mikes. But it was a long three hours where basically nothing happened; there was no substance, no resolution, nothing to hang a drama on. So our storytelling idea was to take one strand out of all the conversations, a strand that probably lasted only five minutes, and suggest that it was actually dragged out over fifteen hours, thus (rather unfairly) making it seem that the editorial team were hopelessly indecisive. They were working on an article that compared the plight of Chilean refugees in Bristol with what was going on in the war in the Falkland Islands. Having apparently debated this all day, night has fallen and the bloke who'd been working on the headline suddenly laughs out loud at the ludicrous comparison he's making.'

David says, 'We were late on delivering the first set of films, so they didn't make the launch of Channel 4 but were transmitted a year later in their first-year anniversary week, one a night across the week at 9 p.m., opposite the BBC news. The impact of this slot was quite dramatic!'

Despite the challenges of finding the ideal raw material for *Conversation Pieces*, Peter concedes 'The films were striking, and they were different and that led to an avalanche of opportunities'. Peter and David would once again be finding themselves in the right place at the right time.

* * *

'As soon as they were broadcast, there was a great flurry of interest from the world of advertising,' Peter recalls. 'We'd had just one approach from the ad world before that, based on the positive reaction to *Down and Out* in 1979. We met these two successful young 'creatives', as they were known in the advertising business, and we talked at some length about doing an ad for John Smith's lager for them. We were still gaining experience and didn't have the equipment or the skills really to take on a major commercial project that the time. We did some storyboarding and design – but never got the gig. I bet the people at the agency were scared off by our relative inexperience. Still, I remember the excitement of going to a London agency. It was clearly a hugely prosperous world. There were young people with Filofaxes at their desks, which was very cool back then. We knew this was a world we aspired to, but for now it was still out of our reach.'

The agency for whom those two young agents worked, Boase Massimi Pollitt (BMP), later gave Aardman regular work in creating commercials for them. BMP was a major, well-regarded agency; it famously had strong client relationships with both the Labour Party and the TUC.

In the wake of the Channel 4 films, which were broadcast in October 1983, Peter and David felt better prepared to work with the ad industry, which was by now already experiencing a boom. It was also alert to fresh talent: David remembers that 'our phone started ringing the day after the first transmission'.

'We never had any misgivings about doing ads,' Peter stresses. 'Pragmatically speaking, the Morph series, for all its success, seemed to be a dead end. No one was saying to us: "Let's have another twenty-six episodes." So, great though it had been, it had stopped. Then, of course, Channel 4 came along at exactly the right moment. There'd been some filling in with any job we could get for a time, but then after that chunk of work for Channel 4, with those five films finished, I don't think we had full order books. The only orders we had were more one-minute episodes of Morph for *Take Hart*. So, someone coming along, brandishing a cheque book and asking for commercials got a very warm welcome. At first, quite a lot of the commercials we did were at an advertising office right by Paddington,' Peter remembers, 'so there was the excitement of coming up to London from Bristol by train [as opposed to coach, which was cheaper]. And then, just 200 yards from Paddington station, entering this ridiculous, wonderful, dreamlike otherworld that was advertising.'

David and Peter routinely joked that London ad agency offices – sleek, smart and spacious – could boast larger toilets than Aardman's entire office space. David adds: 'Those films for Channel 4 were seen by people in the advertising industry, to whom our sort of work seemed to be new. And that was what led us into doing commercials. They were very lucrative, because there was a lot of money sloshing around advertising – and frankly we thought we'd be out of fashion quite quickly, chewed up and spat out. But we decided to make hay while the sun was shining and dived into advertising headfirst. As it turned out, it was a great opportunity for us. It gave us new knowledge, a lot of training and directing opportunities, and a chance to plough money back into the business, buy more gear and re-equip. One great thing about commercials? Your work is on-air every day. It became a drug. It was like people putting four-course meals in front of us. And what capped it all was, once we'd started doing that work, it continued onward at a steady rate.'

And so the commercials work began. One of Aardman's first efforts in this new field was a thirty-second ad commissioned by agents for the Kimberly-Clark corporation, a global brand that produced mostly paper-based health and hygiene products, including Kleenex, Andrex and Huggies. The ad was set in the boardroom of a small company in which a group of executives were contributing their ideas for cleaning products.

The people at Kimberly-Clark's London agency had clearly been impressed by the naturalistic dialogue of the Channel 4 films; one of them told David and Peter: 'We want that vox-pop thing you do so brilliantly.' He then produced a script that had been written for the ad – which seemed totally at odds with making the dialogue feel spontaneous and overheard, in fly-on-the-wall style.

The Aardman founders travelled to London to record the dialogue with the voiceover actors playing the executives. They read their lines off the page and delivered them in turn impeccably, like accomplished professional actors in a play. There was no overlapping each other's speech, no stumbling or repetition, and no hint of the rough-and-tumble of unrehearsed, natural conversation. It felt stilted – and a far cry from *On Probation* or *Late Edition*.

David ordered a ten-minute break, gathered up all the scripts and disposed of them. He then asked the actors to do the scene again, from memory. It worked; the dialogue felt more spontaneous and the desired result was achieved in just two more takes. It was much more like 'that vox-pop thing' they did. No one would be nominating the ad for any awards, but Aardman was making its presence felt, and taking its first tentative steps into a new line of work.

Some of the early ads by Aardman around this time proved to be both hugely inventive and big hits with the public. To accompany them, the agencies frequently used popular songs and adapted their lyrics, which routinely stuck in viewers' minds.

Thus, Jimmy Dean's 1960s hit 'Big Bad John' became 'Big Bad Dom' for the Domestos campaign, its ad featuring a character who magically evolved from a bottle of bleach and looked like a lawman from a cowboy movie. The featured song in the ad for Access credit cards was Louis Jordan's earthy 1944 hit 'Is You Is or Is You Ain't My Baby', the lyrics changed to 'Does You Do or Does You Don't Take Access'.

Millions of people in Britain today who recall those commercials still hum them without realising the company that shot those ingenious ads also brought them Wallace and Gromit, Shaun the Sheep and *Chicken Run* in later years.

The campaign for Lurpak butter had become hugely popular as a result of its use of the jaunty song 'Spread a Little Happiness', first written for a British musical comedy from 1929 but revived by Sting, who enjoyed a chart hit with it in 1982. Three years later, an agency approached Aardman with their concept of a little man made of butter, springing out of a crumpet singing, 'Spread a little creaminess'. This little man, later named Douglas, starred in Lurpak's commercials right through to the end of the century. Peter designed the character of Douglas and did much of the animation.

The major technical problem was to make Douglas look as though he was really made from butter: 'Plasticine was out of the question. It's too dull-looking,' says Peter Lord. 'So we experimented with all kinds of modelling materials and ended up using German beeswax. We spent a lot of time on getting him to look translucent and slightly shiny.'

In fact, the character of Douglas was a subtle tribute to Morph, who in his early years would famously emerge from Tony Hart's table fully formed. A group of younger creatives at the ad agency, Gold Greenlees Trott, had been Morph fans in their teens and wanted a Morph-inspired character for their Lurpak commercials. Interestingly, Douglas's face was designed by a youthful Nick Park, and bears a faint resemblance to his creation Wallace. The agency got two animation icons in one.

'We also did a commercial for Hamlet cigars,' Peter recalls. 'Remember "Happiness is a cigar called Hamlet"? And we did Scotch videotape with a skeleton saying 'Re-record, not fade away' over and over again. That was the voice of the actor Deryck Guyler.'

All these ventures were relatively straightforward compared to the attention to detail required for the most spectacular commercial produced by Aardman in this period – an ad for the innovative Enterprise 64 computer, which had been developed by a British company called Intelligent Software. It boasted a 64-kilobyte memory (a lot in those days!), and the advertising agency wanted to stress its modern, groundbreaking qualities with a commercial that compared it to other computers, which would now seem obsolete.

The Enterprise 64 production was another indication that the workload for Aardman was beyond Peter and David alone. Neither of them would boast that they were born salesmen or businessmen, and around this time they started taking on employees.

Peter and David had also just hired their first animator-employee, a young man named Richard Goleszowski, who had just graduated with a degree in Fine Art from Exeter College of Art and Design. He had specialised in animation, of course. Twenty-three years old, of Polish ancestry, he was smart, creative and intuitive. He had a sardonic sense of humour and talent to burn. In later years, he changed his name to Richard Starzak, though in Aardman circles, where he enjoys almost legendary status, he is universally known as 'Golly'. He seemed to fit in with the company ethic from the word go.

Golly played a crucial role in the look of the Enterprise 64 commercial. The ad agency had had the idea of representing older computers as skeletons. Golly sketched his version of a modern museum, sleek and abstract with black granite-style plinths, and inspired the idea of placing the old skeletal computers on the plinths in stark contrast to the Enterprise 64.

To the accompaniment of the old spiritual song 'Dem Bones', these ancient skeletal computers prance around the modern museum; one of them literally crumbles into dust. The voiceover emphasises the point: 'Some home computers are already obsolescent – their memory limited, their performance slow.'

And then came the punchline: 'The Enterprise 64 ... could be obsolescence, built out.' It very well could have been, but, in a savage twist of fate, the company behind the Enterprise 64 – which doubled its memory and became the Enterprise 128 – went broke around the time the commercial was first broadcast.

Still, that was no comment on the quality of Aardman's work, which was widely praised. It had been an incredibly complex commercial to shoot, requiring a twenty-strong crew – including (among others) a director of photography, a camera operator, focus puller, four modeller-puppeteers, a producer, floor manager and two set riggers, not to mention Pete, Dave – and Golly, who animated it. Aardman received £35,000 for it – an astronomical sum in those days. (Peter and David had submitted a budget of £15,000 to the agency, only to be gently told by the agency producer that it was not enough to produce the commercial. She revised it for them and more than doubled it.)

To put this amount in context, and to highlight the difference between the worlds of television and advertising, Peter and David had shot an entire series of *The Amazing Adventures of Morph* – twenty-six episodes totalling 130 minutes of film – for £60,000. Now they were receiving £35,000 for a thirty-second commercial. They shook their heads in bewilderment, but they couldn't deny they were rather pleased.

* * *

While it may initially have happened almost by accident, creating commercials has continued to be a significant part of Aardman's range of activities right up to the present day. Certainly, it helped that Peter not only liked the work it involved, but also found it pleasurable to be rubbing shoulders with a new industry with a glamorous veneer and a fast-paced work schedule – very different from Aardman's culture.

'I really enjoyed it,' he admits. 'To my surprise, I found I liked pitching for a job. I found my inner salesman. In those days, the ad agency would fax you a script, you'd look at it, work it out, do some drawings pretty informally – and then you'd go to London to meet the client at the advertising agency. And you'd sell the idea – you'd say the right thing, you'd schmooze. I loved that feeling – of winning the job, clinching the deal.'

David also found this work extraordinarily stimulating – and quite scary: 'Suddenly we found ourselves shooting on 35 mm (without any formal training) with the expectation of very high production standards. All very challenging.'

Peter recalls: 'The advertising world was fascinating, and so was the manner, the way people in it behaved. We grew up in the world of independent animation, and that was where I felt most at home. But here was another tribe, of which we were at least honorary members. I say "honorary" because it was such a London-centric business, and the fact that we lived in Bristol seemed bizarre to many of them.

We met a man called Dave Trott [a partner in Gold Greenlees Trott] when we first did the Lurpak commercials.

He was an impressive man, a kind of barrow-boy entre-preneur figure and an incredibly smart bloke. Once we got over being impressed, we became good friends. We ended up doing lots of jobs with his company, but we always met him in London. He was shocked at the very idea of coming to Bristol. So we never felt completely in that tribe, but it was fun. I enjoyed the whole thing. And then of course there was the money . . .'

Up to that point, Peter and David had made solid progress as the founders of Aardman, and each of them had managed to buy a house on the strength of what they had achieved. But, essentially, it had been an austerity career – neither man was making a fortune from it. Whereas the advertising world paid remarkably well.

'It's not surprising, really,' David reflects. 'There were now two commercial channels on British TV – ITV and Channel 4 – and they were both commanding large audiences, so there was the chance that any one commercial could poten-tially make a huge impact.'

'It's true,' Peter admits. 'I think Dave and I both now believe that the level of profitability and loot in advertising set us up – to buy equipment, employ who we wanted or needed and, later on, to make some films just off our own bat. We were able to fund them entirely ourselves, because we had the money lying around.'

Yet Peter and David, with their left-liberal upbringings, were not so voracious that they would work on any com-mercial just for monetary gain. They had to agree between themselves that the content and the message chimed with their own ideals, and more than once turned down the offer of producing commercials for products that didn't align with their values.

This was an era of hard work for them both, and David especially found himself handling a greater range of responsibilities. He and Peter already had a sense of their different skill sets, which basically came down to that old producer/director divide: generally, before they brought in a full-time producer, David would liaise with the ad agencies, supervise budgets and shoot the commercials, and Peter would storyboard the agencies' scripts, design the characters and animate. Both Peter and David directed commercials individually as more came their way.

Apart from anything else, it was sheer fun. 'In the '80s,' Peter recalls, 'advertising was a simpler business. The ad agencies really held the creative whip when it came to TV commercials. They could tell the client what would happen, and the client would just go along with it. Back then, there was very little in the way of formal research, whereas now every idea is researched to death. I don't think it's as much fun as it was.' To this day, however, commercials work remains a crucial part of Aardman's business.

It's entirely likely the two men were attracted by what they saw as a maverick quality in the best advertising agencies, which had the boldness to dream up and then create commercials with a certain edge and flair. Aardman itself was already a company similarly ploughing its own furrow.

4

NICK PARK

Early in 1985, Nick Park was living a spartan existence. At twenty-six years old, he found himself in a no-man's land between student life and part-time employment. He was broke, on the dole, and living in Cricklewood, north-west London, where he could barely afford the 60p Tube ticket to the centre of town.

'I felt poor,' he recalls. 'I finally got myself a really cheap bike just to get around. I could never afford to go to a restaurant. My parents up in Preston were worried about me. I'd call home once a week, but it was difficult to talk for very long – I barely had enough coins for the phone box. My dad would send me the occasional fifty quid, which he could ill-afford.'

Still, he wasn't as desperate as this brief outline of his circumstances might suggest. Nick had a mission to fulfil – a long-term film project he had embarked on that he was determined to see through to the end. If that involved living a hard life for a spell, then so be it – that was the choice he had made.

Since 1980, when he graduated from Sheffield Polytechnic, Nick had been a student at the National Film and Television School in Beaconsfield, Buckinghamshire. His tutors held him in high regard as a talented animator – one who had taken the unusual decision to work in stop-motion, using characters fashioned from Plasticine.

This was the medium he had chosen for his final-year project at the NFTS – a short animation film called *A Grand Day Out*. Its premise was delightfully whimsical, and revolved around Wallace, an eccentric, cheese-loving inventor, and his faithful, resourceful dog Gromit, all set in an unnamed northern town of England. In the story, Wallace runs out of cheese and so decides to build a rocket ship in the basement of his home that will be able to take both him and Gromit to the moon. After all, everyone knew the moon was made of cheese, and maybe together the pair would find some there.

Nick had been toying with these characters since his days in Sheffield, where he had sketched them in his notebooks. They had evolved gradually: originally, they were 'a cat and a bloke with a moustache'. Eventually the cat became a dog (with a mouth at first), the man's moustache was removed and he was given the job of inventor.

Nick had devised the story with Steve Rushton, a friend from art school: 'We sat down in a pub in Notting Hill Gate one night and began working on the script,' he recalls.

Despite all this, there was a big drawback: making the film was a painfully slow process, one that Nick had first embarked upon in 1982. He worked mostly alone; other NFTS students had their own projects to concentrate on, though they gave him some help with models, props, camera and even little bits of animation. Nick laboured for long hours, tweaking his two clay characters minutely by hand, frame by frame, to convey the slightest movement or even a change of facial expression.

Fortunately, he was not short of raw materials with which to model his characters. Shortly after he started his work at the NFTS, he wrote to Harbutt, a company near Bath, whose founder, William Harbutt, had invented non-drying clay back in 1897, and asked if he could have some clay for free in return for a mention in the credits of his film. 'They agreed, on the condition that I arranged for an enormous box of various colours of Plasticine to be collected,' he recalls. 'I used that same block for years.'

Still, the work was slow-going, and he had a problem: the NFTS would not allow students to graduate until they had finished their final-year project, which the school itself was funding. It was now early 1985, however, and well over four years had elapsed since Nick entered the school, so his three-year student grant had long run out. Worse, he had only completed a grand total of seven minutes of *A Grand Day Out* – rather less than a third of its eventual length. He passionately wanted to complete it, but it was arduous, lonely work in a small studio, and each day he was commuting 25 miles by bus from his tiny flat in Cricklewood to the film school.

'I remember thinking: *Where am I going? How am I ever going to finish my film?*' he says now. 'I was trying to cope with all this, but I knew I'd have to keep going.'

Yet, unbeknownst to him, Nick had already planted the seeds of his eventual salvation. Early in 1983, he had invited Peter Lord and David Sproxton to the NFTS to give a talk to students about animation.

At that stage in their careers, Peter and David regarded themselves simply as a Bristol-based animation company, landing steady work for the BBC (notably Morph), but largely unknown quantities in the wider world. Yet within Britain's small animation community, the two men were regarded with huge admiration. Nick had already met Peter Lord briefly at an event for animators and was very impressed by the fact that he was sporting a Morph lapel badge. 'I thought, *How cool is that?'* Nick recalls. 'You wear a lapel badge – and it's of a character you've created yourself!'

Peter and David accepted the invitation to travel to Beaconsfield to share their experiences with students. Afterwards, they inspected some of their work, and Nick showed them the early stages of his efforts on *A Grand Day Out*. Back then, there wasn't a lot to see; Nick had drawn storyboards, constructed the set of Wallace's basement, shot part of the rocket-building sequence – and that was about it. Yet both the Aardman bosses could see that the film potentially had great charm and originality. 'It was obvious Nick was good,' says Peter, 'but we little realised *how* good.'

After their departure, they invited him to Bristol for the next two summers, offering him a month of paid holiday work each time. While he was there, he shot occasional Morph sequences for *Take Hart*, and helped with a set of curious spin-off characters called the Tin Pots who lived on a shelf in Tony Hart's art studio. Early in 1985, Aardman was suddenly in great demand; Peter and David were starting to make commercials, and they found they had more work and more TV commissions than the two of them could realistically handle. They desperately needed new animators to join them, and they now offered Nick a salaried position; it would make him only their second animator-employee. Aardman was also in the midst of preparing an animated film called *Babylon* for Channel 4, which featured a large cast of characters. David reflects that this was the real reason for bringing Nick on board.

It seems astonishing in retrospect, but Nick turned their offer down – simply because *A Grand Day Out* remained unfinished. 'I kept resisting full-time work,' Nick remembers. 'I felt if I stopped making my film – and I was still only part of the way through it – I didn't know whether or when I'd ever finish it.'

They were at an impasse, which David broke by phoning Nick and suggesting an intriguing compromise: if he were to join Aardman as a full-time employee, the company would give him a dedicated space in the studio to continue and complete his work on *A Grand Day Out* whenever any spare time between commissions became available. They said, 'Bring your sets and models for *A Grand Day Out* and we'll help you finish it.'

It felt like an elegant solution – the equivalent of throwing Nick a lifebelt. 'It was a real godsend,' he reflects now. 'I couldn't believe it.' He had enough presence of mind to sound cool and collected on the phone as David outlined his offer, however. 'That's very interesting,' Nick told him. 'I'll certainly get back to you on that.' In his mind, of course, he already knew he would leap at the chance.

* * *

As with many artists, the precise nature of Nick Park's talent is directly linked to the place and time of his formative years. Preston, where he grew up, shaped him, his art and his sense of humour. In his childhood, much of it looked like the popular idea of a northern town, with cobbled streets lined by tiny houses. But Preston was already changing, and there was a population shift from the old centre to newer houses on the outskirts of town.

Another change was the decline of its traditional industries – cotton mills closed down and gave way to engineering and the manufacture of electrical goods. But 'proud Preston', as it is widely known, has a thriving arts and cultural scene, and can boast a remarkable number of listed buildings. Its legendary football club Preston North End were founder members of the Football League in 1888, and its champions in their first season.

Nick was also fortunate in that his adolescent years coincided with a boom in animation on British television. Between 1968 and 1974, popular shows in this vein included *The Clangers* and *Pogles' Wood* (created by Nick's heroes Oliver Postgate and Peter Firmin), as well as Bob Godfrey's *Roobarb*. Godfrey also hosted *The Do-It-Yourself Film Animation Show*, which lived up to its self-explanatory title and greatly

influenced Nick. He also revered the established animators like Terry Gilliam and Richard Williams, who would
make guest appearances on Godfrey's show to explain their
animating techniques. *Blue Peter*, the famed children's TV
series with an ethos of encouraging children to be creative
and make things, sometimes strayed into the field of animation too.

If the timing of Nick's childhood was fortunate for a
young animator, his luck held as he moved into adulthood.
His higher education had included an arts course at Sheffield
Polytechnic, followed by film school. By the time he finally
left the NFTS, animation in Britain had become a boom
industry on several fronts.

As we have seen, the UK's second commercial TV channel,
Channel 4, was launched in 1982, and its executives swiftly
latched onto animated content as a distinctive programming
source. Around that time, too, the advertising world seized
on animation as an amusing, effective medium for TV commercials. Across the Atlantic, the embryonic channel MTV
(launched in 1981) soon realised that pop videos featuring
groups lip-syncing their new hits had become tedious –
custom-made animated films to accompany three-minute
singles could be an entertaining departure.

Though all these elements were fortuitous in easing Nick
into his destined career path, his family was perhaps the
most crucial factor. Nick was the third of five Park children –
'the one in the middle', with two older brothers, a younger
sister and his youngest brother. 'I was always the quiet one,'
he says now, 'the one that didn't say much.' Instead, he simply

got on with things – which even from a very young age often meant drawing.

'My parents were quite aspirational people,' he recalls. 'They didn't fit in with what they were supposed to be. They weren't showy or anything – they just liked to do things in their own way.'

Both his parents were blessed with creative gifts. His mother, Celia, grew up in the cotton-mill area of Preston and left school at fourteen to work as a seamstress. 'She was exceptionally skilled at making clothes and would make wedding dresses for friends. She met my dad after the war. His name was Roger Park. Dad came from Penwortham, which is just outside Preston and therefore rather more sub-urban. He was a professional photographer who worked for a company of architects.' (Significantly, both David Sproxton's and Peter Lord's fathers were also photography enthusiasts and adept with a camera.)

The Parks acquired a TV set when Nick was three years old and, as he says now, 'It certainly worked for me! My mum knew the one thing that kept me happy was to sit me in my high chair and put the TV test card and music on! I also used to like *Watch with Mother*, especially when Rag, Tag and Bobtail were on. I remember thinking they were real creatures with squeaky voices and being intrigued by that.'

The family moved into a bungalow at Walmer Bridge, a village on the outskirts of Preston. 'It meant a giant mortgage for my parents, a lot for their low income back then,' Nick says, 'but they never grumbled because moving out of the town represented a new era for them – and the chance of a positive future.'

Roger Park's passions included photography and also woodwork: 'He would always be creating useful things for around the home,' as Nick recalls. Together with Celia, he converted the house's loft into another bedroom.

Celia, meanwhile, had given up being a seamstress when she started a family, but worked from home creating clothes for friends and family as favours. It sometimes seemed to Nick that in this craft-oriented family, everything in their house was handmade – especially clothes and furniture.

'We four boys were often in the same outfits,' he recalls. 'Mum would find some suitable unique material, so we'd always be dressed the same. She'd make clothes for all of us in various sizes, so you'd then grow up through all those clothes. You lived on hand-me-downs, really. It's as if we'd all swapped clothes one day. There was a definite mentality in my family, which is still there to an extent: "Don't buy anything new if you can make it."'

Nick now admits he had mixed feelings about this at the time – some of his homemade clothes, notably his school blazer, though beautifully made, looked different from those of all the other pupils: 'I longed to be like other people and probably failed to appreciate these things when I was young. Part of me just wanted to fit in.'

Of course, for a young man heading for a career in hand-crafted animation, creating his own characters and sets, this was an unimprovable work ethic around which to grow up.

For years, the Park family went on camping

holidays – though well away from crowded campsites. Then, for several years running, they stayed in a cottage and camped on some farmland in Wales.

Nick now attributes his love of nature to these holidays: 'There we were, in the middle of north Wales, with our own field, having all that experience of the sheepdogs and other animals. It was such a wonderful part of childhood – living out in the wilds and waking up with nature every day.'

Reaching their holiday destination often proved to be an adventure in itself. They would set out from Preston usually unsure if they would reach Wales that same day; they never knew if the family car would survive the journey.

Roger finally graduated from his Ford Popular to a succession of Land Rovers; he bought three, one right after the other. 'We just loved them,' Nick says. 'We could get all the kids in the back and load everything on top. Going on holiday was a bit like going on safari. We certainly weren't your typical family. I remember a friend at school saying we looked like the Beverly Hillbillies.'

When he was around ten, he started borrowing his mother's Standard 8 mm camera; his father had bought it for her and she would lend it to Nick. It had a surprising feature – a stop-motion button that said 'animation'. Roger showed him how the button could be used to shoot frame by frame – a basic principle of animation. After that, Nick started creating his own primitive movies in the attic.

He started making flip-books, and then moved on to animation. His first film was a two-minute short about a character named Walter the Rat; he relied on how-to books from the library to guide him. By this time, he was also experimenting with filming little clay characters.

Though he was a daydreamer at school, he found English and art lessons inspiring. He also discovered that he loved making up and writing stories.

'One day, my homework was to write a story about life as a caveman. In it, I had a pet brontosaurus named "Aarrgh". I got the name from the *Beano* comic, as I loved all those crazy sound effects. The story was ridiculous, but while the teacher was reading it out to the class, she started to cry with laughter. That was the first time I realised I was able to make people laugh through my work. In fact, it was a very *Beano*-like story. I was hugely influenced by *The Beano*. My dream job was to work for it. And that was another way I became interested in storytelling, because I then started to want to become a cartoonist. I liked to draw my own characters. I was very much inspired by comics. Sometimes I'd copy out a whole comic, just to see if I could do it. Or I'd make up a comic character. By the time I was ten, I was drawing cartoons prolifically – filling up sketchbooks and notebooks.'

It helped that both his parents, as we've seen, were creative types who relished making things. Roger was also an inveterate tinkerer; arguably his greatest triumph was building, along with Celia, a small caravan that used to be hooked up to the family car when the Parks took camping holidays. Nick describes it as 'a living room on wheels'; it had wallpapered interior walls and wooden furniture bolted to its floor. In later years, it occurred to Nick that the caravan's interior might have inspired the look of Wallace's living room.

Both Roger and Celia were supportive of his endeavours. When Nick was only thirteen, he started to make puppets for animation, using his mother's cotton bobbins and offcuts from her scrap box.

The boy liked the idea of performance and entertainment, and in his teens he had a few stints operating the spotlight at live shows at Preston's Guild Hall. (He recalls shining the light on such stars as Frankie Vaughan and Demis Roussos, among others.) When Nick was fifteen, he entered a BBC young animators' competition themed for Architectural Heritage Year (1975) with a short film he had devised called *Archie's Concrete Nightmare* (Archie was a castle that over the centuries was surrounded by increasingly ugly modern architecture). The film didn't win, but a clip of it was shown on BBC Two. He vividly recalls seeing it on TV, the announcer introducing it as 'by Nicholas Park of Preston'.

Nick's parents supported the idea of their children making a living from creative endeavours, and urged Nick to apply for a foundation art course that included two A-levels in art. 'It was the best advice I ever had,' Nick recalls. 'It finally made me see that I could do this for a living.' Then, at the age of eighteen, he went on to Sheffield Polytechnic (now Sheffield Hallam University) to study communications arts.

At that early stage, he never really believed there was a career in animation films, but he enjoyed the learning experience and drew little ideas for characters in a notebook that he took everywhere with him.

With a fellow student he had dreamed up an idea for a

possible children's book, featuring a cat named Gromit and Jerry the postman who, it later became clear, bore some resemblance to an eccentric cheese enthusiast who went by the name of Wallace.

Nothing ever came of the children's book, but Nick's course was already set.

* * *

'When I invited Pete and Dave to the film school,' Nick recalls, 'they happened to see what I was doing, the early tests on *A Grand Day Out*, and they asked me to work for them for a month in the summers of 1983 and 1984. I was desperate for the money, but I think they were trying to get me on board because there weren't many other clay animators around at this time to choose from. It was coincidental, there weren't many people you'd ever heard of. There were puppet animators and stop-motion animators, but there weren't many clay animators. So we were like kindred spirits in a large world. I felt thrilled and honoured to be asked, because I already knew Aardman was a company where I'd love to work, the place in the animation world I admired the most. They seemed inspiring and creatively interesting. And that's what I was looking to be part of: doing interesting, cutting-edge projects. I regarded Peter and David as the Frank Oz and Jim Henson [Muppets creators] of animation.'

Nick knew all about Aardman even back in the days when he was a student at Sheffield Polytechnic. And he wasn't the only Aardman fan in his family: around that time, Roger

Park had seen *Animated Conversations* on TV and was hugely impressed by the innovative device of putting the recorded speech of ordinary people into the mouths of animated clay characters. Nick recalls Roger telling him: 'You've got to see this! It's right up your street.'

At the time of his two month-long summer stints, Aardman was just starting to hire full-time employees. 'There were five people there when I came for my second stint,' Nick recalls.

He finally joined Aardman as a salaried employee in February 1985. By this point it was outgrowing its past as 'a small shoebox of a company', as Nick puts it, and, rather than sharing a building with other creative companies, was moving for the first time into its own studio/workshop space behind Bristol University students' union. If it wasn't quite booming yet, Aardman was in huge demand. 'It cost us about £35,000 to adapt it to a studio, but we certainly felt confident enough to take on this building,' David recalls. 'One of the key reasons to move was to make the Channel 4 film *Babylon*, which was pretty big in our terms. And, of course, the increasing demand for commercials.

'They were just moving in when I arrived. It was all just starting to happen for them,' Nick remembers. Peter and David were pleased he had accepted their offer and told him to bring the sets for *A Grand Day Out* with him. Now they had a new, larger studio, he could even have his own space for it.

Initially, the other new animator, Richard 'Golly' Goleszowski, put Nick up in his flat. He was generally made to feel welcome at Aardman – and, as promised, *A Grand*

Day Out had its own little area: in a curtained-off part of the studio in a corner next to the editing room.

He quickly struck up a rapport with both his two bosses: 'Peter and David always looked after the company as a whole, nurturing new talent. They're very different people. Peter is a great animator; Dave has a theatre background – he's interested in drama and theatre lighting, and he's more into the technical aspects: the cameras, the look of a film. They overlap, but they're quite different. They both contribute greatly on script, story and structure, and both of them have analytical minds.'

As bosses, Nick adds, 'they mesh together. They challenge everything in a good way – shepherding and nurturing. They don't pull punches – but they both understand the process.'

Still, as it happened, there was little time for Nick to keep moving forward on his labour of love: '*A Grand Day Out* sat there in that corner for a year. There was always something more important to be a part of when I first arrived. Sometimes I even worked weekends just so I could get back to *A Grand Day Out*. But it was a part-time thing, and there were times when I didn't work on it at all. I was mostly being pulled onto projects where they needed extra animators, so I didn't get around to my film for quite a while. Back then, I was just one of the assistants. No one knew me.'

It was an exciting time at Aardman in the mid-'80s. Peter and David were gaining a reputation as 'the guys who did clay' and were hugely sought-after by advertising agencies. And it gradually became apparent to Nick that his bosses appreciated his work, as they included him in several joint projects. He could not have known it at this point, but his work over the next three years would establish Aardman as a nationally known company – and make him a household name.

5

MOVING ON UP

February 1985 was a key month in Aardman's history. Not only had the company relocated – yet again – to a new headquarters, but, on the very day they moved in, Nick Park, having done two summer stints, began his first day as a full-time employee.

Aardman had previously occupied a smaller space in a building called the Production House, up on Bristol's St Michael's Hill. 'Basically it was a tiny studio and a little office,' Golly recalls. He and Nick had been assistants and had both helped with animating Morph.

The new home, 14 Wetherell Place, was considerably larger – a converted Victorian-era warehouse situated in Clifton. 'It was our first planned and designed studio and we loved every inch of it,' David recalls. 'It looked exactly as I'd imagined a studio-workshop to be.' The new headquarters totalled 2,000 sqft, and it felt unthinkably spacious compared to its predecessors.

Partly, this was because Aardman still comprised only a handful of people. Apart from David and Peter, there were now three full-timers: Golly, producer Sara Mullock and Nick. But on most days several freelancers were around too, including model-makers, puppet-makers, cameramen and electricians. 'We had a great creative atmosphere,' David recalls.

Golly had been at Aardman for just over a year, and was delighted to be on board: 'I'd tried to get animation work in London and Manchester, but hadn't done very well,' he remembers. 'And people said: "You must visit Bristol, they make Morph there." I'd started to make a short stop-frame film in a studio space about a little guy watching his TV and getting sucked into it. I stayed with friends, and I really liked the city. I didn't know it, but a photographer friend of mine knew Pete and Dave and told them about me. So they came in to see what I was doing.

At the time, I was running out of money, so I'd left Bristol for a spell and taken a job in a factory just to earn some more. But Pete and Dave said: "Come and help us make sets." Apparently, they liked my set-building. I remember doing a bit of a fist punch – "Yesssss! I was going to get some work!" – but I really didn't think it was a career. I thought it would be temporary. Basically it was just Pete and Dave. They'd literally just finished doing Morph for TV, and they had a commission for some short films. I came in on the tail-end of it, but I helped build some sets and paint some things up. After they'd given me some work, I thought: *I must learn more about this.* I said to Pete: "I'd love to animate Morph." He said: "Have you done much clay animation?" I said: "No, none at all." I could see his worried look, but I watched how he animated and how things worked, so after a few months I got to do a piece of animation myself.'

As it happened, Golly's timing was good; he was in the right place at the right time: 'I was really lucky, because just as I was working on this, Channel 4 started up, and Jeremy Isaacs visited. I've got a funny little mental picture of him coming in [to Wetherell Place] wearing a camel-hair coat and saying: "Go on, make us some films!" He actually said to Pete and Dave: "I want you to make some films for Channel 4." They did, and on the back of those five short films, all this commercials work poured in. So many commercials! We had this fax machine, and literally every couple of hours there'd be a pile of incoming faxes on the floor. We'd have to sort through job offers. People were desperate to use us. The budgets were enormous, of course, because TV viewing figures were a lot less spread in those days. Commercials were far bigger in the '80s than they are now. I think Pete and Dave started to make money quickly. Nick came as a full-timer the year after me. Looking back, I was fortunate to join when I did. Had I joined four years later, I'd have struggled a bit, because I didn't have any specialist skill. At first, I thought the company changed rather slowly, but then there were more of us, and a lot of freelancers, so it felt very different between day one and two or three years later. And it was very exciting. It suddenly seemed like this could be a career, rather than something fun to do for a while until I found a "proper" job.'

Golly is a candid character, even when it comes to discussing his feelings about Aardman: 'I suppose it's like family,' he says, smiling, 'sometimes it's great and sometimes it can be frustrating! But all my most interesting work has been at Aardman. There have been spells when I was freelance, and I got a lot of projects, but none of them was as much fun as the work I've had here.'

His overall view of the company is overwhelmingly positive: 'I think the great thing about Aardman was they always seemed to be progressing. We learnt how to do things in animation, all the techniques – model-making, set-building, lighting. Everything was more or less created internally. There wasn't any frame of reference, anyone to go to to say: "How do you make a stop-frame animation company function?" It was right from the details of "How do you build a puppet?" to what the company's structure was. It was all self-generating.'

The truth was, as Golly rightly notes, there seemed to be no one else to go to, even though there were two other animation companies in Bristol. These were the Bolex Brothers (Bolex being the name of a 16 mm camera once widely favoured by animators), who had made a sixty-minute feature, *The Secret Adventures of Tom Thumb,* and CMTB, creators of TV's *The Trap Door* series, about a bunch of monsters who inhabit a castle.

'We're all stop-frame,' Golly observes, 'which I thought was extraordinary. That meant there were probably more stop-frame companies in Bristol than in any city in the world. One guy from the Bolex Brothers swore it was because we were living on a ley line! But, the fact is, we didn't mix with them very much in the early days. Over the years there was a lot more cross-fertilisation, but for two or three years I knew these other companies existed, yet I didn't know what they did or where they were. It was as if everyone was in their own little bubble, working out ways to do things – make films and run a business – making it up as they went along.'

Indeed, in the mid-1980s, there was enough creativity within Wetherell Place that Aardman's team had no need to seek out other companies for inspiration. Peter and David were doing plenty to remind the world they were first-rate creators of animated film. And their new animator-recruits, Golly and Nick, were settling in brilliantly, working on a variety of projects and learning enthusiastically as they proceeded. In its new headquarters, Aardman was upping its game.

The range of work being undertaken in this era was dazzlingly diverse – and some of it somewhat startling. Into this latter category would be the film *Babylon*, a thirteen-minute short devised and written by filmmaker David Hopkins. He had written a whole series of stories around the theme of the threat of nuclear holocaust which would become part of a Channel 4 series called *Sweet Disaster.*

It was easily the most large-scale project Peter and David had ever undertaken as directors, and it featured some fifty different characters, all of whom had to be separately animated – a gargantuan task. Most of them are guests at a sinister black-tie dinner for prosperous arms dealers, addressed by their president, who advocates 'peace and profit', gloats about the success of the arms trade, rails against the 'communists' who oppose it, and crows: 'Anyone here who does not believe in profit? We are the real humanitarians.' (The president was voiced by Tony Robinson, who played Baldrick in TV's *Blackadder.*)

But, as his speech progresses, it's clear that something is going wrong. His voice falters, the chandelier in the room starts to shake violently, and one of the guests – a heavy-set man – seems to be growing ever larger as he apparently feeds off the speaker's rhetoric. In the end, this man literally explodes; his white dress shirt flies open, and vast quantities of blood and innards cascade from it, fatally deluging his audience. It's a shocking sequence.

The fatal explosion was shot in live action, and was itself quite shocking. A dustbin-load of imitation offal was tipped through the villain's chest cavity, and the entire studio was splattered with an unholy mix of jelly, food dye, noodles and assorted plastic armaments; the clear-up took several days.

Babylon was not widely seen by the public, but within the industry it burnished Aardman's reputation as an animation studio of great versatility – one more than capable of undertaking bigger, more complex work. (David has pointed out that the size of the *Babylon* project was a major reason Nick was hired in 1985.) It was also invaluable experience for Nick and Golly, who were already on a steep learning curve, though always handling whatever challenges were thrown at them.

* * *

One of the striking innovations in pop culture in the early 1980s was the rise and rise of the music video. Singers and groups had appeared in short films to accompany the release of a record before then but, more often than not, they simply mimed to the lyrics. Not surprisingly, many of these efforts tended to be lame and unadventurous. The landscape was to change radically in 1981, however, with the launch of MTV, a US television channel devoted to pop videos.

MTV was successful right from the outset, and there were enough videos around to fill its programming. Record companies, observing the success of the channel, soon came to see that videos, once regarded as cheap marketing devices, could become a new form of artistic endeavour, as well as a statement by the singers or groups involved.

It didn't hurt that there was a generation of young filmmakers who saw videos as a potential means to further their careers. Even successful Hollywood directors had got in on the act, notably John Landis, who made Michael Jackson's wildly successful video for 'Thriller'.

At Virgin Records in London, an executive named Tessa Watts was in charge of commissioning music videos of the label's artists. She had had several successes in this field, notably with the Human League's 'Don't You Want Me'.

In 1986, Peter Gabriel joined Virgin and released a new album titled *So*. Formerly lead singer with Genesis, he had left the group a decade previously and had bounced around a few other record companies; he was held in high regard without ever enjoying phenomenal success.

Tessa Watts, however, became captivated by a track on

So called 'Sledgehammer'. It was driving, memorable and heavily soul-influenced, with discreetly raunchy lyrics. She knew several accomplished video directors, and approached Stephen R. Johnson, an American who had made the award-winning video for Talking Heads' single 'Road to Nowhere' the previous year.

The 'Sledgehammer' video was to be shot in the UK, and in March 1986 a call came in from a production company called Limelight, sounding out Aardman's interest in the project. Some days later, Steve Johnson, Peter Gabriel and two Limelight executives visited Wetherell Place; they wanted to let Peter and David hear 'Sledgehammer' and show them a provisional storyboard of the proposed video.

Peter's rather esoteric tastes in popular music meant that somehow he'd remained totally ignorant of the career and music of Peter Gabriel. David had to fill him in before the guests arrived: 'Used to be lead singer of Genesis?' 'Oh,' Peter responded, vaguely.

The storyboard they were shown was quite crude, with ideas scribbled all over it. It was crammed with a dizzying multiplicity of arresting images that would disappear from the screen as swiftly as they had arrived. Initially Peter Gabriel would be seen lip-syncing the lyrics with a winning smile, but his image would be pixilated. And then objects would appear in camera at the same point Peter name-checked them in the song – bumper cars, a steam train (which circles his head) and a big dipper. At this time, sophisticated video editing was developing very fast. Many of the effects that appeared in the final film could easily have been cheated by being shot in different layers and then assembled seamlessly. But that wasn't in Steve Johnson's mind at all. He wanted it to be hand-made and real, and he supplied the Aardman team with an interesting brief: he told them that he wanted the video to look 'like a fourteen-year-old had made it in their attic'. As Peter observes, 'Technically, most of the animation in *Sledgehammer* could have been shot in about 1910.'

There would be so much happening visually in the short duration of the video, it looked like a mammoth task. And there was another problem: the single of 'Sledgehammer' was set for release only a few weeks hence, at the end of April. To get this animated, complex, partially pixilated video completed to meet this schedule, they would have just six days of shooting time.

The word 'days' conjures up the notion of nine-to-five shifts, but that was far from the case. As it turned out, the crew worked until midnight for the first five days, and until 4 a.m. on the last shooting day, before it finally wrapped.

It was exhausting for everyone, especially for Peter Gabriel, who turned out to be quite the opposite of a spoiled, bratty pop star. He was thirty-six years old when the video for 'Sledgehammer' was shot, and he remained patient and helpful throughout. He turned out to be a man with an inquisitive interest in the artistic process, too.

It was not easy for him. At one point in the video, Peter's head seemed to be encased in a lump of ice, which was then smashed, revealing him beneath it. In the course of the shoot, he had to spend a total of sixteen hours lying under a sheet of glass. Then, to achieve the sequence in which a blue sky with clouds would pass across his face, which would itself also turn blue, he had to be daubed in blue paint, which irritated his skin.

The 'Sledgehammer' video was an exciting, stimulating, sometimes nerve-racking time for everyone concerned – and an invaluable learning experience for Nick and Golly, still relatively speaking Aardman's 'new boys'.

Nick drew the short straw and had the challenge of working with the two infamous 'dancing chickens' that appear in the video: you see an egg on what looks like the stage of a theatre in front of a red curtain, then the egg is cracked. One of the chickens – dead, plucked, but as yet uncooked – goes into a dance routine on stage, and is then joined by another, whereupon they do a high-kicking dance in unison. Nick – an apparently shy man who can be a ham actor when the occasion calls – worked out the chickens' routine by going through a few dance moves himself between takes. David reports that Nick did a great job, 'but didn't enjoy having to work with the real chickens at all. He wore rubber gloves, a white paper suit and had a fan blowing away from him – he was worried about getting some horrible disease as the flesh of the chickens began to go off.'

The talent in Wetherell Place that particular week was not all Aardman's. Steve Johnson had invited the Brothers Quay, identical American twins based in England who were well-respected avant-garde animators, to join the crew – and they animated a stop-motion sequence involving vegetables and fish. The perfectionist twins were reportedly dissatisfied with their endeavours, but no one else had any problems with them.

Everyone's efforts paid off handsomely. *Sledgehammer* became the most-played video in MTV's history, and it swept the following year's MTV video awards, winning nine – the most awards a single video has ever won. And the video did no harm to the sales of the single, either – it topped the US charts and climbed to the number-four spot in the UK.

All in all, not a bad week's work.

* * *

Aardman was going from strength to strength, and it wasn't as if things went quiet after the frenetic activity of *Sledgehammer* and the gratifying reaction to it.

Within a few weeks, another juicy offer came in, ironically from Broadcast Arts, the American animation firm Peter had for a while considered joining. Though he had decided against it, they had gone their separate ways on good terms, and now the Americans thought of Peter as they worked out how best to handle a new job.

Broadcast Arts had been asked to produce a new children's TV series for America's CBS TV network, which was to be broadcast on Saturday mornings. *Pee-wee's Playhouse* was a direct descendant of the successful comedy film *Pee-wee's Big Adventure* the previous year. Its star was actor Paul Reubens, who had originally developed the character of Pee-wee Herman for a stage show five years previously. Pee-wee was an enthusiastic, childlike, slightly camp but innocent figure in a too-tight suit, with a playful, slyly amusing line in patter.

It was fast-paced and garishly coloured – and Pee-wee took time to preach the values of kindness and tolerance to kids. The show was equally popular with the watching parents, who almost certainly saw in it echoes of old children's TV shows from their own childhoods.

The show required a large number of animators to create the animated inserts for the thirteen episodes of its first season – which was where Aardman came in. Its first episode was scheduled for broadcast in September, just four months away, so a decision was needed swiftly. Peter and David felt the Broadcast Arts offer was more than worthwhile, so they took a radical step and agreed to effectively empty Wetherell Place of all its animators – shipping themselves, Golly and Nick to Manhattan for four whole months – with producer Sara Mullock holding the fort alone. *Pee-wee's Big Adventure*? It felt more like *Aardman's Big Adventure* to the team ...

David and Peter went out to New York first and stayed in an artist's loft apartment on fashionable Lafayette Street in Lower Manhattan. Nick and Golly were initially not so lucky. They were booked into a grim, run-down hotel in Washington Square, back then a notorious haven for drug-dealing. This was the dark underbelly of New York City, and they were soon sprung out of there and moved into a marginally safer apartment a little further uptown.

Shooting took place at the Broadcast Arts studio on Broadway, in the old garment district. It was a hive of fast-moving industry, with brusque American staffers talking loudly and clearly getting the work done efficiently.

Aardman's role in all this became clear after talking with Reubens. They helped him create a little six-year-old-girl character named Penny (she had pennies for eyes), who was made out of clay. The Bristol contingent's task was to animate her adventures.

It didn't seem like much of a challenge, and they were slightly underwhelmed by it. Then, after two weeks, Steve Johnson, who had directed the 'Sledgehammer' video, turned up; he was to be the new director of *Pee-wee's Playhouse*. The Broadcast Arts crowd were less than thrilled by Steve's arrival, but the Aardman quartet felt on surer ground after their *Sledgehammer* experience – especially when Steve, who knew their strengths, advised them to rethink Penny. Instead of animating short scripted stories, he suggested going back to Aardman's roots and deriving Penny's adventures from real, spontaneous recordings. This was a return to the technique and the spirit of *Animated Conversations*, and a natural fit for the Aardman team.

Accordingly, a handful of bright, sparky girls of Penny's age were placed before a mike as they talked about anything and everything in their lives that came into their heads – all for lip-sync purposes. Nick designed Penny's face and gave her blonde pigtails that stuck horizontally out of her head. To the amusement of the Aardman contingent, she looked a little like a young, female version of Wallace, mainly because she had a large, wide mouth. Peter, David and Golly teasingly gave her the nickname Walleena, and suggested she

112

was Wallace's young cousin. For all that, Penny was popular with young audiences, and though the British contingent only stayed to animate the show for that first season, she remained a feature of *Pee-wee's Playhouse* until the show ended in 1990.

Of the Aardman quartet, only Peter, with his three children, was a father, which made his long stay in New York doubly difficult. He had agreed with Karen that he would alternate between four weeks in America, then four weeks at home.

At weekends, the other three would roam the city, often separately. Nick gravitated to outdoor spaces, including Central Park, and marvelled at the abundance of nature in this huge metropolis; Golly (who swears he trod on Andy Warhol's toes at a flea market) wandered through its maze of streets and alleyways, coming across markets and various small specialist shops; while David sought out music in obscure record stores and jazz clubs.

He recalls hearing 'Sledgehammer' in Manhattan's huge, brand-new Tower Records store, while watching Aardman's video on massive TV screens as it played. Without doubt, it was the coolest record of that summer; one night, in a bar with some Broadcast Arts people, they asked David what his previous gig had been. He pointed at the bar's TV screen, which happened to be playing 'Sledgehammer', and said: 'That!' – which immediately made him the most popular guy in the bar. Everyone wanted to buy him a drink and have him relate his experiences of Peter Gabriel. 'A nice feeling,' he says now.

* * *

The team were reunited that autumn back in Wetherell Place to find that precisely no one had forgotten about Aardman during their absence. There were commercials to be shot, though the main item of business was to make five more short films for Channel 4; it had been three years since the first batch of five that had gone under the title *Conversation Pieces.*

Because the pool of talent had now grown, Peter and David took the decision to give everyone a chance to direct. Alongside Nick and Golly, the team was joined by Barry Purves, who had previously been an animator/director at Cosgrove Hall in Manchester. All three were given the opportunity to develop a short film under the series title *Lip Sync.* Originally it was intended that all five films would use real recorded soundtracks, in the manner of *Conversation Pieces*, but corralling all the artistic talents proved to be a challenge. In the end, Peter directed two films himself, both based on interviews. One was *War Story*, in which an eighty-year-old Bristol man, Bill Perry, recounted his memories of the Second World War and especially the blitzing of Bristol. The other was *Going Equipped*, a poignant piece of social realism in the vein of Aardman's earlier *Down and Out*. A young repeat offender talked very movingly about life inside and outside prison, based on a real-life taped interview. Its title is a legal phrase, which means carrying tools that are useful in committing a break-in or burglary.

Golly worked on *Ident*, a rather dark little tale about human identity. It features a colourless man living in a colourless house. He dons different masks when confronted by different social situations – but who is he really? The one splash of colour in all this is the man's dog, who would appear later on in Golly's work in his own series, *Rex the Runt*.

Barry Purves's contribution was *Next*, an animation tour-de-force in which an animated William Shakespeare auditions on stage for a bored theatre director, acting out and miming each play he has written, each in a few seconds, with multiple props. Barry, in particular, heroically resisted the limits of the *Lip Sync* title. *Next* is almost entirely in mime with a grand total of seven spoken words.

And that fifth film in this series? Nick's *Creature Comforts*.

Of the five, this was the one that got people talking: a stunningly original, moving piece in which animated zoo animals bemoan their lot and confess they sometimes feel depressed, bored, or cold in the British climate. Nick recorded the voices of ordinary people in Bristol with help from a journalist friend – some from old people's homes, some off the street or in a corner shop – and asked them to talk about their own lives and living conditions. He then synced their comments to the mouths of clay animals in a zoo, giving them subtle body language with his animation to underline what they were saying.

The biggest hits were a family of polar bears – two parents and their talkative young son – and a jaguar from South America, voiced by a Brazilian student living in Bristol. Straddling a section of tree trunk, the jaguar gesticulates eloquently, while bemoaning the cold weather in Britain and the lack of 'space' – a word he repeats frequently in his distinctive accent, making it sound almost like 'spice'. 'We needs space to live,' he insists, 'to feel we are part of the world – and not like objects in a box.'

'*Creature Comforts* got all the limelight,' Nick reflects. '*A Grand Day Out* got finished around the same time. It was enjoyed, but it was completely overshadowed by *Creature Comforts*, which made a much bigger splash. Even though *A Grand Day Out* eventually won the BAFTA, I was being nominated for both films at that point, and it was *Creature Comforts* that seemed to get all the attention. Channel 4 had bought *A Grand Day Out* from the National Film School – but still it was *Creature Comforts* that everyone was talking about.'

It's certainly true that Nick had felt frustrated by his inability to finish *A Grand Day Out*; other Aardman projects had deadlines which *A Grand Day Out* didn't. And it was equally true that *Creature Comforts* was grabbing everyone else's attention; on seeing the rushes for the first time, even the normally sanguine David Sproxton blurted out: 'That's fantastic!' David recalls now: 'Everyone in the cutting room felt the same.' The praise was welcome, but it almost made Nick feel that *A Grand Day Out*, for which he harboured almost protective feelings, was being overlooked.

Yet Golly offers a more measured viewpoint. He has great admiration for his colleague, and credits Nick with 'bringing a completely different feel to stop-frame animation. Suddenly a film could be comedic, or it might be like film noir. Then again, it could have the same tension and drama

116

as a live-action film. And I think that turned everyone's head, really. When Nick made *Creature Comforts*, he changed something. It sounds pretty obvious now, but Pete and Dave had already made seven vox-pop films, for which they had already recorded people's voices. But those films were always recreations of what had happened – or they were close to what the vox pops had been about. And then Nick came along – he interviewed people and put their words into the mouths of animals. When you do that, it has a power and energy to it. Nick created a completely different beast from the short films Pete and Dave had made. And once he had done that, it seemed obvious: of course you can take some amazing sound recording and subvert it by putting it somewhere else. But when it was first done, and you saw it, it was like, "Wow!" It's also the case that Nick's a very good animator, so you could really believe the animals were thinking as well as talking. He made sure of that.' It was David who suggested to Nick that he try recording ordinary people, then putting their words into the animals' mouths.

A Grand Day Out and all the *Lip Sync* films, including *Creature Comforts*, received their first public screening in November 1989 at the Bristol Animation Festival, and were received enthusiastically. The festival was an important event for Nick, who was finally seeing his work watched by an audience.

In the case of *A Grand Day Out*, this moment had been more than seven years coming, from the time he first began his work on the film. 'I'd always had this vision for it,' he says, a little ruefully. And, as for *Creature Comforts*, the experience

helped him realise that his five-minute film was a spectacular hit. Aside from *Archie's Concrete Nightmare*, the little
amateur film he had made as a fifteen-year-old schoolboy
which had been shown on BBC television, this was his first
taste of public recognition.

Even after the audience applause died down, there was
more to come. The guest of honour at the Animation Festival
that year was the legendary Ray Harryhausen, whose
ground-breaking animated films such as *Mysterious Island*
and *One Million Years B.C.* had made him one of Nick's
childhood heroes. Harryhausen approached Nick after
the screening and told him: 'I've never seen claymation so
smooth!' His praise, Nick would say later, 'was beyond my
wildest dreams'.

The acclaim didn't stop there. Shortly afterwards, Terry
Gilliam, another animation hero of Nick's since his younger
days, appeared on a TV programme to review his favourite
films from the festival. He singled out *Creature Comforts* and
praised it to the skies. Nick, watching this, remembers thinking to himself: *Is that* me *he's talking about?* And then, with a
surreal, Python-esque touch, Gilliam blurted out: 'Nick Park
should be made God tomorrow!'

All Nick's efforts, then, were rewarded. *A Grand Day Out*
would go on to become a signature Aardman film – the
public's first glimpse of Wallace and Gromit, who became
national treasures in Britain. A year later, Alan Yentob at
the BBC contacted Aardman through the corporation's
Bristol animation unit, arranged a meeting with them and
announced he wanted to see more of Wallace and Gromit.

The BBC, he added, would also be happy to acquire *A Grand Day Out* from Channel 4 – an ironic change of fortune for a project that for much of four years had remained behind a curtain at Aardman, sometimes untouched for months on end.

As for *Creature Comforts*, it is regarded to this day as a ground-breaking classic in the annals of animation history. And both these films had been created by a company that, in the eyes of the wider world, had seemed to spring from nowhere.

From any point of view, Aardman was clearly flourishing on several fronts by the end of 1989. The previous five years had been a remarkably fruitful period, during which the company had grown from a tiny concern and become more established, taking on a reasonably sized space and buying more equipment, with two stellar young animators in Nick and Golly. The major projects had come in thick and fast and, though challenging, had been executed brilliantly – *Babylon*, *Sledgehammer*, *Pee-wee's Playhouse*, two series of short films for Channel 4 – and now the double whammy of *Creature Comforts* and *A Grand Day Out*.

None of these films made much money, but still the company seemed to be on an upward curve. No question about it – Aardman was on a roll.

119

6

OSCAR FEVER

There is very little about the profession of clay animation
that can prepare a person for the experience of attending
an Academy Awards ceremony – especially as an awards
nominee. There is no trace of glamour about the day-to-day
life of such an animator: no requirement to dress smartly, be
witty and amusing, act sociably towards colleagues – or, for
long periods of the day, even to speak. It's a profession for
introverts – for people who thrive on a form of creation that
gradually takes shape through hours and hours of seemingly
repetitive work.

True, Nick had had a foretaste of awards ceremonies the
previous year, when, in March 1990, *A Grand Day Out* won
the BAFTA for best animated short film of 1989. This was
the first major awards event that Nick had attended. It was
a lavish affair at London's Grosvenor House Hotel on Park
Lane and, as is usual at the BAFTAs, there were stars galore
in the audience.

He found the experience thrilling. In the course of a

somewhat dizzying evening, he met – among many others – Princess Margaret and also David Puttnam, at that point arguably Britain's most influential film producer.

It was a triumph for Nick – and for *A Grand Day Out*, his remarkable labour of love. His Aardman colleagues were genuinely and justifiably delighted. It felt like a breakthrough for the company, a clear sign of industry-wide recognition that burnished all their reputations. It also didn't hurt a bit that the BAFTA award –a gilded mask – would look good and impress visitors to their relatively modest accommodation in Wetherell Place, which Peter affectionately characterised as 'a glorified shed'.

Several months later, however, the Aardman team were left slack-jawed in amazement when the nominees for the forthcoming Academy Awards were announced. In the category of animated short film, there were just three nominations – and, incredibly, two of them were from Aardman. Both *A Grand Day Out* and *Creature Comforts* were in the running, along with the distinguished Italian animator Bruno Bozzetto's new film, *Grasshopper*. It was stunning news; clearly Nick was in with a major chance of picking up an Academy Award on behalf of Aardman.

Aardman had two US distributors – one of which was a team called Spike and Mike, who organised an annual Classic Festival of Animation that toured short animation films to American festivals and colleges. This year, Spike and Mike had included both *Creature Comforts* and *A Grand Day Out* as part of their programme, so Nick had agreed to fly out to Los Angeles a whole week before the Academy Awards and travel with them as part of their show before heading back to LA for the main event.

Peter and David joined him a few days later, and soon the three men found themselves – rather implausibly – in the stunning setting of Malibou Lake, some 30 miles north-west of LA. A gorgeous, peaceful spot, surrounded by mountains, it had been a popular location for movies ever since the 1920s. Now it was the venue for a delightfully bizarre alfresco party to celebrate the British Animation Invasion before the Academy Awards ceremony the next day. Everything about the party was 'British-themed', meaning that it was unlike any event ever staged in the home country. Baked beans, bangers and mash, and mushy peas dominated the menu, with Watney's Red Barrel to wash it all down. But the central event, in tribute to the visitors, was a croquet tournament – a game few of the visiting Brits had ever played.

Still, the Aardman trio threw themselves into it – Peter especially seeing the funny side of attempting croquet for the first time in his life, wearing a Union Jack bowler hat, and laughing himself silly at his limited skills. David, wearing his old Oxfam striped blazer, won his game with a miraculous freak shot.

This ambitious party was hosted by Terry Thoren, Aardman's other US distributor. He was showing some of the company's work as part of a package of Academy Award-nominated animation films to be shown in art-house cinemas across America. Terry and the Spike and Mike team would share hosting duties during the week of the Academy Awards; today's activities in Malibou Lake represented Terry's turn.

Not that the British Animation Invasion party was closed to outsiders. Some American animators known to the Aardman group showed up, including Steve Johnson, from their *Sledgehammer* days. Peter, David and Nick greeted them warmly, and out of curiosity also went over to meet another local animator who seemed to have a crowd hanging on his every word.

This turned out to be Matt Groening, who was already a big name in Los Angeles as a cartoonist; his comic strip *Life Is Hell* had been a must-read feature of the alternative weekly paper the *Los Angeles Reader* since the start of the 1980s. Groening went on to create the legendary Simpsons family, who had started life with a regular short spot on *The Tracey Ullman Show* in 1987. When that programme folded, Fox TV gave the Simpsons their own half-hour slot, which by this stage had been running for just over a year and was already hugely popular. It had not yet been screened in Britain, so there was little the Aardman trio could talk about with Groening, but, over time, he and Aardman came to share an enormous mutual respect – and he would go on to reference Aardman's work in several *Simpsons* episodes for years to come.

The evening ended with a splendid dinner for nominees, at which Nick was seated beside Bruno Bozzetto. Nick was thrilled to find himself in the company of a man whose work he had long admired as a young animation student. Bozzetto, now in his early fifties, had created his first animation three whole decades earlier, and his short films, which often had a political or satirical slant, had made him famous across

Europe. He was so popular that his best-known recurring character, a little underdog of a man named Signor Rossi, had become the hero of three full-length feature films in the '70s.

'He was so kind and nice to me,' Nick says now. 'He told me very humbly and sincerely: "You're going to win, and it would be very deserving."'

* * *

The big day finally dawned and, for the Aardman contingent, seemed to go on for ever. They had been booked into the historic Roosevelt Hotel, slap bang on Hollywood Boulevard; appropriately so, as it had been the venue for the first-ever Academy Awards back in 1929, becoming a favourite destination for a host of Hollywood stars since, including Monroe, Gable, Chaplin and Shirley Temple among others. After lunch, it was time to take out the tuxedos, don the dress shirts and tie the bow ties – activities the Aardman team did about as often as they played croquet.

Spike and Mike, never given to understatement, had made sure their four-car convoy to the awards ceremony at the Shrine Auditorium would stand out – and that it most certainly did. Dismissing the conventional option of stately black limousines, they had hired four striking classic cars from the 1950s, including a pink Cadillac and a beautiful white '58 Chevy convertible, which was chosen to carry the Aardman team. The wild cheers from the crowds lining the streets as they passed by confirmed this as a terrific publicity stunt.

They arrived, stepped out onto the red carpet and immediately walked into a seething mass of humanity – camera bulbs flashing, fans yelling and shouting, photographers screaming at them to look their way. It turned out they were following hard on the heels of Michael Douglas and his retinue, so there was an even more heightened sense of hysterical excitement in the air. Peter, David and Nick walked through it all, feeling distinctly dazed by the noise and confusion. The flashbulbs kept popping at them all the way to the door of the Shrine.

Inside, they had a quick drink before splitting up – Peter and David to the balcony; Nick to his seat in the stalls with his girlfriend. His seat was quite far forward and right on the aisle; had he been a regular Academy Award-goer, he might have known enough to have taken that placement as a good omen. Instead, he surveyed the people around him and felt uneasy, fretting about the fact that he might actually have to go on stage and speak to them all.

It's a fair bet that Nick Park was perhaps the shyest person in the Shrine stalls that evening, sitting among such stars as Michael Douglas, Sophia Loren, Dustin Hoffman and Robert de Niro. As the awards got underway, he began to worry about remembering who to thank if one of his two films turned out to be the winner.

The evening drew on, and suddenly Chevy Chase was on stage, along with Martin Short, to present the animation award. They were joined – in cartoon form – by Woody Woodpecker, in celebration of the fiftieth anniversary of his first appearance on film (in *Knock Knock*). It was Woody who

read out the result: 'And the winner is ... *Creature Comforts.*
Nick Park!'

On the aisle in the sixth row, Nick rose from his seat and
made his way to the podium. Smiling shyly and nervously,
he said, holding his Oscar statuette: 'Umm ... I'd like to
thank Aardman Animations in Bristol, England. That's Peter
Lord and David Sproxton, and all the team in Bristol. Also
Channel 4 TV. And, er, thanks to Spike and Mike for bringing me here.'

His speech had lasted just fourteen seconds. And, with
that, he walked off to face more photographers backstage,
with flashbulbs popping and reporters (mostly British ones,
for this was decidedly a British success) shouting questions at him.

Afterwards, he returned to his seat to find an unknown
'seat filler' had replaced him while he was on stage (usual
protocol, in case the cameras happened to locate an empty
seat in the auditorium). The seat filler swiftly gave way to
Nick and his statuette, however, and he was left to enjoy the
amazing sensation of the moment in peace.

* * *

The Academy Award for *Creature Comforts* was a phenomenal
success for Aardman. Peter Lord says: 'We were delighted
that Nick made a film in the 'Aardman tradition', but the
credit is entirely his. *Creature Comforts* was sort of spectacular
in its simplicity. He had a great idea and he put it together
beautifully, choosing the best bits of dialogue and adding

some unforgettable sight gags. It was technically simple, in that the camera was always locked off and the characters moved very little.

But those characters proved to be totally irresistible to an audience, especially the Brazilian jaguar, who is an absolute showstopper. It simply worked on people on a level we had never seen before. It got shown a lot at film festivals, and it *always* took the prize. Everyone was astonished by it.

'And that's because Nick has always had this extraordinary instinct for comedy. Now some people are very funny, some stand-ups are *really* funny. But there aren't many animators like that. The word is overused, but Nick is a true genius when it comes to comedy. But the fact that Nick was nominated for two Academy Awards – that really was extraordinary. And *A Grand Day Out* got similar reactions. There was obviously a magic to it that you don't see until it's finished. Everyone could see the Wallace and Gromit pairing was full of good ideas and great gags, but that they should come together quite so well and be so irresistible was still a surprise. So, seeing that no one could resist Nick's work and because we had seen it succeeding wherever it was shown, sweeping the board, we weren't that surprised to find ourselves going to the Academy Awards – even though the whole thing turned out to be like a fantasy dream.'

Peter acknowledges the irony in the fact that Nick was Academy Award-nominated for a film that took him several years of hard slog to complete, whereas the film that won the award only took him a few months.

'Yes,' he says. 'Not a bad irony, though.'

127

* * *

Receiving his Oscar was by no means the end of the evening for Nick. After the ceremony he reunited with Peter and David, and they first headed to the Governor's Ball, blissfully unaware that stars and nominees tended to give it a wide berth back then, preferring to attend private parties. Afterwards, they tried to locate a quiet bar in which to celebrate their success. Passers-by, having seen Nick collect his Oscar at the ceremony, would ask the predictable question: 'How does it feel?' Nick didn't say much – but it felt amazing. Later that evening they headed back to the Roosevelt, but by then its bar had closed. Fortunately, a waiter, spying Nick's statuette, reopened it for them.

Nick was a huge story, especially in Britain, and he was obliged to do press interviews solidly over the next couple of days. He was left pretty much alone in the hotel, talking to the media on the phone, while his colleagues went out and enjoyed the delights of Los Angeles. One invitation he did accept, however, was to tour the animation departments of the Hollywood studios. Intriguingly, while there, he met Jeffrey Katzenberg, then head of Disney Animation.

At this point, Katzenberg was riding high at Disney, having brought to the screen hugely successful animated films like *Who Framed Roger Rabbit* and *The Little Mermaid*. Another massive hit, *Beauty and the Beast*, was only months away from release.

They chatted amiably, Katzenberg at his most relaxed and

approachable, congratulating Nick on his Oscar, discussing his work and casually asking what his future plans might be. Nick had the sense he was being courted and was astonished that Katzenberg knew so much about his and Aardman's work. For his part, Nick was totally unaware of the pecking order among Hollywood's major moguls – and knew precisely nothing about Katzenberg.

With Katzenberg, Nick was non-committal, but made it clear he regarded himself as a loyal part of the Aardman team and would need to chat with Peter and David. Katzenberg listened, smiled charmingly, and they ended by expressing the hope that they might run across each other in the future. Little did Nick know that Jeffrey Katzenberg would come to play a big part in his life – and Aardman's – in the years to come.

* * *

After all the fuss and brouhaha over their success at the Academy Awards had finally died down, much of the world probably assumed that Aardman would take a break until work on their next award-winning film got underway. Instead, they got back to the side of the business that remained relatively hidden from public view (at least in terms of recognition): commercials.

The work was coming in thick and fast, and now 14 Wetherell Place, which had seemed so spacious when Aardman had moved in only six years previously, suddenly felt cramped and inadequate. The company had already had to rent an additional unit in Bristol's city centre for shooting.

David and Peter had concluded a whole year earlier that it would soon be time for yet another major move. They had even seen a place that would suit them perfectly: a 1960s-era warehouse owned by Fyffes, who used it for banana ripening and packaging. It was situated on Gas Ferry Road, right on the harbourside, in the heart of what had once been Bristol's dockland. Like other companies at that time, Fyffes had moved its business operations to Avonmouth, where the new breed of large container ships could access the deep-water Royal Portbury Dock that had been built in the 1970s.

'It was 1991, at the height of a recession,' David Sproxton recalls. 'This was a property that was too big for small-scale stuff, and far too small for the way warehousing was going. The docks had closed, all the big warehousing was happening down at Avonmouth, so this was lying fallow. It was a brownfield site, in a bit of a no-go area.'

The size of the building totalled 30,000 sqft (fifteen times the size of Wetherell Place), and it looked ideal for Aardman's varied purposes. A quarter of it was taken up with a central space of some 8,000 sqft, where in the Fyffes era the bananas had actually been ripened in refrigerators. David and Peter could immediately see its potential as an ideal studio.

The problem, however, was the price – some £1.2 million, which was simply beyond their budget, even with the money from commercials (50 per cent of which, thankfully, was upfront) continuing to pour in.

Aardman asked Fyffes if it would consider leasing the

building. They accepted the idea in principle, but a valuation was needed before a formal agreement could be reached. The valuation came back at a surprisingly modest £750,000, and Aardman's accountants suggested they try a low opening bid of £600,000. Fyffes accepted their offer. 'They were obviously keen to get rid of the old shed!' David recalls. In the end, they paid £650,000 – the extra £50,000 for the land surrounding it, which in later years would become the site for a custom-made Aardman HQ.

It felt like an absolute bargain – a deal that would have been far more difficult to pull off in a bigger, glitzier location. Indeed, David believes that being removed from powerhouse cities such as London and Los Angeles has helped to shape the company that exists today.

'We started out doing commercial work around the same time as a London company called Passion Pictures,' he recalls. 'They had a base right in Soho for a while. We'd talk to them about our businesses and how they were going, and I always recall thinking they had a big overhead. Now *our* overhead, our basic rent, was always pretty low – simply because we were in Bristol. And that allowed us, in our earlier years – the Channel 4 days – not to be so concerned with having to make money *per se*, just to pay the landlords ... So I think all that helped us. We didn't get sucked into that crazy media frenzy, that vortex.'

As a result of this, Aardman has been less constrained than it might have been because of chasing cashflow, allowing it to take on work that feels exciting and desirable, rather than being forced to take on projects purely for financial reasons.

Their philosophy, then, has served them well. And, in strategic terms, the Gas Ferry Road building had proven to be a shrewd investment. As David says: 'At various times, bits of land around the building came up, formerly British Rail land, so we ended up extending the estate in the 1990s, knowing we were sitting on something of a goldmine. Meanwhile, all these luxury flats had started going up around us.'

A couple of days after moving into Gas Ferry Road, an Aardman contingent was off to London for another ceremony – this time the British Advertising Awards, held at the Grosvenor House Hotel on Park Lane. They swept the board, returning home to Bristol with an armful of awards for Aardman's Heat Electric campaign, originally designed along the lines of *Creature Comforts* and directed by Nick Park, which added to the several industry awards Aardman had already won by this time.

As before, members of the British public had been recorded doing the talking for various animated creatures. The campaign's star was the lugubrious Frank the Tortoise, who sprawled on a carpet in the middle of a living room, heater in the background, and hilariously explained: 'It's good to come back into a warm flat after you've just done a run . . .' He was 'a very busy person' who doesn't have much time, so his heating needed to be 'easily turn off- and on-able'.

The company seemed to be carrying all before it: cleaning up at the BAA, winning an Oscar and taking ownership of bigger, better premises – all in a matter of a few weeks.

They finally moved into Gas Ferry Road in January 1992, and Aardman's general manager, Mary Lowance, orchestrated a 'Hollywood premiere' to mark the occasion: 'We had lots of outings and parties in those days, but for this, I wasn't entirely sure what kind of event Pete and David wanted,' she recalls. 'I didn't even know them that well back then.'

She hired a troupe called the Natural Theatre Company from Bath ('the Naturals' for short), who specialised in street theatre and comic interactive performances: 'They set up a scenario in which the studio would be opened by some big Hollywood producer. He was one of the actors, and he showed up in character, in a big limousine. He was a guy dressed in a fur coat. Underneath, I think he may have been wearing a gold bikini,' Mary remembers.

'Two of the actresses came as policewomen. They cordoned off the road to prevent regular traffic from using it, and then they got all the Aardman people to stand off and wait outside until the limousine arrived, so this guy could get out and officially open the studio.' The local press and TV stations showed up and faithfully recorded the event. 'On that first day, when we moved in,' Peter recalls, 'we couldn't believe the space we had. We ran around like kids, revelling in the fact that it was possible to get lost.'

After the fun of day one was over, the employees settled back into their work, the majority of which, as we have seen, was on commercials at this time. Nick had already announced that he wanted to make another half-hour Wallace and Gromit film, and now found himself working alongside Peter and Golly in what came to be known as the creative department, where the three animators could draw up the storyboards for their various forthcoming projects.

Before Aardman left Wetherell Place, Peter had already completed a short film called *Adam*, which was an affectionate, wordless spoof of the Creation story. It featured a naked little man who had been scooped from the clay of the earth's surface and given shape by a large omnipotent 'hand of God' who places him literally on top of the world. The little man, Adam, ambitiously tries dashing around the planet, only to find himself back at the same place. He is constantly reminded that he is in thrall to a superior being.

He then senses that the hand is about to provide a new companion for him. He smartens himself up – a bow tie and a bunch of flowers appear from nowhere – as if for a first date. The companion arrives, but turns out to be ... a penguin. It's an anticlimax for Adam and another reminder that there's a power greater than himself, though the short film ends with Adam and the penguin locked in what looks like an amorous embrace.

Adam was deliberately designed to be like an extended Morph story. 'It was disappointing that Morph's adventures hadn't made more of an impact outside the UK, or in festivals. Somehow, because they were 'just for kids', even the best stuff that Dave and I had done wasn't taken seriously. So, in *Adam*, I made up my mind to reimagine Morph for an adult audience – with Tony Hart being replaced by God.' At six minutes long, it is a little masterpiece – and it served to remind the animation community in Britain that Peter was not just one of the bosses of the wildly successful Aardman, but remained a great British animator.

This was borne out when awards season came around

and *Adam* was nominated for a BAFTA in 1992 and for an Academy Award the following year – which meant that this time Peter was on the red carpet in his own right, as a nominee. Acclaim for the film was completed at the Animation Festival in Annecy, where it won the audience award. This last honour felt genuinely special to Peter. 'I've always had a special fondness for the world of independent animation. It's a community where I feel very much at home.'

* * *

Involvement in Nick's new Wallace and Gromit film was hotly contested between Channel 4, which had originally backed *A Grand Day Out*, and the BBC, which had then acquired it and placed it in its Christmas schedules, with huge success. Peter and David decided to let Chris Moll, who had produced *Adam*, take care of the negotiations in the bidding war.

It soon became clear that the BBC was better equipped to handle the next Wallace and Gromit film. For one, it felt a more suitable channel for family audiences, at whom the film would be targeted. Also, the BBC now had a Bristol-based animation unit, headed up by producer Colin Rose, who had already expressed interest in the project. To cap it all, the BBC had yet another ace up its sleeve: its international distribution arm, BBC Worldwide, would inject extra funds into the budget, which stood at a substantial £650,000 – easily the largest for any Aardman venture to date.

Aardman also had to do a deal with the NFTS for the

rights to Wallace and Gromit as they effectively owned the property, having funded its production. This was a win–win situation: it gave the NFTS an income stream from one of their films, while Aardman secured the underlying rights to Wallace and Gromit and the rights to *A Grand Day Out*.

The new film was to be called *The Wrong Trousers*, and clearly it was unfeasible for Nick to make it on his own, as he had done over so many long years with *A Grand Day Out*. That had been totally his creation, but this time around it was felt he would need a screenwriter working alongside him to shape and refine the story – and to move production of the film along a lot faster.

Aardman chose a well-regarded veteran writer named Bob Baker, then in his early fifties, who had a long list of credits going all the way back to *Z-Cars* in the 1960s. He was best known for his long stint writing for *Doctor Who* in the following decade, contributing to a total of thirty-eight episodes. Bob could also take credit for creating K-9, the robot dog in *Doctor Who*. And, crucially, Bob had been a script editor on various TV and film projects; he was an expert at forging coherent stories from ideas that were inspired but lacked structure.

The company also realised that valuable time could be saved in the making of *The Wrong Trousers* if another animator could be hired to work beside Nick. This role fell to Steve Box, who had started out with another Bristol animation studio, CMTB, creators of the TV series *The Trap Door*. Steve was a skilled animator who had moved to Aardman in 1990, and it was certainly helpful that he and Nick got along well.

They tried to split their duties, with Nick animating Wallace and Gromit, and Steve working on scenes involving a sinister penguin.

For all that, the making of *The Wrong Trousers* turned out to be hard graft, since it needed to be completed as fast as possible in order to capitalise on the success of *A Grand Day Out* and *Creature Comforts* and deliver on a BBC budget and schedule. There was a full-time crew of just ten people, and Nick recalls everyone feeling 'ill and overworked' by the end of shooting *Creature Comforts*, because of the BBC's desire for a Christmas screening.

Some of Nick's early ideas for the plot of *The Wrong Trousers* were discussed with Brian Sibley, an author and radio dramatist who was also an expert on the history of animation. Ideas truly started flowing, though, when Nick and Bob Baker began looking at Nick's old sketchbooks from his student days.

Nick had been an inveterate sketcher since he was a schoolboy, and routinely doodled in his exercise books. He has described a sketchbook as 'a great storage place for ideas', a place where you can 'download them from your brain'.

He and Bob together came up with an idea for *The Wrong Trousers* that made them both laugh: the mechanical 'Techno-Trousers' – massively bulky, like the bottom half of a space suit, and self-powered, so they effectively did your walking for you once you put them on. They also had adhesive shoes, so the wearer could walk up the side of a vertical building. Nick began storyboarding *The Wrong Trousers*, and though this film was a big deal for Aardman – the eagerly awaited follow-up to *A Grand Day Out*, no less – there were plenty of other projects moving forward in the new building. As the main studios were occupied by work on commercials, some of which required large sets, much of *The Wrong Trousers* was shot in an out-of-the-way upstairs space with a low ceiling, though the film's legendary train chase was shot in the main studio later on.

It may not have taken up much floor space, but that did not detract from the quality of *The Wrong Trousers*. Nick and Bob's collaboration had resulted in an outstanding script. At one point early in the proceedings, Bob had been looking at Nick's early notebooks and had noticed a sketch of a villainous-looking character and a chase scene involving a stolen diamond. 'What you've got here is a classic heist film,' he told Nick, and that formed the bedrock of the detailed story that ensued.

The two men approached *The Wrong Trousers* as a piece of suspenseful film noir. Accordingly, Nick's long-time friend Julian Nott, who he knew from his days at the NFTS and who had written the music for *A Grand Day Out*, supplied a score that echoed the mood of an Alfred Hitchcock thriller. The film's moody lighting came courtesy of Dave Alex Riddett and Tristan Oliver, both of whom have gone on to enjoy distinguished careers as directors of photography.

The new film was also crammed with the same amount of visual detail as its predecessor. In its opening sequence, for example, which shows Wallace and Gromit serenely having breakfast at home, surrounded by Wallace's self-invented 'handy gadgets', the headline in the newspaper Wallace is reading exclaims: 'MOON CHEESE SHARES SOAR!' – a cheeky reference to the amazing success of *A Grand Day Out*.

There's also a somewhat darker element in the way Wallace treats Gromit, buying him the Techno-Trousers for his birthday. It's a selfish gift – they enable the trousers to take Gromit for a walk, saving Wallace the trouble. And when Wallace finds out he's broke and advertises for a lodger – 'a paying guest' – he turfs Gromit out of the spare room and he is forced to sleep outside. Gromit is visibly hurt and saddened by this rejection.

Yet it all serves the plot. The lodger turns out to be the sinister penguin named Feathers McGraw, who is silent with expressionless eyes. (Feathers, an outstanding creation in the Aardman pantheon of characters, owes a lot to the skill and ingenuity of Steve Box.) Gromit, being by far the brighter of the two protagonists, is immediately suspicious of Feathers, and follows him to the City Museum, where he seems to be preparing to steal a precious showpiece diamond. The film climaxes with a breathtaking chase, featuring all three characters on a model electric train set that runs through the ground floor of Wallace's house. 'This scene was hugely ambitious,' Peter recalls, 'it was all hands to the pump, and I was called in along with other animators to help Nick and Steve get it completed. Dave Alex Riddett excelled himself with the camerawork, given the sequence energy and excitement.'

The film took just over a year to complete and was screened to great acclaim both at the Annecy Animation Festival in June 1993 and the London Film Festival the following October. It also received a standing ovation at the Venice Film Festival, almost unprecedented for a short. It had its British TV premiere on BBC Two, on Boxing Day 1993, and once more the response was wildly enthusiastic.

Nick Hilditch, reviewing it for the BBC, noted: 'The finale in which they hurtle around the house on a model train [is] as thrilling as any in live action blockbusters. Gromit is the most expressive cartoon dog since Snoopy, and without uttering a word he carries the story through its all too brief thirty minutes.'

Stephen Holden, film critic for the *New York Times*, was equally effusive: '*The Wrong Trousers* has everything one wants from a half-hour cartoon: sharply defined characters, a story that is clearly told, many light joking touches and endless technical ingenuity. With its clay characters frisking through richly detailed sets, it has a storybook realism that is not often found in family cartoons. And in the part of the story where Gromit plays sleuth, it even achieves a mood of Hitchcockian menace.'

Given all this wild acclaim from critics and audiences alike, it was no surprise that *The Wrong Trousers* was nominated for an Academy Award, in the animated short film category. A great honour, of course, but now Nick had to consider the possibility of picking up another Academy Award, and somehow getting through the ceremony once again ...

7

GROWING PAINS

Given the extraordinary reception it received from audiences and critics, it was no surprise that *The Wrong Trousers* was so widely acclaimed and duly showered with awards. Inevitably, however, its success got Peter and David thinking about the different paths Aardman might take.

Should it stay as a relatively small-scale operation, bolstered by revenue from commercials while continuing to make films for the small screen? Or was it time to attempt a leap into a different, bigger league altogether? Their world seemed to be rich in potential and possibilities, and yet still the idea of making a full-length feature film was a daunting one.

It was already apparent there would be huge demand for a third Wallace and Gromit film, but to get it made effectively would require more money and more personnel; *The Wrong Trousers* had left everyone who worked on it – Nick and Steve especially – feeling exhausted.

Still, these considerations could be shelved for a while at least, as the Aardman team returned to the Academy

Awards in March 1994. This time around, Nick seemed to approach the daunting ceremony in a less nervous state of mind. The day before, he went to a stationer's in Los Angeles and bought himself some shiny wrapping paper in a bright, garish green, a roll of Sellotape and a length of cardboard. From this he designed a comically large bow tie that seemed to stretch out halfway to his shoulders.

The Wrong Trousers duly won the animated short film Oscar, so Nick took to the stage in his comedy bow tie, which, as well as the congregated audience members, was seen by hundreds of millions of people watching on TV worldwide. (Incidentally, it wasn't the first time he had worn a home-made bow tie to an awards ceremony, but the sheer size of this one made it noticeable.) But not everyone loved Nick's bow tie – the *San Francisco Examiner* described it as a 'travesty of taste'.

It was a delightfully theatrical touch – and it was a light antidote to several of the speeches, some of which had been necessarily serious. Tom Hanks, who won Best Actor that night for his role in *Philadelphia*, delivered an impassioned acceptance speech on behalf of the gay community in America that brought many in the audience to tears.

Nick's appearance, then, somewhat lightened the mood. Peter was in awe of his protégé's sheer nerve in donning the cartoonish bow tie: 'I'm a bit of a show-off myself, but I would never have dreamed of doing something like that. He was surrounded by people wearing the fanciest *haute couture*, people who'd spent all day in hair and make-up, and he turned up on stage wearing this comedy tie that he'd made in ten minutes. What a charming, subversive, comic act of showmanship.'

Nick admitted later, 'It looked a bit strange, but it turned out that at the parties afterwards, loads of people recognised me. Tom Hanks actually came up to me and said: "Good speech!" I thought, *Blimey, mate, what about yours!?'*

The famed bow-tie incident became one of the many memorable moments in Academy Awards history: 'People mention the bow tie to this day,' Nick reflects.

The stunt may also have suggested he was by this time a little more comfortable in the presence of Hollywood's movers and shakers; indeed, this much was apparent from the contrasting ways in which he accepted his two Academy Awards. This time around, his body language was far more confident; when he was announced as winner, he walked along his row of seats, smiling and shaking hands with well-wishers. He still read his speech a little nervously from notes, but within seconds he acknowledged the audience's laughter by touching the bow tie, smiling and saying: 'Thank you!'

His speech, too, was both thoughtful and diplomatic. He won applause with his tribute to the Academy 'for still supporting the short films category', and ended by pointing out: 'Many directors here started out by making short films – so thanks for giving us a chance.' A cheeky 'Bye-bye!' were his parting words. His speech lasted all of thirty-five seconds – more than twice the length of his first. Nick was getting the hang of accepting Academy Awards.

Watching from above, Peter looked on admiringly: 'Nick

has this knack of getting it right, an ability to charm his audience,' he said later. 'Yes, he's shy – but in his quiet way amazingly audacious.'

* * *

Back in the 'real' world in Bristol, once the moment had been savoured and the last champagne toast had been drunk, Peter and David turned their minds to the challenging question of Aardman's expansion. The success of *The Wrong Trousers* had confirmed Wallace and Gromit as a compelling 'brand', and several companies were now in touch to ascertain if the two characters could be used in commercials. David, Peter and Nick were all concerned about tarnishing the reputation of Wallace and Gromit by allowing them to advertise dubious products. And a small in-house team would have to be hired to supervise the marketing of the characters and deal with the thorny issue of rights and worldwide sales. It would be new territory for them – as would merchandising, another area that had never been on the agenda when Aardman was simply an animation studio.

'We had decided from the very beginning that we would only approve first-rate merchandise to match the quality of our films,' David says. 'We didn't want to tarnish Wallace and Gromit's reputation by allowing them to be used to advertise products with a dubious parentage.' As a result, Aardman opted to hire people in-house to keep an eye on quality control: 'We felt we'd always be better at judging all that ourselves, rather than handing it over to an agent.

The issue was much more about developing a small team to market the characters.'

Given that he had created Wallace and Gromit, Nick had the last word when giving the nod to any given piece of merchandise – along with Liz Keynes, who had been appointed as head of worldwide sales.

As it turned out, merchandising came to represent a sizeable revenue stream for the company, requiring the creation of a separate merchandising team under the Aardman umbrella. The company was reorganised, with Aardman Holdings (which owned land and property) at the top level, with Peter and David as co-owners. The second tier was Aardman Animations, a trading company with Peter, David and Nick as its directors.

Nick regards his title as one of the company's directors as largely honorary: 'Peter and David have the burden of looking after the whole company, and I don't seem to have that. People may want my opinions sometimes, but my responsibility is to keep coming up with projects, really – and films that entertain, and help the company in that sense. I see it as a creative role, really. I'm not very good on business. It's rare that someone like me has an identity within an umbrella organisation, and Aardman is responsible for many things. I just happen to have created several brands within it.' Peter adds, 'Nick's crucial role has always been as a filmmaker and an ideas person. Dave and I have always respected that and tried to give him as much space as possible to do what he does so brilliantly well. He isn't a natural businessman – why should he be?'

Aardman was looking inward to effect necessary change for its expanding businesses, but it also needed to look outward and consider its position within the film industry. It was buoyant with the success of its award-winning short films and was now a recognisable name not only in Britain but in America. So, was now the time to start thinking about its first feature-length stop-motion film? And, if so, would that inevitably mean joining forces with a Hollywood studio?

Peter and David had discussed this between themselves and a few close confidants, and they both believed making feature films could form part of a prosperous future for the company, yet they were also shrewd enough to be wary of the prospect.

The two men had seen British film companies rise and fall like shooting stars – dazzling successes one minute, sunk without trace the next. 'We always had one eye on the long term,' Peter recalls. 'We wanted to build something sustainable, which is why we didn't rush into tackling a feature film. But we had that target in our sights.'

The truth was, a few Hollywood studios had already been sniffing around Aardman, exploring the prospect of a deal. 'We understood that Hollywood can be a brutal place,' David explains. 'We didn't want to be chewed up and spat out. We relished our independence, so getting a deal right was important to us.'

Disney, the world's biggest animation company, had even proposed a three-movie deal – and confirmed it in writing. It was tempting, but Peter and David were canny enough to spot the pitfalls it entailed, the biggest of which being that

Disney would own the intellectual property rights to any future idea that emanated from Aardman. In theory, that could even apply to a new Wallace and Gromit film, which would obviously star Aardman's home-grown characters. Peter and David were both keen to make a full-length British animated film (*Watership Down*, from 1978, had been the last one of note) – but not at any price. 'We understood Hollywood was a brutal place,' says David, 'and we didn't want to be chewed up and spat out. We also relished our independence, so getting a deal right was important.'

They both sensed that fulfilling this ambition would take time, and felt it was worth hiring someone who, among other tasks, might find ways to make it happen. They were impressed by Michael Rose, a bright, urbane man in his early thirties who was working in acquisitions at Channel 4 Television. He was a programme buyer, specialising in TV series and short films that he felt would work for the channel.

They hired him, as he recalls, 'just after *The Wrong Trousers* had won its Oscar. There was a sense that Wallace and Gromit were developing as a brand – so there was already talk of a third film with them that became *A Close Shave*. Added to which, Peter and David clearly had a desire to get into feature films.'

It's worth noting that, at this point, Aardman, for all its success and fame, was still essentially a small company. Michael recalls: 'When I joined in 1994 to work at Gas Ferry Road, there were just twelve full-time people there. I became Aardman's thirteenth employee.'

He was replacing Chris Moll, who, after six years as senior

producer at Aardman (he had overseen *The Wrong Trousers*, *Adam*, and the Heat Electric commercials, among many others), was now moving on.

Michael started with the title 'Head of Development': 'The idea was to progress the Wallace and Gromit projects, develop new ones, but also help Aardman to break into feature films.'

He explains: 'So you had this studio, which was a cottage industry, with lots of creativity. They'd done commercials, they'd done the early short films, and then *The Wrong Trousers*. But it was quite an inward-looking place. It didn't feel as if there was much connection with the outside world. And I think my role was to be a bridge between the creativity of the studio and the marketplace outside – to find ideas within the studio and connect them with the outside world, and vice versa. I think that's how I saw it. And, of course, alongside all that was a long-held desire to make a feature film, and they had on the table this offer for a three-picture deal with Disney.'

This last point was made clear to Michael on his very first day: 'When I arrived there was a message on my desk on a single sheet of paper headed: "Deal with Disney". I think in the classic Aardman way it had been lying around for months.'

As he skimmed the details, it was clear the word 'Deal' was being used as a noun rather than a verb; the one-pager simply outlined Disney's proposals. 'Chris Moll had advanced the negotiations around [the deal], but then he'd left, and no one could get it over the line because it didn't feel comfortable to Aardman.'

Michael knew enough about recent developments at Hollywood studios to skim the one-pager and realise Disney's proposal sounded somewhat familiar: 'It was almost identical to the deal Pixar signed [with Disney] before *Toy Story*. We didn't sign it because it was written, in classic Hollywood legalese, in such a way so that you would make the three films together – develop them all – and, until the third was finished, Disney would be in control of everything, and would keep all the rights. Now, Wallace and Gromit would have been involved in all that. So there was a real unease – and rightly so – that it would tie Aardman in knots legally.'

Michael Rose observes that Peter and David have never run Aardman in any textbook manner that might be taught to business school graduates: 'The studio was unstructured. It grew in a higgledy-piggledy way. But then again it has become hugely successful, so obviously there's something in their method that does work. The basic things are really smartly done. That ethic of theirs, wherever it came from, meant they looked at the one-pager about Disney and simply said: "We'd lose control." To me, the great thing Pete and Dave have done is that, from the earliest days, they learnt to own their rights, on the basis that you never know where the value lies. Look at Morph: he was very popular in the 1970s, but then pretty much dormant throughout the 1990s. And now they've revived him again. They were able to do that because they'd bought back the rights to Morph from the BBC in the '70s. They don't own the Tony Hart shows, but they own all the Morph footage from those shows. Even

149

when they were young stars, they hung onto the rights of that footage. And that was why they could repurpose it. They own the intellectual property in Morph, so they can always repackage that. They did this at a time when everyone else was just selling – not thinking about rights, just taking the deal. And, over time, they've reinvested their revenue in their facility, which meant they could rent their own equipment out for commercials, so they were just incredibly smart.'

* * *

The year 1994 marked the beginning of a seismic shift in the world of Hollywood animation. Until that year, Disney was the only game in town when it came to animated features or musicals. This would change when Jeffrey Katzenberg left Disney and started DreamWorks with co-founders Steven Spielberg and David Geffen. However, by year's end it wasn't clear what DreamWorks' plans might entail.

According to Michael Rose, he persuaded Peter and David to go to Los Angeles with him, telling them: 'Look, this piece of paper has just been lying around here. We've got to do a deal with Disney – or do something different. We can't just do nothing. Let's go there, sit down with them and see if we can make it work.'

Peter and David had already been to Hollywood and talked with a studio keen to make a half-hour TV series of *Creature Comforts*. It was clear they didn't understand the unstructured, 'vox pop' essence of the film.

Still, they agreed to Michael's idea, and arranged a

meeting with Peter Schneider and Tom Schumacher, then running Disney's flourishing animation department, along with some of their colleagues. The issue of the proposed deal was raised, but the atmosphere soon turned chilly.

'The meeting must have lasted all of twenty minutes,' Michael recalls. 'There was an exchange of views, and then we said: "What happens if these projects don't go forward? What happens to the rights?" And they said: "If you're going to get married you have to sort out the divorce arrangements first." We said that didn't sit comfortably with us. So they said, "Okay, what you need to do is go and talk to John Lasseter, who's making *Toy Story* with us, or to Henry Selick, who did *The Nightmare Before Christmas*, up in San Francisco. See what they have to say. And if you don't sign this deal, you'll never make a movie in this town." And then, as one, they just got up and walked out. For all of us, that felt just wrong. It wasn't the Aardman way.'

'They told us more or less that they were the only game in town,' Peter recalls. 'There was an arrogance about Disney that didn't sit comfortably with us. We didn't like what they had to say, and we didn't like their controlling instincts. They were impressive, of course, even intimidating, but we certainly had no desire to be in business with them. But when we were put off so comprehensively at Disney, remember, it was Schneider and Schumacher; it wasn't Jeffrey Katzenberg.'

Despite this setback, the Aardman contingent did take one piece of the Disney animation bosses' advice: they decided to meet John Lasseter, then in the middle of making *Toy Story*, and Henry Selick, an approachable personality who was working on the animated film version of Roald Dahl's *James and the Giant Peach*. With both men they discussed their experience with Disney. Meeting them in San Francisco, Selick recommended a man named Jake Eberts, who had helped finance *James and the Giant Peach*. 'Jake's the man to talk to about this,' he told them persuasively: 'You need to meet him.'

Canadian-born Eberts lived a globe-trotting existence, dividing his time between Los Angeles, London, Paris and Montreal. He was well-known in Britain, having founded Goldcrest, the most high-profile British studio in the 1980s until a series of hits was followed by massive box-office flops, and the company's attempted entry into British television proved unsuccessful.

On the same trip, the Aardman trio had a meeting with Warner Bros. executives about a possible feature deal. Michael recalls: 'They offered the earth. They said, "Any deal you want." They said, "Don't go to Disney." They gave us the whole studio tour; they threw everything at us. But when it came to doing a deal with them, everything came back as "No, no, no." And what they actually offered us in the end was similar to Disney.'

The Los Angeles trip was turning out to be disheartening.

'What this all taught me is that we were operating at a kind of mini-mogul level,' Michael Rose reflects. 'We didn't quite have the clout to be talking at the right level – in other words, to studio bosses.'

* * *

When David and Michael met Jake Eberts in LA, he immediately struck them as someone who could help them. Tall, angular and handsome, with frizzy grey hair, gold-rimmed glasses and an amused twinkle in his eye, he inspired affection and radiated quiet authority.

Eberts was totally different from the Hollywood executives they had met; more relaxed, with a broader, more humorous view of the world. Yet those same industry bosses knew him and greatly respected him.

They dined at a smart, delightful restaurant in Venice Beach in West Los Angeles. Eberts had originally been an investment banker but was fascinated by films and so had started to invest in them, reinventing himself as a producer. He was instrumental in reviving the struggling British film industry in the early 1980s with such titles as *Chariots of Fire* and *Gandhi*. And, more recently, in Hollywood, he had been executive producer on *Dances with Wolves* and *Driving Miss Daisy* – both box-office hits and multiple Oscar-winners. In short, he was a man to reckon with.

He even liked animation, and was familiar with Aardman's work – as it happened, his children were Wallace and Gromit fans. He now outlined an idea that might finally help Aardman get a feature film off the ground.

Jake's plan was to arrange some 'development money' – that is, funding for the preparatory stage of a film before shooting starts, including the screenplay, when ideas for the film are created. He could do this through his own company, Allied Filmmakers, and it would be bankrolled by the French film company Pathé, based in Paris. He would put up $5 million to develop the script and get the project moving.

Once that was sorted out, Jake promised to arrange meetings between Aardman, who would now have a stronger hand, and the 'top table' of bosses at several studios. It would represent a huge leg-up; no wonder David insists: 'From the moment we met him in LA, it felt like Jake had been heaven-sent.'

Peter Lord echoes that view: 'Jake was terribly helpful to us. It was useful that he'd already produced a stop-motion film – *James and the Giant Peach* – but the man was more important; we liked and trusted him instinctively. Jake was a gentleman, in a slightly old-fashioned way, but he was no mug – he was a very smart fellow. He was a great help to us and steered us eventually to DreamWorks. He was the enabler.'

By this time, there was a kernel of an idea for Aardman's debut feature film. Peter and Nick took time away from the office, using David's basement kitchen as a relatively peaceful haven, to see if they could convert that idea into a storyline. Nick had originally come up with a single drawing as a starting point – a comic image of a chicken inside a wire fence, clearly trying to escape by digging a hole with a spoon. The more the two men thought about it, the more they realised that this could be the seed of an exciting, hilarious story – it would be a POW escape movie involving chickens.

Inevitably, they kept returning for inspiration to *The Great Escape* – the 1963 film starring Steve McQueen, James Garner

and Richard Attenborough – which felt like the classic example of a prisoner-of-war escape film. Both Nick and Peter had
loved it as boys: the brilliant improvisations, the disguises,
the heroic men – they were inevitably all men – fighting
against overwhelming odds, the derring-do, the stiff upper
lips the life-and-death stakes – it was delicious to take all
these elements and to replace the heroic male characters
with female chicken protagonists. There were, as Peter puts
it, 'glancing references' to the original, but he and Nick did
not borrow from the actual story so much as its atmosphere,
its richness of characters and the way it generated suspense.

Working on another kitchen table in David's basement, the
two men sketched and doodled, exploring visual gags – long
an Aardman trademark – as they tried to devise a compelling storyline. But they were unfamiliar with the challenges
of film story and structure. Quite simply, they were playing
with too many storylines to be pared down to a strong single
narrative that would form the film's backbone. Ideas came
and were developed and cherished before being abandoned.
As Nick recalls, what they had written would be four hours
long on screen. It badly needed to be shaped and crafted.

Peter and Nick took time out from their labours to join
David, Michael and Jake in Paris, where they enjoyed a truly
memorable lunch in an out-of-the-way backstreet bistro with
Jérôme Seydoux, head of Pathé, along with a handful of
his executives.

Peter recalls dreamily: 'There haven't been many great
meals in Aardman's history, but this one stands out as quite
exceptional.' While a typical Hollywood lunch would be

teetotal, efficient and brutally short, this was a splendidly French celebration of food and wine. As Peter recalls it, they talked about the proposed film for no more than ten minutes during that long, genial afternoon. A relationship had been forged, however, and the sense from the French contingent was that if Jake Eberts approved of these Englishmen, they must be okay.

Still, it was one thing to be partnered with Pathé for European rights, but, as Michael Rose points out, 'the question was: what would it mean, working with a Hollywood studio? What does it mean to the creative process, the story-telling? Do we have to start doing fast-cut Hollywood pacing, lots of songs, wham-bam jokes? All those other animated hit movies out of Hollywood were musicals, but Aardman were adamant that this would be a film without songs. Nick and Peter wanted it to be comedy-drama. So I think we were coming at it in quite an interesting way.'

There was still some nervousness within Aardman about throwing their lot in with Hollywood, but, as Michael remembers it, feelings were mixed: 'We also thought that if this is our first feature movie, it's got to play to the world, and the only way that would happen is through a partnership with a Hollywood studio. So there was this real ambition to be up there. We were trying to find the right approach – and that's where I think Jake was very instrumental in navigating the right partnership and the right sort of deal, which we would never have achieved on our own.'

* * *

Despite all this heady talk of Hollywood and feature films, elevating Aardman as a company to have a truly international reputation, there was still plenty of work to be done back on the home front. The third Wallace and Gromit film, *A Close Shave*, had to be shot, and it continued the increasingly familiar pattern of its predecessors: requiring a bigger crew, a shorter deadline and a higher budget. Colin Rose, head of BBC Animation, met with Aardman in April 1994 and expressed huge enthusiasm for *A Close Shave*, but was insistent that it needed to be ready for broadcast on BBC television over Christmas the following year. That left just eighteen months for writing, storyboarding, animating and shooting the film.

In terms of its content, it also marked a few departures from Nick's two previous films. For one thing, Wallace and Gromit are now running a window-cleaning business, which provides the context for Wallace's meeting of the amusingly named Wendolene Ramsbottom, a wool-shop owner in the same town with whom he engages in a tentative romance, voiced by veteran actress Anne Reid.

Again, however, just as there had been in the last film, there was a somewhat darker aspect to the story – notably when Gromit is suspected of sheep-rustling and thrown in jail, as well as the introduction of Wendolene's fearsome dog, a brutish creature named Preston. Key animator Steve Box was brought on board once more and took responsibility for Wendolene, and also supplied some 'edge' and menace to Preston, as he had done with the villainous penguin Feathers McGraw in *The Wrong Trousers*.

A Close Shave also featured a surprisingly attractive new minor character in the form of an appealing, initially nameless little sheep who gets mixed up in a sheep-rustling subplot. 'I think we'll call him Shaun,' says Wallace, who, like his human creator, cannot resist a pun. (For Shaun, think 'shorn'.) No one could have guessed at this point that Shaun the Sheep would become one of the most popular and successful of Aardman's animated creations.

There was a delicate balance to be maintained in all of this. The charm of Wallace and Gromit films was that they looked and felt like the creations of one person: Nick Park. But, whereas Nick had created almost all of *A Grand Day Out* himself, and *The Wrong Trousers* with only a dozen or so collaborators, *A Close Shave* was of necessity a bigger production in every way.

Apart from Steve, three extra animators were now brought in to work alongside Nick. Knowing he wouldn't be able to animate very much himself, he provided a fortnight's special tutoring in the art of animating Wallace and Gromit before production started. Much attention was devoted to the delicate art of animating his beloved characters' eyes and brows.

Nick's own animating was largely restricted to some crucial scenes featuring Gromit – especially the ones that showed him in jail. For almost all other scenes, though, he oversaw the work of his colleagues – just as a live-action film director would give instructions to actors. As for the script, he and Bob Baker started virtually from scratch; Nick basically knew he wanted another comedy-thriller, but with a romantic element.

In total, *A Close Shave* required a crew of more than thirty, which included more camera crew and model-makers, as well as animators. By Aardman's standards at the time, this was a huge crew and was a significant factor in pushing up the budget to the £1.3 million mark. Importantly, though, it was also a crucial part of the preparation for more ambitious productions.

As an indication of its scale and ambition, Nick's old friend and regular composer Julian Nott worked in Prague with a 65-piece orchestra (unheard of for a short animation film) to create the score, which subtly referenced old movie thrillers such as *The Third Man* and, in one scene between Wallace and Wendolene, evoked the bittersweet romance of *Brief Encounter.*

Even though actual shooting did not start until November 1994, the film was completed eleven months later – in time not only for a Christmas broadcast on the BBC, but for its world premiere at the London Film Festival the month before.

The question was, would the new film retain the familiar feel of the first two? Could it survive being made under a more industrial process? It was important that it did, because, as Michael Rose observes, *A Close Shave* was regarded within Aardman as a dry run for the full-length feature the studio wanted to make in the near future. 'We knew we needed to scale up our operation to enable our schedules to be more reasonable,' says David. 'Otherwise it was hard for the crew to see light at the end of the tunnel. Keeping morale up is critical in keeping energy up on production.' Thankfully, they needn't have worried.

Viewers found *A Close Shave* as beguiling as the two Wallace and Gromit films that preceded it. It attracted a huge TV audience, while the critics raved about its ingenuity. It was a palpable hit.

There was also a delightful, unforeseen consequence to its success. Wallace, of course, is a notorious cheese-lover, but his romance with Wendolene finally founders over this very issue. 'Won't you come in?' he asks her as she passes by his house. 'We were just about to have some cheese.' 'Oh no, not cheese,' she responds. 'Sorry, it brings me out in a rash. Can't stand the stuff.' The camera zoomed in on Wallace's horrified face and, after gulping in disbelief, he asks, 'Not even Wensleydale?' Then, later, brooding on the subject, he asks Gromit: 'What's *wrong* with Wensleydale?'

It so happened that Wensleydale cheese was made by the long-established Yorkshire-based Hawes Creamery, which had been struggling financially. After *A Close Shave* was broadcast, the dairy churned out special Wallace and Gromit-branded truckles (cylindrical wheels) of Wensleydale by the tens of thousands, and sales went through the roof, securing the dairy's future, says David: 'The film certainly helped increase demand and led to an early licensing deal – which proved very worthwhile for Hawes Creamery.'

* * *

By this time, Aardman had received an intriguing invitation for *A Close Shave* to be screened at the Sundance Film Festival in January 1996. This was a flattering proposal; Sundance, once a haven for regional American filmmakers given to making earnest documentaries about social issues, had gradually established itself as a festival that welcomed innovative young creatives from New York, Los Angeles – or anywhere else for that matter. Robert Redford, who lived near the festival's base in Park City, Utah, was its founder, which gave it both authenticity and a sprinkling of Hollywood glamour. (It didn't hurt that Jake Eberts was a friend of Redford's, and served on Sundance's board.) Steven Soderbergh, then only twenty-seven, became hugely famous after his sensational *Sex, Lies, and Videotape* was screened at Sundance in 1989, while three years later Quentin Tarantino got his first big break with *Reservoir Dogs* after it was screened at the festival to an audience that included several influential Hollywood agents.

Despite all this, Sundance did not seem an obvious destination for *A Close Shave* – or for Aardman. There was another factor to consider, however, in that during the seven years when young talents like Soderbergh and Tarantino were 'discovered', the January festival had become a favourite destination for Hollywood studio executives and talent agents from both coasts, who jetted in to check out the new filmmakers in town with a view to signing them up.

Jake Eberts was swift to see the advantages for Aardman in having a presence at Sundance that particular January; it could easily pave the way to meeting high-level studio contacts who could green-light their first feature film. It was decided that Peter and Nick (who had conceived of the story for the proposed film and would jointly direct it as well as producing it with David) should make the journey to Sundance, along with Jake and Michael Rose.

Jake secured meetings in Park City for Aardman with the Hollywood studios currently showing an interest in animation – including Warner Bros. and Fox. The one relevant studio without a presence at Sundance in 1996 was DreamWorks, which had officially opened for business the previous year and was already making its first animated feature, *The Prince of Egypt*.

Jeffrey Katzenberg had by this time finally quit Disney and was now jointly running DreamWorks along with music industry tycoon David Geffen and the legendary film director Steven Spielberg. There was therefore no urgent reason for any of these men to be in Park City to talk up a potential deal with a British animation studio.

When Jake contacted Katzenberg, who headed up the animated division at DreamWorks, and told him Aardman were going to Sundance, Katzenberg swiftly came up with an irresistible idea. He would have the DreamWorks private jet fly up to Salt Lake City, the nearest airport to the festival, pick them up and fly them all back down to LA to dine that same evening with him ... and Steven Spielberg.

Finally: the top table. Jake had worked his magic and delivered on his promises. Peter and Nick had been talking about this for well over a year, and finally the chance had come: they could look two Hollywood moguls squarely in the eye and pitch them an idea for a film. It would be known as *Chicken Run*.

8

A PITCH IN TIME

By this stage of their lives, Peter and Nick had already experienced great success, enjoyed a degree of fame and known the pleasure of receiving awards. Neither of them was still young enough to be wide-eyed and impressionable, but this trip to Sundance was turning into a heady adventure, one they would always remember.

'Beware when they send a private jet for you,' Michael Rose says now about the Hollywood clique, with a broad smile. 'Yes, it was quite a gesture, and a way of showing DreamWorks were genuinely interested in us. But for us, it was also: "Let's be on our guard here."'

Still, for ninety blissful minutes, Peter and Nick could sink back into the cream leather seats of the DreamWorks jet and simply luxuriate in the experience. Peter recalls thinking to himself, *Now we're talking. This is how showbiz is meant to be!* They sat back as cocktails and canapés were brought to their seats, and then paid a visit to the cockpit, gazing down on the bright lights of Las Vegas over the pilot's shoulder. Michael was enjoying the experience too, while Jake Eberts,

163

the fourth member of their party, looked calm and relaxed; he had obviously experienced this particular form of high life often enough.

On the plane, Jake and Michael checked with the others which idea they were planning to pitch, and Nick showed them a piece of paper with the words 'Chicken Run' on it. Everyone agreed.

After the jet touched down in Los Angeles, the luxury travel merely continued in a different form. An enormous DreamWorks limo was standing by to whisk them from the airport to the restaurant where they would be dining that night.

They got there before their hosts, but two of them soon arrived – Jeffrey Katzenberg himself and Walter Parkes, a close associate of Spielberg's who had been president of his Amblin Entertainment company, and who, with his wife and business partner Laurie MacDonald, had been called upon to help create DreamWorks. Parkes, calm and urbane, was a heavy hitter in his own right; beyond question, the Aardman group would be spending the evening with Hollywood royalty.

As for Katzenberg, his track record was formidable. As Disney's former CEO, he had helped turn around the company's ailing fortunes with a remarkable string of hit animated musicals: *The Little Mermaid* (1989), *Beauty and the Beast* (1991), *Aladdin* (1992) and *The Lion King* (1994). All of them were probably too saccharine and sentimental for Peter and Nick's tastes, but you couldn't argue with their astronomical box-office returns.

There was certainly nothing saccharine about Katzenberg himself, either. Famously straight-talking, he had fallen out with Disney, quit the studio and was at that time suing them for money he felt he was owed; some reports claimed he had settled out of court for $250 million.

Spielberg was running late, and would not join them for dinner, so they moved to their table. Ironically, given the subject of the film they were about to pitch, the speciality of this high-end restaurant was ... chicken.

'So we look at the menu,' Michael recalls, 'and then – this is a very Hollywood thing – they say: "You have to have the chicken! The chicken's great! The chicken's out of this world! Okay, everyone's having the chicken!"'

They ordered, and Katzenberg filled them in on the latest developments at DreamWorks, as well as the company's aims and ambitions for the future. The chicken arrived (which lived up to expectations), then, as everyone was finishing up, Steven Spielberg walked in.

It was an understated entrance. He was dressed informally in a casual shirt, jeans and a baseball cap, and had you not known this was the world's most successful and famous film director at the time, you would never have guessed. He went around the table, shaking hands with the British visitors with a surprising hint of shyness.

Gratifyingly, he was aware of Aardman's track record, and congratulated Nick on his awards successes. Everything was going well. Then Jake Eberts said gently: 'You've got an idea, haven't you, gentlemen? Why don't you pitch it?'

Peter and Nick had discussed this moment. Nobody

had ever coached them in making the classic Hollywood pitch, but they knew – or at least they hoped – that a perfectly honed ten-word pitch had the power to unlock the doors to the movie world. They looked at each other; Nick took a deep breath, glanced around the assembled moguls, and out it came: 'We want to do *The Great Escape*. With chickens.'

There was a moment's silence as the idea sank in, followed by a burst of spontaneous laughter on the part of the DreamWorks team. It helped that Spielberg in particular seemed delighted by the idea. 'I love it,' he said. 'That's perfect.'

He admitted that when he was growing up *The Great Escape* had been one of his very favourite films, and he recalled that, in his college days, he had found a way to project the film onto his own stomach. (He was vague about the details.) He also revealed to the dinner party that he owned a ranch near Malibu where he kept . . . 300 chickens.

Much of the tension about pitching the film started to fade away, and Peter and Nick now elaborated on their 'chicken run' idea. Sensing potential victory, Peter warmed to the theme: 'Think about it. Look at a chicken farm: there are rows and rows of wooden huts – in a compound surrounded by a chain-link fence. It really does look like Stalag Luft III from *The Great Escape*.'

Now he and Nick began playing off each other, picking up each other's cues and pressing home the pitch to their receptive audience, who leaned forward intently. These were some of the film's characters; this was how the story would play out. Around the table the surprised laughter from the DreamWorks team had subsided, but they were still smiling – and looked impressed as Peter and Nick outlined their idea.

Peter remembers: 'Nick and I grinned at each other – we couldn't have hoped for a better response. Now Nick told them more, explaining about how our courageous chickens were locked up by brutal farmers, who acted like the camp commandant and guards: "You've got dogs, wire fences and a whole host of heroics. Finally, the chickens build themselves a mechanical plane, and that's how they escape. That's the climax to the film."'

At one point, Nick felt confident enough to take a conversational detour: 'I remember telling them about what had inspired me,' he recalls. 'It was a story, almost like a fable, from India perhaps, of a man who found the egg of an eagle. He took it home and it was reared by chickens. It grew up thinking it was a chicken. It scratched in the dirt and would occasionally look up at the sky. He saw an eagle and said: "What's that?" His fellow chickens said: "That's an eagle, the king of birds. But we're chickens, we belong down here." So the eagle lived and died a chicken, because that's what he thought he was.'

He smiles at the memory: 'I remember Steven Spielberg was very touched by that. I had a copy of the story with me and he took it home and read it to his children before they went to bed. They all loved it. That wasn't what *Chicken Run* was about eventually, but it was part of our inspiration.'

It was finally time for the two sides to part company, and it was clear by then that Spielberg, Katzenberg and Parkes all genuinely loved the story.

'It all seemed to gel,' says Peter now. 'I knew we were going to do the deal with DreamWorks. Everybody in the room was positive, convinced of our ability to pull this off. Though Jeffrey, as usual, was all business all the time, and asked immediately: 'So, guys, when can we see the script?' The Aardman team would come to learn this was merely par for the course with him.

Peter recalls: 'At the end of the night we all shook hands, and even though this was just the first pitch, it really felt as though we were sealing the deal. There are some scary things about Hollywood, but this is the very best of it: people with the certainty, the power – and the money – to make a deal on a handshake. If you've got studio heads saying yes, you know everything else will follow. And who wouldn't want to make a film with Steven Spielberg's new studio? It was all so fantastically thrilling.'

Back in his room at the stylish Shangri-La Hotel in Santa Monica, Peter called David to tell him the pitch had been received enthusiastically. He then called Karen to let her know he'd been schmoozing with Steven Spielberg – with an excellent outcome. Peter found it hard to sleep that night, feeling both elation at having pitched *Chicken Run* successfully, and trepidation at the challenge ahead: making Aardman's first feature film – and for a Hollywood studio no less. Who knew how long it all might take?

Peter and Nick returned to Aardman like conquering

heroes; now it was time to share the news with everyone else. Peter was aware there had been rumours about their frequent trips to the States. Aardman had never been a secretive place, but, until the deal was real, there had never been a story to tell. Now it was time to 'address the troops' and engage everybody in the new adventure.

Aardman employed close to sixty people by this time, and all of them, along with a handful of more-or-less-permanent freelancers, crowded into the Gas Ferry Road canteen, which could comfortably accommodate only about half as many. Standing on a chair to make himself seen, Peter addressed them.

He told them of meeting Katzenberg and Spielberg, that DreamWorks loved the idea of *Chicken Run* and was prepared to finance it, which meant Aardman was now branching out into the feature-film business.

Peter was honest enough to admit he did not know all the ramifications of what this meant: 'We're going to need lots more people, more space and whole new ways of working. Other than that, I've got absolutely no idea!'

Nevertheless, he promised it would be 'an adventure of the highest order – and since we're all pretty much in the dark, we're all going to have to pull together for this enormous and extraordinary enterprise'. He pointed out this would be the first British animation feature in stop-motion: 'So we'll be building something unique and, I hope, creating something none of us will ever forget.'

* * *

David Sproxton had known for a while that if *Chicken Run* received the thumbs-up from a Hollywood studio, it would trigger significant changes within Aardman. A feature film was such a big undertaking, and relatively speaking Aardman was still a small company.

'It was decided early on that Nick and Peter would co-direct,' he says. 'We'd learnt from discussions with Hollywood animation studios that when it came to directing animated feature films, two heads were better than one. There's a massive workload, and it's a long haul.'

It certainly helped that Peter and Nick got along well, and hugely respected each other. Interviewed later that year and asked about animators who had influenced him, he Nick: 'If I have to cite someone, I should say Peter Lord; I've always been challenged and influenced by him.'

Still, if Peter was to be occupied full-time on *Chicken Run* for an indefinite period, it would be necessary to restructure Aardman's management. At this point in its history, it still remained true that no one within the company's ranks had any business training at all. As general manager, Mary Lowance was doing sterling work, but, as David puts it: 'Michael Rose may have done some business studies, and I had an economics A-level – but that was it.'

Yet this did not mean there was a lack of strategic thinking: 'I think we could consider our very determined aim to get into feature films as a strategic move,' David reflects. 'The same applies to continuing with commercials, and bringing on new talent.'

For his part, David rather relished the variety that his role as co-founder had brought him. Peter had never had much enthusiasm for the business side of things, but David was interested in addressing the bigger picture for the company's future, while keeping one foot in production with lighting and camera work.

But now the time had come to make a decisive change. With some reluctance, he told Peter to concentrate solely on getting *Chicken Run* made, with Nick beside him. While they did so, he would attend to the business end of Aardman and find ways to keep it viable and flourishing in the long term. 'I wasn't assertive about it,' David recalls. 'But things like this did tend to default to me.'

It wasn't just making a major feature film that needed attention – there were commercials, broadcast work, rights management and the growing need to engage constructively with the emerging digital world. All of these areas required strategic thinking, not just day-to-day remedies.

David was prepared to help make that happen, but felt unable to do it alone. He needed an adviser and mentor, and brought in John Savage, CEO of the Bristol Chamber of Commerce, on a consultancy basis. They already knew each other as both were on the board of Bristol's Old Vic theatre.

'John understood the need to support our creative work, while introducing systems that would keep our finances on track,' David says now. 'He had a great deal of business experience and was keen to help what he could see was a growing company that was bringing real value to Bristol and the UK.'

From its very modest beginnings, Aardman had evolved simply over the years, adding people to the payroll as they became necessary to keep the company moving forwards; technicians, administrators, assistant producers etc. There was no conventional structure to the company – no board of directors, and certainly no external directors to help guide and shape it.

This organic approach had served it adequately for years, and Aardman did have longer-term plans for Wallace and Gromit and series work like *Rex the Runt*, but now a business plan that stretched beyond the next week, month or even year felt not so much desirable, but imperative.

The problem was that David and Peter felt differently about this subject. They both took the view that the quality of Aardman's work was key – but what would that work be? Additionally, Peter tended to be suspicious of 'non-Aards' – people from conventional business outside who wouldn't understand the unique creative culture of the company.

John Savage certainly fell into that category; he was an outsider, and Peter was wary of him, even though as a consultant he was of no possible threat to the position of anyone inside Aardman. However, David insisted he needed help, resigning himself to taking care of all pressing company matters while Peter was tied up with *Chicken Run*.

David did so with something of a heavy heart. It felt like abandoning his craft, losing out on the camaraderie, banter and joint problem-solving with the crew on the floor, as well as the artistic satisfaction of being directly involved in creating memorable images.

Still, he couldn't do it all, and being a jack of all trades was already feeling stressful. Finding a managing director would be time-consuming – and what were the chances that one could be found who would easily slot into an unconventional company like Aardman? There was another pressing argument, too: could Aardman even *afford* a new MD?

Weighing up the pros and cons, David finally reached a decision: it would be have to be him or nobody.

The truth was, there was little time to linger over this decision. *Chicken Run* would definitely go into production, but where would it be shot? Gas Ferry Road had certainly grown, but was nowhere near big enough as it was. Aardman tasked a company of architects to draw up plans for a new studio on the Gas Ferry Road site that would be suitable for feature-film production. They came back with a scheme that would have cost a mind-boggling £25 million to implement. It was time for a major rethink.

In the end, John Savage proved his value to Aardman by finding a suitable alternative. He put out feelers to industrial estate agents and found a huge industrial shed on a frankly ordinary-looking 1970s-era business park called Aztec West, which was nevertheless convenient for the M4/M5 interchange.

It was being vacated by Mattel, the toy manufacturer, and was a massive 80,000sqft in area – more than enough space to shoot a major feature film. The conversion would cost money, but then the money from DreamWorks would take care of that. Moreover, the facilities would be available to Aardman long after *Chicken Run* had been completed as the lease was in their name.

* * *

It was March 1996, the time of year when Nick made what was starting to seem like his annual pilgrimage to the Academy Awards. *A Close Shave* was one of five films nominated for best animated short – and duly won: Nick had become something of an Academy Awards darling in this category and *A Close Shave* was the hot favourite. Thanking his voice stars Peter Sallis and Anne Reid, as well as his parents and everyone at Aardman, he concluded: 'We did it again.'

They certainly had. In the space of just six years, three of his films had now received Academy Awards and a fourth had been nominated – a rapidly achieved record not even perennial Oscar favourite Meryl Streep could match.

9

LOST IN NEW YORK

If there was ever any doubt about the affection in which Wallace and Gromit were held both in Britain and America, a curious incident in 1996 settled the argument for good.

In October, Nick Park and Aardman's publicist Arthur Sheriff flew to New York for three days to promote the American DVD release of *A Close Shave*. Sales of Wallace and Gromit DVDs in the States had been modest, and so a press reception for Nick had been organised at the Tavern on the Green in Manhattan's Central Park.

Since the film features sheep-rustling, some executives from BBC America, responsible for releasing the DVD, had arranged for live sheep to attend the reception. Sheriff concocted a plan to let one of these sheep 'escape' – hopefully into the main streets of Manhattan, creating havoc. In his mind, he conjured up a best-case scenario: press photos of burly New York cops chasing a sheep down Madison Avenue, all because Wallace and Gromit were visiting the United States.

Arthur Sheriff had become intrigued by Aardman and its

work since he had attended the Bristol Animation Festival in 1990, and approached Chris Moll, who would later be a producer on *The Wrong Trousers*. Aardman was at the point where it needed some well-orchestrated publicity, and Sheriff was already experienced in the field; he had handled PR for CBS Records in London and worked for the flamboyant pop impresario Robert Stigwood, who produced *Grease* and *Saturday Night Fever* and also managed the Bee Gees. Adept with the media, he could handle both tabloid reporters chasing a breezy headline as well as broadsheet journalists who wanted more detail and context for their pieces. Above all, he was enthused by what Aardman had already created in Bristol; it was clear to him they were 'a good story'.

When they landed at JFK, Nick was clutching a black wooden box containing models of Wallace and Gromit in their motorcycle and sidecar combination – something he brought with him on all publicity occasions. They were an irresistible 'prop' and the press everywhere liked to photograph him with them.

As it happened, their plane was three hours late. A heavy storm had dumped 4 inches of rain on Manhattan that very afternoon, and the driver of their chauffeured car had clearly given up on them. After a long wait to find a yellow cab to take them to Manhattan, they found that trees had been uprooted by the storm and had partially blocked the roads; it was an exhausting end to an already long day. In torrential rain, they finally reached the hotel; its doorman grabbing their bags from the boot of the taxi while Nick dashed inside and Arthur paid the driver. They joined up again in the hotel lobby, whereupon Nick asked Arthur if he had the box that contained the Wallace and Gromit models. Arthur had assumed Nick had picked them up with his bag. They dashed back onto West 54th Street, which was full of yellow cabs. Nick vainly chased one of them, but it was not theirs. He was saddened and in disbelief. In the mix-up, they hadn't obtained a taxi receipt, so couldn't even contact the company to attempt to retrieve the valuable cargo.

Both soaked to the skin, they met up with Jane Ayer, Aardman's publicist for the West Coast, who had flown in from Los Angeles to handle the New York event. Over dinner, after being told about the tragic loss, she had an idea. She suggested they release what American police call an APB – an 'all-points bulletin', which typically alerts officers about a wanted criminal or person of interest – to all media outlets in New York, telling them Wallace and Gromit were missing.

It was headlined (delightfully, in New Yorker font): 'HAVE YOU SEEN THESE OSCAR-WINNING FILM STARS? To accompany it, Nick drew a picture of the characters aboard their motorcycle and sidecar. The message below read: 'Wallace & Gromit were mistakenly left behind in a New York City yellow cab Saturday evening, October 19, at 10 p.m., en route from JFK to the Rihga Royal Hotel. The clay animation characters are urgently needed for a special event and television appearance at the Virgin Megastore at Times Square on Tuesday. Owner/creator Oscar-winning director Nick Park is offering a REWARD. Please contact Jane Ayer at the Rihga Royal Hotel if you have any information.'

New York's legendary all-news radio station 1010 WINS immediately broadcast the story, appealing to all taxi drivers to check their vehicles. By the time Arthur got back to his room, the phone was ringing; it was CNN, asking to interview Nick. Arthur told them he would get back to them and put the phone down – whereupon it immediately began ringing again. This time it was the *New York Post*, desperate to get the facts. During the five minutes he was talking to them, the hotel switchboard reported seven more calls to him, all from media outlets. It was a red-hot story.

Nick did a few phone interviews that night: 'I feel as if I've lost my best pals,' he told reporters forlornly. The next day, Arthur took over interview duties for him, but by the time Sunday afternoon New York time rolled around, British news desks had woken up and were just as interested. A man at *The Times* told Arthur it was 'a slow news day' and so he called every national news desk in the UK, gave them the full story and arranged for all the British newspapers to have bikes sent to his office in London to collect Wallace and Gromit pictures.

On Monday, *The Sun* made the story its front-page splash: 'LOST IN NEW YORK' read its enormous headline. That same morning, BBC Radio 4's *Today* programme followed it up, and their item elicited yet more calls, starting with ITV's *News at Ten*. By this time the news coverage had gone worldwide.

The search ended – suddenly, and to everyone's relief – with a simple explanation: the taxi driver who had taken Nick and Arthur to the hotel had had enough of driving in the rain on Saturday evening, and had decided to call it a day; it had been his last fare. He had first heard about the story only when he'd clocked in at work again on Monday morning, whereupon he checked his trunk and found the black box. He then returned it, with Wallace and Gromit safely inside, to the hotel.

There was a general sense that if there was anyone in Britain or the United States who had not heard of Wallace and Gromit up to this point, they certainly had now.

It had been a fraught, exhausting trip – but one with a happy ending at least. When Arthur and Nick boarded their British Airways plane home at JFK, they settled into their seats with a sense of relief. They had brought their characters on board as hand luggage, inside their black box, and as a flight attendant helped Arthur with his W&G-branded bag into the overhead locker, she told them cheerfully: 'Have you heard? They found them!' Arthur and Nick simply smiled at each other.

Then, just before take-off, the captain addressed his passengers: 'We're delighted to welcome Nick Park on board today. And you'll be relieved to know Wallace and Gromit are safely on the plane too.' At which point it seemed every passenger on board spontaneously joined in a round of applause.

Astonishingly, the media could not get enough of Wallace and Gromit, and the story rumbled on for a few days longer, culminating in a spoken-word opinion piece on the religious 'Thought for the Day' segment on BBC Radio 4's *Today* programme. Nicknamed 'the God slot' by critics, it featured speakers who often sought to find a biblical parallel with current news stories.

The controversial commentator Anne Atkins, a regular contributor, used her five minutes bizarrely, recounting Wallace and Gromit's adventures in New York, asking listeners to imagine the 'feelings' of the two lost puppets, and expressing her empathy with Nick, their creator. She ended with a biblical quote: 'Suppose, Jesus said, you had a hundred sheep, and lost one of them, wouldn't you leave the ninety-nine and go and look for that one lost sheep until you found it?'

As Arthur Sheriff liked to say afterwards: you couldn't make it up. Yet all the hullabaloo had only underlined the extent to which the public cared about these two improbable clay heroes.

10

CHICKEN RUN

The Academy Award triumph for *A Close Shave* was a source of delight to DreamWorks, who were now more eager than ever to get their Aardman film into production. Jeffrey Katzenberg's words from the night of 'the Big Pitch' now echoed in Peter's brain: 'So, guys, when can we see the script?'

The short answer: 'Not yet.'

Peter and Nick had given it some thought, but neither of them had really gone through the process of identifying a suitable screenwriter who would meet with them and work towards delivering – possibly after several drafts – a script that was fit for purpose. In this particular area of the film business, they were still novices.

They made a bright start, however, choosing Jack Rosenthal as a strong candidate for the job. He was both a screenwriter and an admired playwright, with an impressive, varied list of credits. During his long career, Jack had written the delightful TV drama *Bar Mitzvah Boy*, more than one hundred episodes of *Coronation Street* in its earlier days, and the well-received TV play *Spend, Spend, Spend* about Viv Nicholson, the glamorous, reckless wife of a big winner on the football pools. Most remarkably, he had also collaborated with Barbra Streisand on the screenplay of her 1983 film *Yentl*.

By the time they met Jack, he was in his early sixties, still prolific and at the height of his writing powers. They soon commissioned him. He was funny, accomplished and versatile – just the kind of writer they were looking for.

Peter and Nick first met him in a hotel in London and talked over their idea for the chicken story, after which two more meetings followed in Bristol. A lot of talking and swapping ideas was involved, and then Jack went away to write a first draft.

'Jack told us he couldn't write gags,' David recalls, 'but that was okay with us. We needed a story structure and an emotional backbone to the story.'

There was nothing technically wrong with Jack's first draft, but it felt like a million miles away from what Peter and Nick had envisaged in their heads. They were both used to an extended collaborative process, but they had clearly failed to get across the gist of the story they wanted. In retrospect, it dawned on them that they should have taken note of the good things about his script – and there were many – while persuading him to work with them and refine his story, bringing it closer to what they had in mind. At this point, however, they simply did not know enough about the writing process to do anything along those lines. Feeling more than a little embarrassed, they decided to look for another writer. But who?

Once again, Jake Eberts proved to be an invaluable source of advice. He recommended Karey Kirkpatrick, who had the script of *James and the Giant Peach* among his credits. Maybe he could do something similar on behalf of *Chicken Run*? Jake duly arranged a meeting between them and Karey at a deli in Santa Monica.

Karey, an Anglophile and a fan of British comedy, was enthused by the idea. He flew over to Britain, and Peter and Nick swiftly whisked him off for an intensive writers' retreat.

They had decided by then to set *Chicken Run* in a post-Second World War Britain, specifically in rural Yorkshire – and so they headed north. While they were out walking, they were startled to realise they were almost on the doorstep of Hawes Creamery, the Wensleydale cheese factory, and decided to drop in for a visit.

The reception the employees there gave Nick and Peter was welcoming, to put it mildly: 'They might as well have thrown down palm leaves in front of Nick as he walked in,' Peter recalls drily. 'It was like Christ coming into Jerusalem.' It wasn't so surprising – Wallace's renowned love for this particular cheese ('Not even Wensleydale?') had not so long ago saved the company from closure.

Later on, the creative trio sat down together and analysed what they had agreed upon so far. They didn't know it at the time, but this would mark the start of a creative journey that would take four years to complete.

* * *

Broadly, *Chicken Run* was envisaged as a parody of every prisoner-of-war escape movie ever made – from *The Great Escape* to *Stalag 17*.

The British chickens (almost all female) are the helpless inmates of Tweedy's Egg Farm, banged up in this bleak, scary place ringed by fences and subject to military discipline. The 'camp commandant', so to speak, is Mrs Tweedy: a harsh, greedy woman obsessed with the chickens' egg-laying rate. One egg a day is the minimum, and any one of them who fails to meet it suffers mortal consequences. (This was the fate of 'Edwina', named after the ex-government minister Edwina Currie, who had been sacked from her post after she claimed that much of the nation's egg supply was riddled with the salmonella bacteria.)

Mrs Tweedy's husband, the hen-pecked Mr Tweedy, routinely spies on the chickens, convinced they are 'up to summat'. But his formidable wife insists they're 'stupid chickens', barely bright enough to hatch an egg, let alone a plan.

Yet Mr Tweedy is right. One of the chickens, a passionate, plucky idealist named Ginger, yearns to be free, and has attempted some ingenious escapes in the past. In an obvious nod to Steve McQueen's character in *The Great Escape*, she routinely gets thrown into a coal bunker (i.e. 'the cooler') for her pains. Nevertheless, she constantly urges her comrades to free themselves. In practice, however, it's not that easy. The guard dogs are on constant watch; most chickens are too fat to squeeze under the fences; and scooping earth from beneath them with a spoon turns out to be a futile exercise.

The chickens feel doomed. And now they learn that Mrs

Tweedy is considering a change of career, forgetting eggs and instead turning the chickens into meat for pies.

Hope arrives in the form of Rocky Rhodes the Flying Rooster – a smooth-talking but unreliable American cockerel who has managed to escape from a travelling circus and ends up landing in the chickens' enclosure. Believing him to be a professional flyer, Ginger realises Rocky could be their salvation and threatens to turn him in unless he teaches them all how to fly.

Will he agree? Can he train the plump old birds to take flight before they're tossed into Mrs Tweedy's pie-making machine? In short, can Ginger persuade Rocky to become the saviour the chickens all desperately need?

* * *

Working with Karey turned out to be intriguing. In this instance, it helped that he was American rather than British, and thus had a different reaction to the story in cultural terms. For instance, he strongly believed that *Chicken Run* needed a romantic element – and that would be the relationship between Ginger and Rocky.

Encouraged by David and others at Aardman, Karey came to think of himself as the 'guardian' of the story. He wanted the 'heart' of *Chicken Run* to be given more emphasis and was always stressing the emotional aspect of the script, pressing for it to be made more prominent.

Peter admits now he was surprised by Karey's viewpoint: 'When we started on the project, the last thing we imagined was that *Chicken Run* would have a really strong rom-com thread running through it. Romance is one thing that definitely doesn't feature in *The Great Escape*!'

It certainly doesn't: but then it hadn't blossomed much in Aardman films, either. Take *A Close Shave*, in which Wallace's romance with Wendolene Ramsbottom immediately comes to an end after her innocent admission that she can't stand cheese.

Peter adds: 'I'm famously unsentimental and, left to our own devices, we might well have forgotten to put in anything deeply emotional at all. At the outset, we just assumed that the chickens would want to escape. Well, of course they would; that's what people want, don't they, in prison movies?'

For his part, Nick has voiced his distaste for sentimental, saccharine stories in animation. In this same year (1996), he was interviewed by director Kevin Macdonald for Faber & Faber's fifth *Projections: Filmmakers on Filmmaking* series, edited by John Boorman, and said: 'I get turned off by some of the things in them – the sanitised stories and sickly-sweet characters.'

But this certainly wasn't Karey's approach. As written by him, Ginger was strong-minded, determined and principled – and remained so, even as he built up the story's romantic elements.

Peter now admits: 'Ginger and Rocky's is a classic love story: instant antipathy slowly giving way to admiration and finally to love – which needs to be destroyed, so it can be rebuilt better and stronger. These were the areas Karey attended to, while Nick and I pursued the gags and the overall spectacle. So there was a constant, lively and key debate between the three of us throughout this process: "Was this scene too cheesy?" "Was that line too obvious? Too ... American?" From *Brief Encounter* onwards, Brits have been disinclined to express what is in their hearts too clearly. So how clearly could Ginger express herself? Could she discuss her feelings without it seeming too blatant? We were trying to achieve that precious balance between taking the material seriously enough that you cared without straying into what we Brits perceive to be sentimentalism. In this way, slowly, and through a series of discussions, the film started to become real for us all.'

Finally, they were on the right track.

* * *

Chicken Run was of a different scale to anything Aardman had contemplated before; in comparison, even the complexities of *A Close Shave* seemed minuscule.

The crucial Hollywood pitch meeting with Katzenberg and Spielberg had happened in January 1996. The script itself – in the hands of Karey, Peter and Nick – had started evolving later that same year. Yet it would be October 1998 before filming started, though production, including voice casting and set-building, had begun a year previously. Before any footage could be shot, the whole film had to be storyboarded, which meant hundreds of drawings showing each and every scene.

The process of making the film, when it finally started, was a massive and vastly complex undertaking. Every part of the 80,000 sqft was eventually required for some element of the filmmaking process, but, even so, 'By the end of the shoot,' Peter says, 'we were bursting at the seams and actually had to shoot a few scenes at another site.' Visit the set of an Aardman feature film, and it feels as if you're watching a small city busy at work.

At certain points in *Chicken Run*'s production, there were up to thirty sets or units shooting – each with an animator (a dozen of whom had been trained for the project) backed up by camera, lighting and rigging crews. Dave Alex Riddett and Tristan Oliver gave the film the cinematic edge that the directors were looking for. At its peak, the crew consisted of some 200 people; Aardman proudly let it be known that the majority of them were recruited locally. Before every scene, an animator would 'rehearse' it after a visit from Peter or Nick, who would act out each sequence, including movement and facial expressions. (A good example of why two directors work better than just one on animation films.) The animator would then be expected, with everything set up, to shoot each scene in a single take.

It's an extraordinarily intricate and labour-intensive process. To outsiders it is surprising, or indeed incredible, that an animator is happy to have shot six seconds of finished footage in a week; but that is the 'industry norm'. *Chicken Run* ran for eighty-four minutes – an average length for an animated film – and it took almost eighteen months to shoot.

All this fails to take into account the voice artists, who

recorded their lines, mostly in London, again even before any animation had begun. Peter or Nick would direct the actors, but it often happened that re-recording would become necessary as a result of script changes or subtle new developments of certain characters.

Additionally, of course, because this was also a DreamWorks animation film, Jeffrey Katzenberg had to be kept in the loop. He was keen to know the state of production at all times: 'He would fly into Filton every six or eight weeks,' Nick remembers; he'd arrive on his private jet at Bristol's modest Filton airport, bringing his support team with him, so he could visit Aardman and check up on the story reel in person.

Because of Katzenberg's often tempestuous personality, there were those who anticipated his flying visits with trepidation, but David Sproxton was full of admiration for his professionalism and thoroughness: 'Jeffrey was brilliant. He was always right on top of production,' he recalls. 'In some ways, he's like the last of the great Hollywood moguls.' And Peter adds, 'He's the hardest working, most driven person I've ever met. He'd put in a full week's work back in LA, then fly to Bristol and back over a weekend, without a rest, and pick up on his productions over there.'

Nick saw the funny side of his Aardman colleagues' reaction to Katzenberg's impending visits: 'It was like he was Mrs Tweedy storming into the chicken coop, trying his best to catch us all out! But in fact, I got on with him rather well. It was new and exciting – and having DreamWorks behind the film, it was a real learning process.' Indeed, Katzenberg would deal with Nick directly: 'He wanted a personal relationship,' he recalls.

'There was a problem in that we wanted *Chicken Run* to feel as British as we possibly could – and of course Jeffrey wanted to make sure it could be understood by American audiences.'

This difference between the two cultures came to a head when Katzenberg objected to a line in which Mrs Tweedy uses the northern slang word 'wazzock' (meaning a stupid, annoying person) to berate her husband. No one in the US would understand it, Katzenberg argued. Peter and Nick countered that it was clearly an insult – and, besides, it was simply an amusing word in its own right. Having made his point, Katzenberg conceded.

That was how it was between Aardman and DreamWorks: some battles were lost, some were won. But it was always clear that there were two separate factions within this partnership, each with its own distinct agenda and ethos.

* * *

Peter, Nick and Karey had by now created a whole cast of characters for *Chicken Run*, and it was imperative to find the right voice actors to play them.

'From very early on we had created Ginger as the passionate one, the ringleader who wants to free her fellow chickens,' Peter says. 'We even referred to her as Miss X, after Richard Attenborough's role in *The Great Escape* – he was Bartlett, the master organiser of the escape known as

"Big X". Quite how she evolved, I can't tell you – because creating characters from scratch is a great mystery. Stories build characters, and characters lead to narrative – they're irresistibly linked. Ginger was the strong, visionary one, surrounded by a crowd of comic eccentrics, and it was difficult to find her. But Karey was very influential in giving her dimension until we had a voice to work with – when, of course, she really took off.'

Julia Sawalha, already famous for playing Jennifer Saunders' sensible daughter Saffy in TV's *Absolutely Fabulous*, was chosen as the voice of Ginger. 'We loved her youthfulness and vulnerability and intensity,' says Peter. Jane Horrocks, star of the film *Little Voice*, was recruited as the dim-witted chick Babs, and used her native Lancashire accent to great effect. The versatile, sought-after Imelda Staunton played the pragmatic, slightly fearful chicken Bunty.

Karey had originally created a pair of twin chickens, but they never made it to the final script: their places were taken by Fetcher and Nick, a pair of unscrupulous rats played by Phil Daniels and Timothy Spall.

The role of the one remaining male chicken in the coop, Fowler, went to Benjamin Whitrow, who played him to the hilt as a 'frightfully English' RAF veteran ('644 Squadron, poultry division!') who disapproves of Rocky and, indeed, of Americans in general: 'Always showing up late for every war. Overpaid, oversexed, and over here!' (This last phrase was in common usage in Britain during the Second World War; Peter had passed it to Karey, who found it amusing and immediately incorporated it into the script.) David had given Karey a list of RAF slang from the period, and some examples of servicemen's wartime banter.

'Casting Rocky Rhodes was crucial, but we didn't realise at the time quite how important it would be,' Peter recalls. 'From the earliest outline, we'd had a chicken living wild and free outside the fence, while our heroes were cooped up inside – the Lone Free Ranger, as he came to be called. In those early versions, the Ginger character met him, but we had no idea how they came together. We knew Rocky was bloke and we knew the chicken farm was basically full of women. We thought maybe he could be a foreigner and talked about making him Irish, but the idea of making him American proved to be a really terrific story idea. The great thing that I didn't realise at first is that it meant American audiences could see the film through his eyes. As soon as he arrives he's making jokes about it: "And what brings you to England, Mr Rhodes?" "Why, all the beautiful English chicks, of course." It meant there would be an American viewpoint in the film, one that fitted in organically and inspired a lot of comedy. Between Rocky and Ginger there's this incredible chemistry. There was already a battle of the sexes; and now we could add a cultural divide as well.'

Of course, if *The Great Escape* was even loosely the template for *Chicken Run*, it followed that Rocky had to be a strong, watchable character – preferably with a touch of Steve McQueen-style charisma – so Peter and Nick tossed around the names of big Hollywood stars who might provide his voice.

Nick remembers: 'It was built into the script very early on

A photograph of David taken by his father a year or two after they moved to Walton-on-Thames, 1957.

Peter Lord as Quasimodo at a fancy-dress party aboard the SS *Chusan*, somewhere in the Indian Ocean, 1966.

Another favourite family photograph of David sharing a moment with a fellow sufferer, 1961.

Peter Lord on a canal holiday with the Sproxtons in his early teens, 1968.

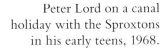

Peter's favourite dressing-
up outfit, Sydney, 1964.

David and Peter in the
Sproxton's spare room
with their homemade
camera rostrum, 1972.

Peter and David moving into
animating modelling clay in the
spare bedroom at Walton, 1973.

David with his student colleagues
Don Wynn and Shah Irani in
the lighting box of the Assembly
Rooms Theatre in Durham, 1975.

Peter animating a shot for *Take Hart* in their first studio in Bristol on Waterloo Street, 1977.

David shooting home movies on his first 16 mm movie camera, 1970.

A posed picture of David in their Waterloo Street studio, 1977.

Peter animating Morph in the Wetherell Place studio in Clifton, Bristol, in the late 1980s.

A posed picture for the BBC during the shooting of the *Blue Peter* sequence, at their Stork House studio in Hotwells, Bristol, about 1981.

Peter poses with Sarah Greene for the BBC while shooting the *Blue Peter* sequence at Stork House, 1981.

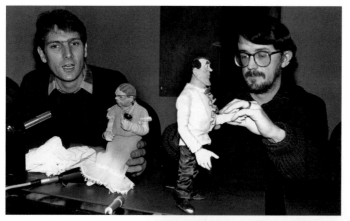

David and Peter on a panel at the Brussels Animation Festival with models from the Channel Four film *Babylon*, 1986.

Nick Park, Richard Starzak (Golly) and David relaxing one night in New York during the making of *Pee-wee's Playhouse*, 1986.

An early drawing of Wallace and Gromit by Nick Park.

EXT. BANANA LANDSCAPE 'A GRAND DAY OUT'.

Peter posing for a comedy portrait at the back of the Wetherell Place studio, 1986.

Richard Starzak (Golly) portrait, late 1980s.

Nick Park portrait, late 1980s.

Peter Lord indulging his love of comics, 1984.

Richard Starzak (Golly) at Wetherell Place. Late 1980s.

Peter Lord's sketches of Morph.

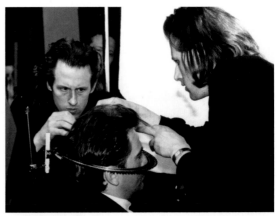

The Brothers Quay, Timothy and Stephen, animating the model train around Peter Gabriel's head at Wetherell Place for the *Sledgehammer* video, 1986.

Peter animating a clay cast
of Peter Gabriel's head for
the *Sledgehammer* video at
Wetherell Place, 1986.

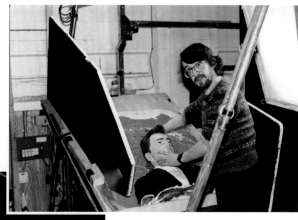

Nick protected himself against
salmonella while shooting
the dancing chickens for the
Sledgehammer video, 1986.

The entire staff of Aardman celebrate
Christmas, 1983.

A staff photograph
taken at the back of the
Wetherell Place studio,
circa 1985/6.

A set up shot in the style of an advertising magazine campaign to inform the industry of the company's move to Wetherell Place in 1985. Shot at the Production House.

Peter animating Morph at Wetherell Place with Susannah Shaw, 1985.

Nick sharing a gag with Peter at Gas Ferry Road, circa 1996/7.

A posed shot of Nick working on *Chicken Run* at the Aztec West studio, north Bristol, 1999.

Publicity shot of the three directors around after the release of *Chicken Run*, 2001.

Peter enjoys a joke with Jeffrey Katzenberg on one of his visits to Aztec West, Bristol, just before the release of *Chicken Run*, 2000.

Publicity shot of Peter Lord on the set of *Chicken Run*, 1999.

Publicity shot of Nick Park and Peter Lord on the set of *Chicken Run*, 1999.

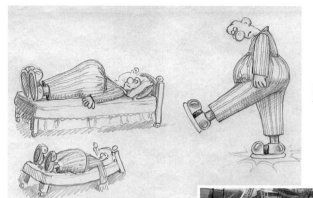

Some sketches by Nick Park of Wallace in *The Wrong Trousers*.

The crew and cast of *A Close Shave* celebrate the winning of an Oscar on board the SS *Great Britain*, with Peter Sallis and Anne Reid in 1995.

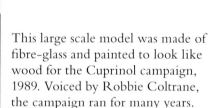

This large scale model was made of fibre-glass and painted to look like wood for the Cuprinol campaign, 1989. Voiced by Robbie Coltrane, the campaign ran for many years.

A still from one of the many Lurpak adverts Aardman produced for Gold Greenlees Trott between 1986 and 2003.

Nick poses on the set of *The Curse of the Were-Rabbit* with his fourth Academy Award in 2006.

Merlin Crossingham animating the van on the set of *The Curse of the Were-Rabbit*, 2005.

Queen Elizabeth II visits the Aardman studios when in Bristol in 1996.

Peter Lord with Andrew Bloxham and Hugh Grant being shown around the model-making department of *Pirates!* 2011.

Imelda Staunton, the voice of Queen Victoria in *Pirates!* 2011.

Martin Freeman in the voice record booth for *Pirates!* 2011.

Peter Lord on the set of *Pirates!* 2011.

Peter Lord enjoys the display at the ACMI Aardman exhibition in Melbourne, 2017.

Part of the Wallace and Gromit ride at Blackpool Pleasure Beach, 2013.

Nick Park at the launch of the Bristol Shaun in the City charity trail, 2015.

A still from the *Shaun the Sheep* series, 2014.

A live show in a Japanese Shaun the Sheep theme park, 2017.

A range of Shaun the Sheep merchandise in Japan, 2017.

Staff in the new Aardman building, 2012.

Fåret Shaun Land at the Swedish theme park Skånes Djurpark, 2017.

Nick with Maisie Williams and Eddie Redmayne on the set of *Early Man*, 2017.

Nick Park and Dave Alex Riddett on the set of *Early Man*, 2017.

A still from *Early Man*, 2017.

Morph in the series funded by Kickstarter, 2013.

Visualise This, a short film by Danny Capozzi, 2017.

Still from a DFS advert, 2017.

The original Aardman.

that Rocky was an outsider, so it felt fitting when Mel Gibson was suggested. He wasn't just your average Hollywood star.' Indeed, though he often played American characters, Gibson was Australian – which made him an outsider of sorts. It helped that he was handsome, dashing – and in his four *Lethal Weapon* cop movies, all of them hits, he had shown a flair for fast-paced, funny repartee with his screen partner Danny Glover. He'd certainly be needing that on *Chicken Run* . . .

When Peter and Nick were in Los Angeles for the Academy Awards, for which Peter's short *Wat's Pig* had been nominated, Jake Eberts had arranged for Gibson to call Peter and invite them to join him at an offbeat location – a cigar club on the top floor of a building on Rodeo Drive, right in the heart of affluent Beverly Hills. It turned out Mel Gibson had a weakness for large Cuban cigars.

He and his producer met them and they all chatted amiably, though it wasn't quite clear why the invitation had been issued. It turned out that Mel's children were great Wallace and Gromit fans, which gave Peter and Nick the leeway to pitch the role of Rocky to him at a later date.

Eventually, the deal was done, and Peter felt reassured whenever he listened to Mel talking: 'His voice was full of colour and character, dark and light. It was a dream for an animation director.'

Mel was clearly on board, and the only drawback – not a fatal one, as it turned out – was that he would not be able to voice his lines in London with the rest of the cast. He would be filming in Canada at that point, so he would need to be recorded in Vancouver. Shooting outside America helped get around the strict rules and rates of the US Screen Actors' Guild, which Aardman could barely afford and which Katzenberg did not want to pay.

To voice Ginger's one-on-one scenes with Rocky, Julia Sawalha was flown out to Canada's west coast to join him. All too often in animation, actors are recorded separately from each other, thus losing the natural chemistry of their interaction. Peter and Nick felt it was crucial to have their two leads in the same room together.

Unfortunately, there was yet another snag. When Peter and Nick flew into Vancouver to meet Mel, they were waved through immigration without a second glance. But Julia, arriving from London, was not so lucky: she was held by customs officers, shepherded into a side room and asked what she, being English, was doing in Canada: 'We've got plenty of actors in Canada. Why are you coming in to record?' Nick tried to tell a customs official that he really wanted Julia Sawalha specifically in their film, but they still held her for a whole hour. Not the most relaxing introduction to Canada, especially after a long flight.

Yet, in the end, everything turned out well, and both Mel and Julia adjusted to the fact that animation directors require multiple takes of each voiced line to give them a variety of choices later on. 'Let's be honest, neither of us had worked in much depth with actors,' Peter remembers, 'considering which, Mel and Julia were extraordinarily patient and tolerant.'

* * *

Back at Aztec West, work continued remorselessly. Making a full-length animated film, they all discovered, is an exhausting process for everyone involved. But for month after month the two directors especially were put through an experience that was wearing in its own unique way. 'What does a director do?' Peter asks rhetorically. 'He answers a question every five seconds – all day, every day.' It's an intense level of non-stop decision-making that can easily induce migraines.

Shooting had begun in October 1998 and it was now April 2000 – just a few weeks away from the world premiere in Los Angeles on 23 June. The end was near, but it had been a long, hard haul.

David recalls: 'And just as we were finishing up on production, Jeffrey Katzenberg asked us: "So what have you got planned for the next movie?" Of course, we hadn't got anything planned.' (At this point, *The Tortoise and the Hare* was in development, but there was nothing definite for Aardman to announce.)

This seemed to be a tactic of Katzenberg's – always to appear to be thinking a step or two ahead of his creative partners, in much the same vein as: 'So, guys, when can we see the script?' If nothing else, it certainly kept them alert and on edge.

The truth was, most people at Aardman had been so consumed with the making of the company's first feature-length film that there hadn't been time for strategic future planning meetings to think beyond it. But this point would soon be addressed.

And, in a sense, *Chicken Run* wasn't quite over even then.

First, it had to be promoted – seemingly to the whole world. DreamWorks, like any other Hollywood studio, wanted millions and millions of people around the globe to know that this film was about to be released.

The filmmakers and some of the lead voice actors hit the road and did dozens of media interviews in various countries – several major cities in North America, as well as London, Madrid, Barcelona, Munich, Paris and Stockholm. Journalists and TV crews would be flown into these locations from other countries to ask questions about the film at press junkets.

Typically, every reporter has just five minutes to fire questions at them, then he or she is ushered out and another immediately steps in and continues the salvo of questions. Predictably, many of the questions are more or less identical, which is handy, because in giving answers, there is no time for thought or contemplation – and certainly not complexity. It's all strictly business: stick to a few brief, memorable phrases, and repeat them to every questioner. And remember, without fail, to mention the name of the film.

After one such session in LA when Nick and Peter were punch-drunk after a score of interviews, they were astonished when the next interviewer appeared in full rooster costume. After a brief 'hola', he gave a five-minute monologue in Spanish and departed, smiling and clearly satisfied. 'Nick turned to me, deadpan: 'Were we just interviewed by a chicken?'

For his part, Peter tried to escape the junkets and wander off to explore each new city, if only for an hour or so, while Nick's method was to retire to his hotel room between batches of interview sessions each day and 'stare inanely at the ceiling, as my brain was so frazzled'.

But then, in fairness, *Chicken Run* would be opening in almost fifty territories across the world in the months to come. Movie fans in all those countries needed to be made aware of that fact. And a certain Hollywood studio needed to make its money back.

* * *

While *Chicken Run* dominated the conversation around Aardman – and a large proportion of everyone's time – in the four years before its eventual release, it would be wrong to assume it was the only creative activity in and around the studio. Other projects had been hatched and saw the light of day during this intense period, too, and Katzenberg's implied criticism in his question 'What have you got planned for the next movie?' failed to take into account a lot of other first-rate work Aardman had been doing.

Even before *Chicken Run* went into production, Peter Lord had been working for a while on a personal project – his animated short *Wat's Pig*. It was eleven minutes long and told the fable-like (and almost wordless) story of twin princes separated shortly after their birth: one remains in the royal castle, while the other is raised by a pig. The brother in the royal household is a weak and pampered boy, while his brother in the countryside grows up resourceful and hard-working. When a neighbouring prince declares war, the brothers reunite to try to save their nation.

In an unusual format choice, the screen is split in half so that it's possible to follow both stories simultaneously. Peter admitted it was a labour of love: 'Short films like this are seldom a commercial opportunity – a polite way of saying that, with the possible exception of *Creature Comforts*, they don't return any significant money.' But this was still in the heady days when Channel 4 were commissioning and funding independent animated films – 'the whole British industry owes them a debt for their support'. As it was, *Wat's Pig* was well received and was nominated for best animated short at the 1997 Academy Awards – just as Peter's earlier short film *Adam* had been four years previously. Another return to the much-loved red carpet was called for.

The late '90s was a creative boom-time for the studio, and for stop-motion animation generally. The year after *Wat's Pig*, Steve Box had the opportunity to direct his first solo film, also for Channel 4. *Stage Fright* was a theatrical fable set in a decaying music hall and it featured the voice of comedian Graham Fellows. It was ambitious and visually beautiful and Steve won a BAFTA for it in 1998.

Then there was *Rex the Runt*, an amusing series with deadpan humour directed by Golly, who had introduced the title character in his short film *Ident* some years previously. It featured the dog Rex and his three family members, all of whom somehow knew they were on television and devised adventures to entertain their viewers. A total of thirteen ten-minute episodes were broadcast on BBC Two, starting from Christmas 1998, and a second series began in 2001. It was a pioneering animation series, still much loved by a young-adult audience for its anarchic and subversive humour.

Away from Aardman and working for the BBC, Golly also directed *Robbie the Reindeer*, whose protagonist was the son of Rudolph the red-nosed reindeer – except that fact could not be specifically mentioned for copyright reasons. In what became an inspired running joke, the word 'Rudolph' was replaced by the phrase 'Robbie's dad', and if any characters started to say his name, they were swiftly interrupted. Robbie himself was a lazy, physically out-of-condition reindeer, which did not prevent him from aspiring to become a member of Santa's dashing reindeer team.

Robbie the Reindeer was filmed in aid of Comic Relief, and Richard Curtis was its writer and executive producer. It comprised three episodes, each around seven minutes long, all shown on BBC television in 1999, 2002 and 2007.

Angry Kid represented something of a departure. Devised by Darren Walsh, it was a series of sixty-second films about a sweary teenage boy with red hair and a whiny, grating voice who is extraordinarily rude and gets himself into all kinds of scrapes. With scores of substitute face masks to create lip sync, it's a revolutionary technique unique to Darren.

It was originally commissioned by Channel 4, but they demanded online rights – just at a time when the potential of online exposure was starting to become clear. 'We had a hunch *Angry Kid* would be ideal online content,' David says now, 'so we told Channel 4 we'd be happy for them to have the TV rights, but we'd insist in retaining online rights.'

That marked the end of that deal, but then Aardman

entered discussions with Atom Films, one of the US's pioneers in providing entertainment alongside content for
emerging smart-phone platforms including the new '3'
network. Atom embraced the idea of short-form content and
largely targeted an 18–35 age demographic. They were the
perfect environment for *Angry Kid*.

Tentatively, Aardman sold Atom ten *Angry Kid* episodes,
and they immediately took off, appearing on Atom's 'most
watched' charts. The TV industry took notice of this, and
BBC Three came in with an offer – for more money than
Channel 4's original bid. As David observes: 'If we'd taken
the Channel 4 deal, we would have waited several years to
earn back our costs; under the BBC Three deal, we recouped
in about eighteen months.'

Angry Kid has enjoyed surprising longevity. A total of sixty
episodes were shot, spread over several years from 1997, with
the latest CGI version being made in 2015. It still features on
Aardman's YouTube channel, having maintained its popularity after all this time.

Apart from these shorts and television programmes, there
was plenty of other change within Aardman that had nothing
to do with film. The lucrative advertising industry was proving to be the main growth area, and the company had landed
a major account with the huge American gasoline company
Chevron. David discussed the deal with the company's
executives in Los Angeles while he was there to attend the
1994 Academy Awards ceremony, and what clinched the deal
was the series of Heat Electric ads, based on Nick's *Creature
Comforts* films, which had become so popular on British TV.

In the same vein, the commercials featured talking cars, each with a different personality. There was Pickup Pete, who tows horses to their barn every night; a car whose housewife owner uses it for shopping expeditions and has a habit of denting it; and a car that boasts of its many 'options' on a service station forecourt, with a dog faintly resembling Gromit attending to it. This turned out to be a major, long-running account; to this day Chevron remains one of Aardman's advertising clients.

It wasn't only the States that clamoured for the Aardman touch in their commercials, either. After an approach from Japan, the company shot some spots featuring Wallace and Gromit for a product called Glico Pudding, a sort of custard. In one of the best-known in the series, Wallace and Gromit are seen enjoying Glico Pudding on the surface of the moon.

There was sound business logic behind this decision. In Japan, famous stars appear in TV commercials as they are regarded much more highly compared with the UK and the US. So the mere fact of Wallace and Gromit appearing in Japanese TV adverts confirmed they had already reached star status there.

* * *

The seemingly endless pre-release phase of *Chicken Run* was almost over. Peter, Nick and their lead actors had done literally hundreds of interviews for TV and print media. Having completed a whistle-stop tour of several European capitals, Peter and Nick were crisscrossing the States, visiting major cities to gain the film yet more exposure. They had even sat in on pre-release 'test preview' screenings – Nick in Portland, Oregon, and Peter in Long Beach, south of Los Angeles – so they could see how a local audience would react. 'Watching the very ordinary, very American families drifting into the cinema at Long Beach, Peter remembers realising with a shock: 'These are our audience! These people with such utterly different lives and experiences. What on earth are they to make of a film about chickens in '50s Yorkshire?' Would they enjoy being transported to a world they'd never seen before? Or would the film just leave them baffled? In fact, the Long Beach crowd responded well to the film. They gave it excellent scores and reviews, leaving everyone feeling relieved and confident.

It genuinely seemed that nothing was left to chance. Following the test screenings, DreamWorks had been doing 'tracking' for the film: asking members of the public if they had heard of *Chicken Run* and whether they planned to go and see it. Unhappily, the figures were moderate at best. At this point, Katzenberg had two choices: he could either reduce the studio's press and advertising spending (known in the industry as 'P&A') in an attempt to cut DreamWorks' losses before the film even opened, or he could go for broke, roll the dice and increase the P&A, backing a film in which he believed in the face of possible losses. To his great credit, Katzenberg chose the latter course.

But though he acted decisively, the outcome was still uncertain. At the end of their promotional tour, Peter and Nick found themselves in his company, once more aboard the DreamWorks jet, heading back to LA for the film's long-awaited weekend opening.

During these journeys, Jeffrey routinely buried his head in business; but now he looked up from the script he was reading and became confidential. Turning to them, very seriously he said 'This weekend we're going to be jumping off a cliff. This may work – or it may not work. So we'll just hold hands and jump together.'

Given his usual unassailable confidence, this was disconcerting to hear. Peter recalls his feelings at the time: 'Not really being aware of what was going on behind the scenes at DreamWorks, this came as a real surprise. And not a pleasant one. I now realise he might have been thinking of the whole future of his company. I don't believe I ever saw a chink in his armour before that or afterwards.'

This is surely the right analysis. Up to that point, DreamWorks' animation division had released films like *The Prince of Egypt, Antz* and *The Road to El Dorado* – all of which achieved high grosses, but had been expensive to make, and therefore did not make much money.

'They'd had four pretty moderate successes,' Peter recalls now. 'They'd got a sort of vestigial Disney audience going to see them. But it wasn't an audience that was passionate about them. *Chicken Run* had an entirely different appeal – it was irreverent, it was funny. So if he were now to have only a moderate success or a flop with us, that might have been disastrous for DreamWorks.'

David has another viewpoint that helps explain Jeffrey Katzenberg's worries: 'He knew that no one in Hollywood had succeeded in opening a new movie studio since 1938, and at the time of *Chicken Run*, DreamWorks had its financial problems. We were in business with them for ten years, and in that period they had to refinance three times, so there was a lot of anxiety around that place in its early years. The *Shrek* films were the turning point for DreamWorks [the first was released in 2002] and they were a long time coming. I thought Jeffrey gave it a bloody good shot.'

As it turned out, the climax of the *Chicken Run* story was a happy one. Quite simply, it was a big hit. Sometime during its opening weekend in America, Jeffrey managed to track Nick down by phone while he was on holiday in a remote croft in Scotland. He was keen to break the news that *Chicken Run* had just passed the $12 million mark at the US box office, which was significant: this was the industry's 'make or break' figure that determined whether a film would be successful. In fact, to the delight of everyone at DreamWorks, it ended up grossing over $17 million over the whole of that opening weekend and went on to break the $100 million mark at the US box office, ending up at around $106 million. In the rest of the world, it grossed a further $118 million.*

True, other DreamWorks films had grossed more, but then their budgets were vastly more than Aardman's $45 million: *Antz* and *The Road to El Dorado* had cost twice as much. *Chicken Run* could thus boast healthy profits.

Chicken Run has found its place in the record books: eighteen years after its release, it remains the highest grossing

* Figures courtesy of Box Office Mojo.

stop-motion animated film in history. But even with their success, Peter found himself uncomfortable with the way Hollywood studios release their films: 'I hate it that the first weekend's takings determine the destiny of a film. It hardly gives a film a chance to find an audience.'

Never one to dwell on success too long, Jeffrey told Peter and David: 'We should make a sequel.'

'Now, as I remember it,' Peter recalls, 'this wrong-footed us, because in our innocence we hadn't expected it. Franchising films [making several sequels of a hit film] hadn't really started back then. And in terms of *Chicken Run*, I certainly hadn't thought of it. I thought the story was done! We told Jeffrey we couldn't do it at that point. It would have been five years before we'd have anything to show.' And, in fairness, the prospect of working immediately with chickens for another five years was not tempting.

11

A FABLE TOO FAR

By the turn of the century, Aardman's fortunes had broadly followed a gentle upward curve. Since the days when Peter and David had founded it as teenagers, it could boast a number of substantial achievements: the creation of memorable, beloved clay characters like Morph, Wallace and Gromit; a reputation as a company that produced not only ground-breaking animation like *Creature Comforts* but also eye-catching, lucrative TV commercials; a slew of Academy Awards, BAFTAs and other prestigious awards; a gradually growing and gainfully employed workforce; and the completion, in partnership with a Hollywood studio, of the globally successful feature film *Chicken Run*.

Not much to complain about in all that, but over the next few years, Aardman's mettle would be tested by a number of incidents that could only be defined as setbacks.

The first of these had its roots in the company's desire to make another feature film. As we have seen, before *Chicken Run* had even wrapped, Jeffrey Katzenberg had already alluded to this with his brusque question: 'So what have you got planned for the next movie?'

It was time to survey the ideas that had been pitched by screenwriters close to Aardman and see if any of them could be developed into a story that might be appropriate for a feature film.

One promising idea had come from Karey Kirkpatrick, who had written the screenplay for *Chicken Run*. He was hard-working, full of ideas, and had made a good impression on the Aardman team. Through his association with Aardman, he looked a solid talent from the DreamWorks viewpoint.

Kirkpatrick had come up with a story that had a cute, appealing premise. It was based on Aesop's fable about the Tortoise and the Hare, and posed the question: 'What if the hare had won the race rather than the tortoise?' Obviously, that set up the opportunity for a dramatic rematch, with the tortoise clearly cast in the role of the sympathetic underdog. And Aardman could add its distinctive touch to proceedings by shooting it in a style akin to *Creature Comforts*, in the manner of an animated documentary.

Thinking of *Creature Comforts* led them to consider Golly as a possible director. He had long been an admirer of *Creature Comforts*, and eventually went on to direct a whole new *Creature Comforts* series for television. He had gone off staff and freelanced for a spell, but had directed most of the episodes of *Rex the Runt* in recent years, as well as *Robbie the Reindeer* for the BBC and Comic Relief.

Golly showed interest in *The Tortoise and the Hare*, so it was agreed to develop the idea further. Maybe this could be the feature film to follow in the wake of *Chicken Run*.

It seemed like a good plan, and the production machine went into overdrive. Comedian Paul Whitehouse was to play Harry the Hare, while Morris the Tortoise would be voiced by veteran screen legend Michael Caine. Prominent British actors Brenda Blethyn and Bob Hoskins were also assigned substantial voice roles. Models had been designed and sets were built to create an attractive backdrop – a small town that looked remarkably like Bristol; it even had a suspension bridge.

After a number of drafts, Kirkpatrick had produced a good first-draft script – which started off more or less adhering to Aesop's fable. As schoolboys, Harry and Morris run a race. Convinced he cannot possibly lose against a tortoise, Harry takes a nap and loses. The story then fast-forwards to the two characters as young adults, with Harry feeling forever humiliated by his defeat. To regain some of his lost self-respect, he challenges Morris to a rematch.

It all seemed fine on paper, but with one obvious problem: Michael Caine was in his late sixties at this point, and, though loaded with charm, his voice suggested his age and simply didn't sound right in the mouth of Morris, who was meant to be in his early twenties. With many apologies and thanks, Caine would need to be replaced.

There were by now some 160 people working on the $25 million (£17.7 million) film. The story itself seemed workable, so the reel was dispatched to Jeffrey Katzenberg at DreamWorks. And that was where the problems started.

Katzenberg let it be known that he felt something wasn't working. 'I knew what he meant,' Peter recalls. 'And I think we could all feel it.'

David recalls: 'Golly had often said there was a fundamental issue with the story – partly to do with the original fable and partly the new approach to it: where would the tension be if the hare had to win, and the audience knew it from the start?'

So was the basic idea of the story just not good enough? Or had Aardman gone into production before it was ready?

'Both of those things, I think,' Peter reflects. 'Certainly, we went into production when we weren't ready. Absolutely that. We set off making the film when the story was still unresolved. It's a very risky place to be. The story had all the right elements – an underdog hero, an implausible challenge to take on. But it wasn't quite funny or heartfelt enough.'

So now it was all hands to the pump at Aardman in terms of tweaking the story, rewriting scenes and redefining the characters. For all their efforts, however, Katzenberg remained unmoved. In June 2001, he announced that *The Tortoise and the Hare* needed a pause in production: 'Take two weeks and really figure this stuff out,' he ordered.

It was a real blow, and involved sending home the majority of workers on the film for a whole fortnight. Peter, David and other senior Aardman executives tried to comfort themselves that this kind of hiatus had happened with other films that had become massive hits – *Toy Story* and *Shrek* among them.

Part of the problem, however, was that there was a creative tension between Golly and Jeffrey Katzenberg. From their first meeting, the American mogul had been sceptical about Golly, who, when asked if he had read the script, replied: 'Yes, and I don't think it's working very well.' At which point Katzenberg walked out of the room. The two men were opposites as personality types: one fast-talking, supremely confident and unused to being crossed; the other reflective, sardonic and faintly downbeat – no one's idea of a yes-man.

On a later occasion, Golly and Peter flew out to Los Angeles so Golly could pitch Jeffrey an idea he had for salvaging the film's third act. But again Jeffrey, surrounded by his assistants, did not respond positively to the new ideas.

Two weeks came and went, but, despite a huge amount of work from everyone to try to find a solution to the problem, there was something wrong with the story that no one at Aardman or at DreamWorks could convincingly fix. 'I'd done my best to fix it,' says Golly, 'We all had, but I wasn't sure we could ever swim with this particular script.'

In the end, Aardman was forced to lay off ninety staff working on *The Tortoise and the Hare*, which was now to be put on hold for as long as six months.

'We'd never faced failure on this scale before,' Peter admits. He called a crew meeting in the Aardman canteen and tearfully told them the film would not be made; the company had failed them but would not be giving up on the project.

No one ever did give up on it, but after the six months were up, in February 2002, Aardman was forced to admit publicly that the film's production had been postponed indefinitely. As David notes about DreamWorks: 'That decision for them was just money – about $5 million by that point – but for us it meant putting people out of work.' And, of course, $5 million was relatively small change for a Hollywood studio.

'It irks me that we didn't spot the structural crack in the story before going into production,' David adds. 'There was so much going for *The Tortoise and the Hare* – it was a very funny idea and it had a lot of interesting characters. We should have brought in stronger writers earlier to wrestle the problem to the ground. I think in the end it could have been a very good film.'

Reflecting on these events now, Peter admits: 'I have to say the film wasn't good enough and we went into production too early. But now I often wonder: had we just gone ahead and finished it, would it have been so bad? It was bloody painful for so many people when we closed down that film – very stressful and very upsetting. So what if we'd kept going? Because when you *do* keep going, you *do* make it better. It's always the case that you make it better. So I didn't really know what I was doing, honestly.'

Now Golly takes a broader view of why the story didn't quite click: 'I think *The Tortoise and the Hare* worked against the Aardman ethos. Its world was completely populated by animals, which was something no one here had ever done before. With *Creature Comforts*, you're always aware of the human presence – whether it's in a zoo, or on a leash, you're aware these are kept creatures. We based *The Tortoise and the Hare* on this city where animals drove cars and worked in all the shops . . . I couldn't get my head around it. Was this a different world? A different planet? I didn't understand the basic premise of it, so it went downhill from there.'

One positive thing to come from this period in which so many people at Aardman had no work was the creation of Wallace and Gromit's *Cracking Contraptions*. These were ten one-minute films that showcased some of inventor Wallace's more outrageous inventions – such as the Autochef, a robot that cooks your eggs just as you like them, and the Snoozatron, which plumps your pillows, plays restful music and gives you a good night's sleep.

Nick recalls: 'The animators were all in downtime and wanting to have a go at directing, so the idea of making one-minute Wallace and Gromit films was approved. We all realised how long it would be before *The Curse of the Were-Rabbit* and a new Wallace and Gromit film would come to market.'

So, the animators were given the chance to think of ideas, which Nick oversaw: 'This worked as a training programme for the teams to prepare for *Were-Rabbit*, but also to keep everyone busy in this downtime,' he recalls. *Cracking Contraptions* launched on the BBC's site and on Atom Films in October 2002.

Everyone survived to fight another day, however, and Golly would go on to a whole new challenge, overseeing the creation of a *Creature Comforts* series for television.

12

RABBITS AND RATS

If there was one lesson that had been learnt from the *Tortoise and the Hare* disaster, it was that Aardman needed to develop their feature projects ahead of time.

'We weren't very good at being assertive enough during the development process to push hard on potential problems and not let things slide,' David Sproxton observes. 'Development is a long, drawn-out process and we didn't allow enough time for it.'

Nick and screenwriter Bob Baker were already at work on a feature-length Wallace and Gromit movie, the plot for which they had devised together almost accidentally, while tossing around ideas for a Wallace and Gromit book for the BBC.

It would be 'a vegetarian horror movie', in which Wallace and Gromit, their careers as window cleaners now in the past, were working as humane pest controllers somewhere in the English countryside. Their company would be called Anti-Pesto, and its job was to protect the locals' vegetables from marauding rabbits. The mistress of the manor house,

213

the posh, delightful Lady Tottington, hires them, against the advice of the villainous Victor Quartermaine, who has designs on her.

In the course of a long, intricate story, it emerges that a giant rabbit has been devouring many of the locals' vegetables. But who could this enormous 'Were-Rabbit' be? And what is possessing him? All becomes clear towards the end, at Tottington Hall's annual giant vegetable competition.

After a meeting between Peter, David and Nick with Jeffrey Katzenberg on a different topic, Nick took him to one side and sounded him out about the prospect of a Wallace and Gromit feature.

Katzenberg phoned him later that night and told Nick he was definitely interested, whereupon Nick and Steve Box pitched the idea, outlining the bare bones of the story. It was a detailed, intricate pitch that lasted two hours. (At one point, Katzenberg dozed off, almost certainly because he was jet-legged.)

He was immediately concerned it might be too British for American tastes, but he liked the idea and encouraged Nick, Steve and Bob to forge ahead with what would become *The Curse of the Were-Rabbit*.

Nick had taken note of the fact that DreamWorks seemed more comfortable with two directors on feature-length films, and asked Steve Box to co-direct. This was an easy choice for Nick: 'Steve and I had enjoyed working together for many years on Wallace and Gromit and had become firm friends with a similar sensitivity and humour. He felt like a natural choice as a co-director. I admired the way he worked in a hands-on style with the characters and loved the energy and attention to detail that he guaranteed.'

As for Bob Baker, he was Nick's long-term writing partner, who had brought real skills to their partnership – someone who could turn Nick's ideas and drawings into a coherent story. Nick, Steve and Bob huddled themselves away at Wetherell Place, now being used by Aardman as an overspill studio and a development hub, to work up a script. Later in development, Mark Burton, an accomplished TV comedy writer who had supplied additional dialogue on *Chicken Run*, was drafted in to join the team.

The new team proceeded with the story until they were satisfied they could pitch it in full to Katzenberg and his team. He flew into Filton airport, as usual, and headed straight for Wetherell Place, where the pitch would take place – a more modest venue compared to what Katzenberg was used to in Los Angeles.

As Peter recalls: 'At nearly two hours, the pitch was very long and very un-Hollywood. Let's be honest, it rambled. Neither Nick nor Steve's delivery was exactly slick, and Jeffrey, I'm sure, had never sat through anything like it; he was used to something altogether punchier. At one point, Steve even sang a little song on a ukulele. The whole thing was deeply eccentric and unapologetically British. But it was bursting with a sense of fun. It had the stamp of pure comic genius.'

But for all its eccentricities, it was an irresistible idea. The basic decision was settled: DreamWorks would make the *Were-Rabbit* film.

Nick was pleased the project had reached this stage and was feeling benign towards DreamWorks: 'They had a lot of faith in us, this small British company. They were helping to put our work out there and were very much wanting to make an Aardman film – one they felt could be marketable.'

But, as he concedes, that sense of bonhomie did not last: 'Shooting *The Curse of the Were-Rabbit*, there was less of a sense of that good relationship. Instead, there was a lot of fighting over the rights to Wallace and Gromit. Things were starting to go wrong at that end.'

Indeed they were. From Aardman's vantage point, it was one thing for DreamWorks to play tough in negotiations over films they were backing featuring new characters devised specially for that film. But Aardman insisted on a very different deal with DreamWorks from the one they had struck for *Chicken Run*: 'We had to hang on to various rights; we needed guarantees of control over our characters,' Peter notes. 'We didn't just want a standard net-profits deal,' David adds. 'NET really means Nothing Ever Turns up – meaning money.' Aardman also needed some guarantee of participation in the film's eventual box-office grosses.

Michael Rose helped broker the right deal for Aardman, in conjunction with an American entertainment lawyer. They were willing to agree that Aardman would not make a feature film for any other company during the period leading up to *Were-Rabbit*'s release. Crucially, however, Aardman's position was that if DreamWorks were not prepared to accept their proposed deal, *The Curse of the Were-Rabbit* would be made as a one-off TV special, backed by funds from the BBC and other European broadcasters.

In other words, they were prepared to walk away. Nick remembers Michael Rose's phrase was: 'Wallace and Gromit are our Crown Jewels – we can't sell them short.'

It was a laudably tough negotiating stance, and Katzenberg balked at first. But the Aardman team dug their heels in and, without agreeing specific figures, the two sides adjourned, leaving the details to their legal teams.

It worked out happily: *Were-Rabbit* would be a DreamWorks film, but Aardman would get a back-end deal from box-office grosses. And, critically, the company would retain full ownership of the pre-existing characters they had created.

All in all, not a bad day for the 'little guys'.

* * *

Still, it was never exactly easy with DreamWorks, who found fault with a handful of aspects in the film. Nick's original title for it had been a witty play on words: 'The Great Vegetable Plot'. The studio did some audience research on the phrase, however, and it transpired the word 'vegetable' did not appeal to American children. *The Curse of the Were-Rabbit*, on the other hand, with its intimations of a horror movie spoof, received widespread approval on both sides of the Atlantic.

Jeffrey Katzenberg also wondered out loud why the Antipesto vehicle (an Austin A35 van) had been drawn as rusty. 'Is the rust essential?' he asked. 'We sighed a little,' David recalls, 'and said, "Yes, the rust is essential."' He

217

notes that while British audiences tend to favour underdog characters, Americans gravitate towards aspirational social climbers. 'To Jeffrey,' he says, 'Wallace should have had a gleaming pick-up truck.' Needless to say, Aardman won that skirmish.

Another piece of good news was the casting of Helena Bonham Carter as Lady Tottington. Nick and Steve were delighted with her performance. 'Sometimes when actors play someone very posh they can overdo it and it can be off-putting,' he says. 'But with Helena there was something softer and endearing about her voice. She made "Lady Totty" very appealing.'

One way and another, then, *The Curse of the Were-Rabbit* had sometimes been a bumpy ride, but David insists it also represented a learning curve for Aardman: 'We hadn't been spending time – it's not money, it's time – doing enough iterations in the story. Nor that deep rigorous analysis of: "Is this the best we can do?" The finished story reel of *The Curse of the Were-Rabbit* is about 6,000 storyboard frames. We drew about 25,000. It meant every sequence is done at least three or four times to get it better and better. And that's the hard bit. Making it is one thing, but actually getting it to click is hard. And we needed it to click. Towards the end of shooting *Were-Rabbit*, we changed the original ending quite dramatically. They were about six weeks away from shooting it and we were saying, "The ending isn't strong enough." Nick was anxious about it. I remember we were in New York at the time. Jeffrey had flown a lot of us over – Pete, Nick, Golly and our publicist Arthur Sheriff – to do a big promotional event at the Lincoln Center. In the departure lounge at JFK coming back, Nick was expressing his concerns. "I'm not happy with the ending," he said, and we asked him: "What's the issue?" The ending we had at that point was a sort of "false wedding" in which you think Wallace and Lady Tottington are getting married – but they're not. You hear the church bells ringing out, you see the top of the spire – but then the camera pulls back and it transpires that it's Lady Totty and PC Mackintosh who are getting married. Wallace and Gromit wish them well, then they drive off in their van, which is stuffed full of rabbits, which they empty over the county border. Nick wasn't happy about it.' Indeed, he agreed it would be funny if she'd had a crush on PC Mackintosh, but it 'felt a bit random'.

'The problem was that PC Mackintosh wanted nothing to do with this vegetable stuff at all,' David continued. 'He's a huge cynic about the whole vegetable competition. And then there's Lady Tottington, who's the biggest tree-hugger in the town. Yes, it's comic that they'd get married – but they wouldn't. It doesn't play to their character. Nick's development of the new ending worked much better. That was quite a major rewrite very late on. In fact, we held the whole shoot back for four or five weeks. No, it wasn't ideal – but that's what happens, if you're lucky: you find a better ending.'

* * *

During this period, Aardman managed to develop another idea for a feature film that found favour with DreamWorks. It had the working title of *Ratropolis*, and it was the story of

219

Roddy, a pet rat whose owners live in a posh London flat. One day, he is flushed down the toilet and ends up in a sewer, where he finds a city that looks a lot like London but is made out of junk. There he meets a sewer rat named Rita and urges her to return above ground with him.

The idea had come from Sam Fell, a bright writer-director already known to Aardman; he had directed three episodes of *Rex the Runt* for them.

Ratropolis was one of half a dozen ideas Aardman pitched to DreamWorks, and it was the one that Katzenberg immediately liked. In contrast to the *Tortoise and the Hare* experience, there would be plenty of development and preparation time; the *Curse of the Were-Rabbit* team had by now vacated Wetherell Place and the *Ratropolis* team moved in.

There was a sense of enthusiasm surrounding it: a different kind of story from a first-time feature director, and potentially another first-rate film from Aardman, reinforcing its status as the leading exponent of stop-motion animation.

Everything was proceeding smoothly until September 2003, when Peter was on a relaxing walking holiday in a remote area of the Lake District. Even in this inaccessible part of the world, Katzenberg's people managed to track him down. 'At that time, Jeffrey used the phone brilliantly to hold his empire together. He always had two assistants to line up his calls like air-traffic controllers stacking planes up at Heathrow – though with less waiting time. He'd hang up on one high-powered call and instantly pick up the next one. To be out of contact was anathema to him. And there I was, in a cottage halfway up a mountain with no reception at all. I had to travel 5 miles down the valley to a sort of mountain pass where finally I got mobile signal. But, when I got through, the message from Jeffrey wasn't good. 'We've got to make *Ratropolis* in CGI.'

But how could that be? The whole point of Aardman was that it stood proudly as a company that produced stop-motion animation – a tradition that went back to its earliest days, when Peter and David were still in their teens.

Katzenberg elaborated, and his reasons for insisting on CGI were dispiriting to Peter. It seemed he'd heard it on the grapevine that his rival animation company, Pixar, also had a rat-related movie in development. It would be called *Ratatouille* and was about a Parisian rat with ambitions to be a gourmet chef in a five-star restaurant.

It was thus quite unlike the story of *Ratropolis*, but Katzenberg had been down this road twice before with films that sounded somewhat similar. In 1998, DreamWorks' movie *Antz* had lost out at the box office to Disney's release the same year of *A Bug's Life*. And, more recently, DreamWorks' *Shark Tale* had been nowhere nearly as successful as another under-water movie, Pixar's *Finding Nemo*.

Katzenberg was desperate not to let such a thing happen again, and this meant he was adamant that *Ratropolis* had to be completed and released before Pixar's *Ratatouille*.

If *Ratropolis* were to be filmed in CGI at DreamWorks' studio at Glendale in Los Angeles, that would ensure it would open first. The alternative, if Aardman insisted on making it in stop-motion, was to wait until shooting was finished on *The Curse of the Were-Rabbit* – thus missing this newly imposed 'deadline'. To set up a new, dedicated CGI studio in Bristol was simply impossible. Making it in Los Angeles was the clear answer to him. Peter could see another reason for Katzenberg favouring this option: 'With the film being made under his own roof, he could exercise more control over the decision-making.'

Peter resisted the idea initially, but Katzenberg wasn't about to change his mind. On a damp Cumbrian hillside, with a failing mobile signal and watched by a few impassive sheep, Peter debated the pros and cons with Jeffrey. 'Ultimately he made it pretty clear,' says Peter, 'if it wasn't going to be made in CGI, it wouldn't be made at all.'

That in itself caused another problem for Aardman: no other project was in an advanced state of planning, so starting virtually from scratch would mean at least another five years before a new film would be completed.

On the upside, being in production would bring revenue into the company, and Aardman would need to find a bright idea for a new stop-motion film once *The Curse of the Were-Rabbit* was completed anyway. In the interim, *Ratropolis* was retitled *Flushed Away*. Peter and David realised that making this film – even under these less-than-perfect conditions – would at least relieve the strain on the company finances. David could see another consolation in the requirement to make it a CGI film: 'We had expected to make *Flushed Away* as stop-frame, but realised that it was a massive-scale movie, with lots of sets and underground scenes with loads of liquid – all of which would have been difficult in stop-frame. In many ways, making it CGI was a win–win, as we could make the film and simultaneously enter the world of CGI movies.'

* * *

'I love *Flushed Away*, and I'll always consider it a wonderful achievement. Sam Fell and Dave Bowers did a marvellous job. But I can't say I loved the process of making it,' Peter reflects. 'It was hard to enjoy. Not because I didn't like the film – it was just that I regretted that it wasn't made in our own studio. That was the reality. It's our film, but it was made at *their* studio. Sam and I had developed it as a stop-motion film. It would have been glorious to make it that way, at Aardman; but we lost that opportunity, and therefore lost that intimate connection with the film that we'd have felt had it been made here in Bristol. As regards the technique, CGI versus stop-motion, I didn't mind so much. Both techniques have their attractions. But making it in Los Angeles, that was the problem. And, again, I was not prepared – maybe I was being stubborn – to move out there for the whole time. Because that's what Jeffrey would have liked – if not to direct, then certainly to be the Aardman producer on the ground for the whole time. Which I absolutely didn't want to do, because Aardman is my company, and it's here in Bristol. I wouldn't stay in Los Angeles full-time so I travelled there a lot instead. The travelling became a bit of a bore, but, more fundamentally, their way of making films, their studio ethos, didn't really fit with ours. With the Atlantic between us for the first

two films, I always felt we had a good, lively working relationship. But now the film was anchored at DreamWorks, the
dynamic changed. Jeffrey was on top of *everything*, all across
every project. It was undeniable, it was just a fact of life.'

DreamWorks had a process whereby the filmmakers
would put together a storyboard, then a story reel, add temporary voices – and show the result to the studio's executives.

'Great idea; we do exactly the same thing at Aardman.
But at DreamWorks, you do it for Jeffrey above all,' reflects
Peter. 'You show this reel regularly to him and his people –
and immediately they go into conclave. There'd be twenty
people in there – directors, writers, producers – and all of
them diving in instantly, critiquing what they'd just seen.
I don't mind criticism, but in the studio it became a forum
for showing off and generally scoring creative points with
the boss. If Jeffrey said "good note", it was a major accolade.
I hated all that. We wouldn't do that in Bristol. We'd watch,
consider and take our time before reacting.'

For all that, he concedes some elements of the story did not
emerge until late in the shoot: 'It's an interesting thing about
storytelling. We had this story from the first: a privileged
rat named Roddy, living above ground in a state of extreme
comfort, is flushed down the toilet and ends up in a subter-
ranean world which he finds horrifying. All he wants to do
is get home. But down there he meets Rita; there's chemistry.
He does his damnedest to get back to his ivory tower but,
when he gets there, he realises it's all shallow and mean-
ingless without Rita. So he goes back to rescue the girl from
down below. That was the shape, it was there from early on,

but what was wrong in the rat's ivory tower changed a lot. He started out as an entitled, fairly obnoxious aristocrat, yet he ended up more sympathetic. And it turned out that the thing that was wrong in his world was that he was lonely. He didn't have community or friends or family. And that idea, which sounds quite simple, came very late in the process, more than three-quarters of the way through the shoot.

It's interesting how stories stay alive and evolving. You know what happens – but not always why. Did that change come too late? Well, I wish it had come in earlier. We had two excellent characters, hamster butlers played by Simon Callow and Geoffrey Palmer. But when we changed Roddy's story and made it about emotional isolation, it no longer worked for him to have company of any sort. He had to be alone, so, with regret, two great characters were struck from the record.'

Peter felt the reasons for doing so were shaky: 'We were trying to portray Roddy as lonely, and we had a scene on his birthday when the butlers bring him a big birthday cake, and then retire from the room so he can eat it. To us, that suggested how lonely his life was, but the DreamWorks people thought, "No, if the butlers are around, how lonely can he be?" So that was a lot of work wasted.' 'And', adds David, 'thousands of dollars down the drain!'

* * *

In the end, both *The Curse of the Were-Rabbit* and *Flushed Away* performed well enough at the box office – though not

225

quite well enough to keep DreamWorks happy. *Were-Rabbit* received rave reviews from critics and took the top position on the US box-office chart on its opening weekend. It ended up grossing $56 million in the US and around $135 million in the rest of the world, about half of that figure in Britain.

The following spring, Nick and Steve Box went to the Academy Awards, where the film was named best animated feature – a first for Nick, whose previous Academy Awards had been for animated short films.

Nick and Steve both wore big, though relatively tasteful, bow ties, designed by Paul Smith – and, on receiving the award, dug into their pockets and produced two miniature versions of the same bow ties, which they placed around the necks of their statuettes.

One of the films *Were-Rabbit* beat to the Academy Award was Tim Burton's *Corpse Bride*. Coincidentally, his partner Helena Bonham Carter had a voice role in both films, and they were sitting directly in front of Nick and Steve when the award was announced.

Touchingly, Nick paid tribute to Peter Sallis, who had been invited to the ceremony. Noting that Peter had been voicing Gromit for twenty-three years, Nick told him: 'You've been an absolute gem, Peter. You've really sparkled all the way.' Nick then thanked 'Jeffrey Katzenberg and DreamWorks, who also sparkle'. (He now regrets that, in the nervousness of this occasion, he forgot to mention Peter and David too.)

It was a sincere compliment, and a night to celebrate for

all concerned. But the truth was that relations between Aardman and DreamWorks had been somewhat icy in the preceding months. The studio had hoped *Were-Rabbit* would gross more money in the US and the worldwide market than *Chicken Run*, given that Wallace and Gromit were already known entities.

Nick recalls that DreamWorks put out a press release claiming the film had lost money and implying that Aardman had underachieved with a potentially promising idea. 'It looked pretty good from where I was sitting,' Nick says. 'In our personal dealings they were still very friendly, treating us like we were "best buddies" – and then there was this cold, clinical side where it was just "this is business". They tried to make it look to the press like we were the problem.'

At this point, Nick recalls, 'we were right in the middle of making *Flushed Away*, so it was not a happy time'. Yet his personal relationship with Jeffrey Katzenberg had always been a good one: 'I'd seen him give a hard time to other people, but I felt lucky with him. He always had respect for me.'

Yet Nick also concedes: 'Our relationship with DreamWorks started to reach a very strained stage. To my mind the battle over the rights for Wallace and Gromit had probably soured things. They probably weren't used to small studios like ours fighting our corner – and in the end I think they felt aggrieved by the deal we'd struck.'

Moreover, as David observes, DreamWorks had problems way beyond the box-office performance of Aardman's films: 'They weren't happy, and a big factor in all of this was that by the time they were making *Were-Rabbit*, they had run out of money once again. This was the third time they had had to refinance, and now they were clean out of options. So they did the only thing they could to keep the wolf from the door: they floated the company on the Stock Exchange.' The flotation raised more than $800 million, which certainly helped – but now they had investors they needed to constantly appease. David notes: 'The flotation also meant a realignment of the DreamWorks business plan, in which every film the studio made had to achieve big [box-office] numbers. This was a high-risk strategy for any studio. And the market for animated features was now getting more saturated as other studios entered the fray. I think DreamWorks lost confidence in *Flushed Away* and held back a bit on P&A, which didn't help.'

All of this cast something of a shadow over the impending release of *Flushed Away* in November 2006. There was now intense pressure ahead of time in Los Angeles for the film to perform well and reach huge audiences. As Nick puts it, '*Flushed Away* became a football that was being kicked around.'

To be sure, DreamWorks did everything they could to help the film along – even if their methods to lure American audiences seemed foreign to the Aardman contingent.

'We did all these test screenings, showing the film before it was totally completed,' Peter recalls. 'And when you test, the end result is a page of statistics. The companies that run the screenings send out questionnaires on two sides of paper, from which they get the age and gender of everyone responding. They're asked what they liked best and least about the film, which characters they liked most and least, and they're asked if they would recommend the film to friends. These are set questions, and from the set answers they could make calculations and give you a figure – and they wanted most answers to be "excellent" or "very good" and "would definitely recommend the film to other people". From that they get numbers. The clear pressure from DreamWorks was: "The numbers aren't good enough. We've got to get them up to *Shrek* levels." That was the target. So, on we went, working away, changing things about the film quite late on – and indeed, in the last screening, we actually got to the famous *Shrek* numbers. Jeffrey would argue that we got there because of all his constant driving for more and better. And that was great. We thought, *Well, our work is done, what more can we do? The film's just about finished at this stage.*'

But from the DreamWorks point of view, *Flushed Away* performed disappointingly. It exceeded the US total for *Were-Rabbit*, grossing some $64 million in the US and $113 million in the rest of the world, but the US figure fell short of the $100 million that *Chicken Run* had achieved and which DreamWorks now desired.

Despite the intense market research in advance, then, it was never going to be another *Shrek*. 'I was very disappointed it didn't do better,' Peter reflects, 'because I thought we did a really good job on it. All those surveys, all those opinions, all those damn statistics – and it still didn't do well at the box office. So what does that tell you?'

Maybe there were aspects of the film the surveys failed to pick up? 'It isn't a science,' he says, 'that's for sure.'

There's a haunting question that hangs over the film to this day: what if Aardman had won the argument and *Flushed Away* had been made as a stop-frame film rather than with CGI?

Nick has his views on the subject: 'I remember years ago, when with the rise of CGI we at Aardman would often think: *How long can it last, this stop-motion thing we do?* There was a sense we should enjoy it while we could. And in a way that's maybe been the key to our success. We never talk about it, but we enjoy it – I think that's the key. Now there's a lot of CGI, some great films out there – but we're standing out now. It's our identity. It's more there than ever – to stand out against the crowd. It's very competitive out there; everything relies on sassy writing, fast quipping and keeping up with fashions. I feel we can step slightly away from all that, still enjoy what we do – and be different and relaxed about it.'

What's indisputable is that *Flushed Away* would feel like a very different film had it been made in stop-motion rather than CGI. Would it have been more of a commercial success? It's an unanswerable question.

'I think *Flushed Away* lost its way,' says David. 'Because it was made in Los Angeles at DreamWorks, it slightly went out of control – in the sense that DreamWorks were trying to take control. There's some good stuff in it, but I think there's a remoteness about it – Pete was flying over again and again, trying to wrestle it down. I think we weren't clear enough about what the film was trying to say. Whereas *The Curse of the Were-Rabbit* is hilarious. Yet, even with that team – Nick, Steve, Bob Baker and Mark Burton – it took a fair bit of effort to get it there.'

13

Such Sweet Sorrow

It didn't take DreamWorks long – a little less than three months after *Flushed Away* opened in the States – to act decisively. Citing the film's 'heavy losses', the studio announced it would end its partnership with Aardman after ten years.

To film business insiders, this hardly came as a shock. Rumours had been swirling constantly about the future of the DreamWorks–Aardman deal ever since the studio had announced – even before *Flushed Away* opened – that it expected the film to lose money for them.

Many within Aardman, too, were already anticipating such an outcome. It had been noticeable in the run-up to the release of *Flushed Away* that DreamWorks actually cut back on the money they had allotted to press and advertising. They had done just the opposite for *Chicken Run*, helping that film to achieve a flying start at the US box office. But, of course, DreamWorks, having been floated on the Stock Exchange, now had shareholders and investors watching their every move; Jeffrey Katzenberg no longer had the freedom to throw extra money at potentially risky projects.

Diplomatic sentiments were issued from both sides. Katzenberg said: 'While I will always be a fan and an admirer of Aardman's work, our different business goals no longer support each other.'

Maybe one could detect a sting in the tail of that comment – but for Aardman, publicist Arthur Sheriff was impeccably statesmanlike. Stressing that there was no animosity in the split, he noted that DreamWorks was focusing on computer-animated films, while Aardman wanted to continue its long tradition of making hand-crafted 'claymation' movies, while also looking to CGI feature films in the future.

'We always knew America would be a hard task for us,' Sheriff added. 'We're a very English company. We embrace the international market, but we think part of our strength is our English sense of humour, and we want to continue with that.' He went so far as to describe the split as 'fantastic news', because it released Aardman from the Hollywood pressures to make only mega-budget blockbusters. He stressed that there were no plans for lay-offs among the Bristol workforce.

His measured tone could not quite prevent British headline-writers from going to town on the story: 'GROMIT, HELP! CLAYMATION HEROES DUMPED' was how *The Guardian* portrayed it. The *Telegraph* opted for the obvious pun: 'WALLACE AND GROMIT'S FILM DEAL IS FLUSHED AWAY AFTER BOX OFFICE LOSSES'.

Several British papers repeated the incorrect notion that Aardman's alliance with DreamWorks was 'a five-picture deal' that had now stalled. The deal with DreamWorks had in fact been a rolling housekeeping arrangement that went from film to film, and could have ended at any stage.

Arthur's comments accurately reflected the mood within Aardman, however, alongside an acknowledgement that, creatively, the company was always in a very different type of business to that of any Hollywood studio.

David Sproxton, recently reflecting on the fact that Aardman now had up to 150 full-time staff, added: 'I think we have reached a steady state.' He was adamant, too, that if the company took people on, they would always want to keep them fully employed: 'I think of what we saw at DreamWorks; they expanded from 1,200 to 1,500 people in a relatively short time, and it becomes a bit of a monster. Jeffrey had the energy and drive to push a lot of projects through, but if he hadn't been there, I think they would have struggled. At some stage it becomes ... a bit more than a factory perhaps, but certainly a very big machine.'

Mixed feelings about the split were inevitable on Aardman's side – though many of them stayed within its walls. David, on his part, remains clear in his opinion that the experience had been a positive one overall.

'When we left DreamWorks,' he observes, 'we were saying "we need to be our own Katzenberg" – in other words, to be as critical as he was when we're reviewing our own stuff ourselves. It's harder than it seems, but you do need to get these [films] up there to match the creative firepower the Pixars and the Disneys have got. It's huge, and they can spend a lot of money getting it right – and getting the story of a film to where it needs to be before they even start. And we're sort of playing in that pond, so we need to take as much trouble as they do.'

Katzenberg had broken the news to Peter after calling him into his office in Los Angeles, saying simply: 'I think this is probably the time to go our different ways.' Peter was surprised by the suddenness of his announcement, but hardly shocked by the news. 'I can't for the life of me remember the detail, but the meeting was very good natured and civilised. All I can recall with certainty is that, as I stepped outside his office, a tide of relief swept over me. I was delighted.

'When we did the deal with DreamWorks, the focus of our attention was all about making *Chicken Run*. Theirs was the best offer, so we pursued it. But inherent in our pursuit was the notion that getting to Hollywood was the absolute summit for filmmakers. Well, when you're ten, you might sit in a cinema and watch *The Great Escape* or *Mary Poppins* or a Bond movie and think: *This is the acme of popular culture. Wouldn't it be amazing to be part of that world?* It's aspirational to go to Hollywood. And when you get there, you're inclined to think, *I'm at the highest table now.* And indeed it is very thrilling and seductive. But there are other areas, other markets and other audiences that are just as exciting and challenging. For me personally, working on short animated films has been equally important and valid, even though I haven't been actively involved for ages. And though Hollywood always beckons, I don't feel it's our natural home.' David sympathises with Peter's view, but adds: 'The trouble is, there's no funding for short animated films in the UK. There's no realistic commercial market for them, sadly.'

The whole *Flushed Away* experience had been hard. The team in Bristol never felt fully attached to the film because so much of the work was carried out in Los Angeles. Peter had had to spend long weeks in Hollywood, an environment with which he had become increasingly disenchanted; he felt it was too often cold, ruthless and ego-driven. He wanted to be working back in Bristol, a city he loved and felt was his natural environment.

'I'm sure, from DreamWorks' point of view, we were hard work too,' he says, 'making these decidedly British films, always determined to go our own way.'

The 'divorce settlement' wasn't too complex. Aardman had been developing a feature film to be called *Crood Awakening*, its story (an idea based on a book) devised by John Cleese, an idol of Peter's from his teenage years, when he had watched him on *Monty Python's Flying Circus*, awestruck at his comic genius.

The film was about a family of cavemen who were living very basic lives at a time when fire, the wheel and animal traps had yet to be invented or utilised. The basic story was of this family coming to terms with a new, relatively modern life.

Peter had already visited Cleese at his Pacific beachfront home in Santa Barbara, north of LA, where they had spent an entertaining weekend batting ideas back and forth. Cleese was a relaxed avuncular host, reclining on his sofa with a cat on his chest, and spinning comic set-pieces for the movie. For a change of scene, they would wander round his estate, visiting the menagerie of curious pets that had the run of the place. With his amanuensis, Kirk de Micco, Cleese spent eighteen months on *Crood Awakening*, outlining its basic story and writing a funny first draft. But he didn't have the appetite for the slow and rigorous process of producing successive drafts, improving the story little by little. And, by now, Peter knew only too well that this arduous process was an ingredient in every successful animated picture.

The film became one of the bargaining chips in the Aardman–DreamWorks split in that it was decided that DreamWorks would assume ownership of it. (It finally opened in 2013, titled *The Croods*. Co-directed by Kirk de Micco, it was a sizeable hit; Peter and David received 'special thanks' in its credits.) 'We decided they could have the film,' David says. 'They owned it by default anyway, as they had funded its development.' For their part, DreamWorks relinquished any interest in the Aztec West studio in Bristol.

For Peter, at that particular time, when he had spent long spells in the previous year feeling marooned in Los Angeles, it all seemed a price well worth paying – even though the lease of Aztec West, involving significant outgoings, fell to Aardman at a time when it had no deal for a feature film that would put the space to good use.

As for the split with DreamWorks, David can see both pros and cons: 'The deal probably would have come apart anyway. It made us aware that when you're partnered with a huge company like that, even the people you're talking to don't have full control, so it makes you wary of these megacorporations. Also, people can play musical chairs. Suddenly the people you're dealing with aren't there anymore. A new wave has come in – and who are they? How do you prepare for them? That happens quite a lot in this business, certainly. You're aware there's always that bit of turbulence and that things are always liable to change. How do you protect yourself against the consequences of such change? Can you have more ownership of stuff, so if things do change and we don't like what's going on, we can take it elsewhere? In fact, we were lucky with Jeffrey. You spoke to him directly and once you understood how he worked, he wasn't so hard to get on with. He was trying to do the impossible, start a studio from scratch. He must have been under enormous pressure in many ways. And he gave it a pretty good shot, to be honest.'

14

UP IN SMOKE

The first few years of the twenty-first century had so far been a roller-coaster ride for Aardman, and 2005 was no exception. On 10 October, the Monday after the first weekend of the US release of *The Curse of the Were-Rabbit*, and four days before the film opened in Britain, David received an early morning phone call from Kieran Argo, an Aardman staffer in charge of exhibitions and transport for festivals.

In halting tones, he told David that a fire had broken out in the Victorian warehouse near Temple Meads station where Aardman rented space to store sets, props and company memorabilia. Law firms and accountants also stored their paper records in the building.

The fire, Kieran said, had been raging for hours, and everything inside the building had been destroyed – including all the items from a travelling exhibition that had just returned from Japan. The roof of the building had collapsed in the fierce heat, which was intensified by the presence of so much paper within (all those legal and financial documents).

David asked about the company's valuable artwork, but

239

that had fortunately been stored at the studio itself. Still, it was bad enough: a significant part of the company's history had been lost for ever.

Hundreds of little clay characters, including surviving Morph figures and many of the forty-plus Gromits and thirty-plus Wallaces needed to make each animation, were in metal cases. Nearly everything had simply melted in the intense heat, and only a small number of items on loan to an exhibition had survived.

It was undoubtedly a major blaze. At its zenith, the flames were a 100 ft high, and fifty firefighters were required to attend.

Initially, the true story was misreported by the media, thanks to a BBC website suggesting it had been Aardman's studio that had caught fire. News travelled fast, and the company began receiving emails from around the world expressing sympathy for their loss. After a swift intervention from Aardman, the word 'studio' was changed to 'offsite storage warehouse'.

The immediate question was: could it have been arson? The cause was initially unclear, though there had been recent suspicious fires in the area concerning land that was coveted by building developers. The true cause, however, would need to be determined by investigators.

In the first instance, Aardman's most prominent figures reacted to the blaze with perspective and realism. 'To the outside world, it was a disastrous event and a big story,' Peter recalls. 'But it didn't make a great emotional impact on me. I'd never even seen this building before, during or since. It was out of sight and out of mind. Her Majesty the Queen mentioned the fire to us when David and I received our CBEs from her. "A great part of your history," she told us, sympathetically. But I can't remember feeling it at the time.' Now Peter concedes: 'There were some glorious sets and props from *Chicken Run* – notably the Pie Machine and the giant wooden bird that the chickens escaped in. I didn't miss them until years later when we put together a historical exhibition of the studio's work. Then their loss really struck me. And I'm sad that any last original drawings of our first creation, Aardman, were lost. They would have been a fascinating reminder of our beginnings.'

David admits his own immediate reaction: 'When I put the phone down on Kieran, I felt oddly detached. It was shocking and horrible to lose so much of our work, but it was hard to know what to feel when I didn't have a clear idea of what was in the warehouse in the first place.'

Nick, however, managed to put the fire into a philosophical perspective, citing the recent dreadful losses of life from an earthquake on the India–Pakistan border. 'Even though it is a precious and nostalgic collection and valuable to the company, in light of other tragedies, today isn't a big deal.'

As well as a blow to the company, the fire was yet another incident that reflected Aardman's popularity – and its ability to make headline news.

The Sun splashed the story on its front page, turning it into a curious version of an obituary. Surrounded by small photos of some of Aardman's leading star characters, it ran a list: 'Rocky and Ginger – DEAD. Mr and Mrs Tweedy – DEAD.

Tony Hart's chums Morph and Chas – DEAD. Douglas the Lurpak butter man – DEAD.' And so on.

It was certainly an eye-opening way in which to report the event and, to some readers, it might well have seemed tasteless. To many at Aardman, though, the jet-black humour of that front page helped to put the shock surrounding the fire into some kind of perspective. David confesses he laughed when he read it: 'I mean, nobody actually died. Putting it bluntly, it was only stuff.'

The timing of the blaze was ironic, occurring as it did hours after news of a triumph for Aardman from the United States. *The Curse of the Were-Rabbit* had begun strongly on its opening weekend; it was number one in the US box-office charts, taking $16.1 million (some £9 million) in its first two days.

Arthur Sheriff was keen to stress this piece of good news to the press, if only in counterpoint: 'This should have been a day for celebration – and instead everything we have done until now has been destroyed. It was very important to us. It really is a bit of a tragedy.'

In all, some thirty years of props, models and scenery were destroyed. There were a few consolations, however. For one, the destroyed artefacts were all from past projects. Aardman's library of finished films was stored elsewhere, and therefore not affected. Nor was production work on current projects; sets and props from the company's new film, *The Curse of the Were-Rabbit*, had not yet been transferred to the affected building.

It took fire investigators exactly two months to reach their conclusions about the cause. They emphatically ruled out arson. Instead, they established that the fire had started in a ground-floor office of the warehouse.

It had clearly resulted from an electrical fault in the battery charger of a device that held the security guards' walkie-talkies, though Assistant Chief Fire Officer Bill Feeley said the blaze could have been avoided had the building been equipped with a sprinkler system.

Happily, there were no human casualties, and no firefighter was injured in tackling the blaze. Fortunately, there was even insurance cover on the articles returning from the exhibition in Japan. But it was a sad, jolting day for Aardman – and a melancholy reminder that a part of the company's history had been consigned to the ashes.

15

A STATEMENT BUILDING

Shortly after the turn of the new century, it was becoming clear to David and Peter that Aardman needed another radical rethink about its premises. Over the past twenty years, the company had moved to ever larger premises in different parts of Bristol, trying to keep pace with its broadened ambitions and increasing number of employees. But still it wasn't enough; Aardman was spawning scattered satellite premises, so a new building, designed to their specifications, would be highly desirable – and, happily, something the company could afford.

They looked again at their existing site, the old Fyffes banana-ripening warehouse overlooking the river on Gas Ferry Road. It had served them well up to this point, but the truth was Aardman was expanding in terms of both personnel and new departments at a rate they could hardly have anticipated. Several Aardman projects for TV were now being developed, so a standalone broadcast department was a must. As the whole business grew and

Aardman characters, notably Wallace and Gromit, had become phenomenally popular, so rights and merchandising became another crucial aspect of the company's overall business.

'We were bursting out,' David recalls. Aardman's initial response to its own rapid growth had been temporary buildings, constructed on the existing Gas Ferry Road site. The key word, however, was 'temporary', and they survived under a constant threat that their permits would not be renewed. In truth, they were hardly easy on the eye, the site gaining the nickname 'Portakabin City'.

Portakabin City housed the rights and merchandising, accounting and HR departments, which had previously been relocated to Queens Square, almost a mile away. This meant almost fifteen minutes on foot or five minutes for David on his bike – far from an ideal situation.

'We knew we'd bought this land at Gas Ferry Road with a view to eventually doing something with it,' David reflects. But what, exactly? Aztec West, where at any one time between 10 per cent and 15 per cent of the company's employees and regular freelancers worked, would remain as a sufficiently large studio space, mostly for feature-film production. But the new building on Gas Ferry Road needed to accommodate everything else Aardman did. Unquestionably, it would be the company's HQ.

A well-regarded Bristol architect, David Mellor, of the firm Alec French Architects, was recommended to David and Peter; they met him and shared their vision for the building. He responded immediately to their ideas.

245

'He set about trying to understand the Aardman tribe,' David recalls. 'He'd ask: how did we operate? What was the anthropology of the way we operate? And it made me realise, watching him at work: the really good architects are good anthropologists.'

Mellor, who was clearly enthused by the challenge from the outset, told them: 'Mostly we're putting up a school, a hospital or a residential property for a developer. But we don't usually work directly with the people who are going to occupy the building.'

He explained to Peter and David: 'For us to work out how this building's going to work, we need to know how *you're* going to work as a company.' So, they told him at great length why a new building was important to them, what the advantages of one would be for Aardman, and outlined certain aspects of it that they felt were crucial.

'We said we'd all be in one building, which was good,' David recalls. 'We said we'd want our people always to be aware that there are other departments there – and that although ideally it would be one massive open-plan building, we knew we'd have to have it on three floors.'

Peter adds: 'We wanted this to be the ultimate expression of what Aardman means. Commissioning a new building was going to be a massive investment, so it would be a statement of pride in the company and faith in the future. All the places we'd worked in before had been 'the studio' to us, of course – from the room above a shop in Clifton to the banana warehouse – and we'd enjoyed finding an existing building and making it work for us. But this was our chance to make the big statement for ourselves, and the staff and the city. Above all, we believed we could devise a fun environment where creativity could thrive.'

Work started on the site in 2008, and it opened for business the following year.

* * *

Walk today down Gas Ferry Road, approaching what was once the harbourside, and the Aardman building is on your right. From this vantage point a visitor might not expect anything special; one's eye stays at ground level, towards a discreet entrance set on the diagonal.

Once you step inside, however, it's a shock. The building feels vast, and from the lively reception area at its near end – all sofas, stuffed Aardman characters and memorabilia – your gaze is inevitably drawn upwards. There's a lot of pale wood to be seen, which enhances the lightness and calmness of the building, and you hear employees' voices from within, but they come at you softly on the air, faintly muffled, so you cannot quite hear what they are actually saying. There's a feeling of tranquillity about the place, not unlike the atmosphere in some places of worship.

Then, as you stand in reception and take in the building's length, you're inevitably struck by the 'stairway to heaven' – a huge, wide central staircase that ascends to the top floor. It is, quite simply, a breathtaking sight; it dominates without feeling remotely obtrusive or out of place.

Every detail in this spectacular building was the result of

much consideration and consultation with staff, Peter, David and Mary by David Mellor and his team.

'It was really interesting, because essentially you're taking a punt,' David Sproxton says. 'The building is basically two three-storey blocks with a gap between them, and you point them at each other slightly, which creates this triangular atrium. I wasn't sure at first about the atrium. I've seen them in law firms' buildings, in big office blocks, and I'd always felt they seemed an incredible waste of space.' He felt they were often an arrogant symbol of corporate prowess ('Look how big we are!'), but Mellor made a persuasive case, and David admits: 'This one works.'

As for the central staircase, Peter and David had told Mellor that they wanted to make it easy and logical for employees to have 'corridor conversations' – chance meetings between colleagues from different departments from which creative ideas might spring. 'So the staircase needed to be wide enough for two people to talk on it, and for another person to pass them by with ease,' says David.

If this staircase looks as if it might belong on board a ship, that's no accident. David and Peter also stressed they wanted the building, situated as it is beside the river, to reflect something of Bristol's maritime history, including boat-building and the historical engineering of the Victorian era.

'To some extent, we wanted it to feel Brunelian,' adds David – a reference to the legendary nineteenth-century engineer Isambard Kingdom Brunel, an overwhelming figure in Bristol's history. It was Brunel who was engineer of the Great Western Railway, which was to link London to

New York via Bristol, and his great steam ship the SS *Great Britain*, as well as the city's famous Clifton Suspension Bridge and London's Paddington station.

Much of this rich history is subtly acknowledged in the building's staircase. David Mellor recommended a first-rate industrial designer, Mark Lovell, who then worked in Wiltshire. Says David Sproxton: 'He came up with this idea of a laminated staircase, a little bit like one you might find on a boat. It has chromed concrete reinforcing rods. The whole staircase is actually a suspension bridge, pinned at each end and held in tension by big steel bars that run underneath it. It was entirely handmade by Warren Hughes Furniture in Tiverton. I think it was the biggest single job in the firm's history. So there it is – a suspension bridge, with a Brunelian DNA in it. That was the statement bit!'

'And what's even better,' says Peter, 'it bounces. Because it's hanging, and made of wood, it's kind of organic; it gently responds to your footsteps. Stop in the middle for a chat, and you feel it bouncing very softly under your feet.'

It is by no means the only fascinating aspect of the new building, however. For instance, its interior space is semi-open plan, and dividing walls are at half-height: 'So you can see people at work if you look over the walls,' David points out. 'You have a sense of your own space, but you're aware of other departments there.' There is more glass in the walls and doors than in the average building, which also enhances employees' awareness of different work being done elsewhere.

There was a wealth of detail involved in planning the

building to Aardman's exact specifications: facilities manager Tony Prescott and general manager Mary Lowance, once again showing her remarkable versatility, canvassed employees about their wants, needs and preferred options, and spent eighteen months working closely with the architects on the responses.

During the course of their own work, Peter and David had already visited the headquarters of other major creative companies, including Pixar, and observed the careful thought and planning that had gone into designing buildings which would reflect the ethos of those companies. This helped to convince them they were on the right track.

And, at the other end of the scale, they visited Sheepdrove, a small organic farm and conference centre in Wiltshire, which gave them a significant idea for their own project: 'It was a beautiful building, made out of wood, which somehow softened it and gave it a warmth – which I think we now have here,' says David. 'You look up and see all this beautiful woodwork. It's as if you relax into it. I think we've come out of that high-tech steel and glass period in '80s and '90s architecture. This felt a bit more homely.'

The overarching brief for the building was that it should be 'designed to be highly sustainable, in both its materials and use of energy'. It certainly fulfils that brief and, almost as a bonus, it also feels tranquil. On entering it, some people report that they automatically exhale, naturally and involuntarily.

'There's something physical about that,' says David. 'The building is naturally ventilated. It feels calm when you come inside. Our conference room is air-conditioned, but the bulk of the building is not air-conditioned. It's got natural air coming into it – and the way it's designed is to draw air in and vent it at night. As a result, it has a very natural feel. We talked with David Mellor a lot about buildings that are totally hermetically sealed. We didn't care for that idea at all, so we entered into a discussion: what makes a healthy building? A healthy atmosphere? Many buildings have air-conditioning, which feels dry and metallic and "plasticky". That's not true here. There's not even much carpet in this place, so you don't get the smell of synthetic carpet you often experience in new buildings, and I think even that makes a difference.'

Another factor that enhances the ambience in the building is its acoustic engineering: 'Before it was fitted out, the place was a concrete shell,' says David. 'Then the engineers came in and asked, "What would you like the ambient acoustic to be like?" We said we'd like to hear the buzz of industry and the fact that people are talking, but no conversation. And they did exactly that. They absolutely fine-tuned it.'

Other aspects of the building offer more versatile choices: many of its internal walls are not structural but detachable, so they can either be used to separate adjacent work areas or removed to create a larger space. These are known as 'pinboard' walls, useful for holding drawings or pictures during group meetings, but also removable to offer more open-plan space.

'We thought long and hard, and we felt we needed to be flexible,' David recalls. 'All these walls are effectively partitions or pinboard-type walls. We've taken some walls down, put a few more up. We wanted to make it adaptable.'

Then there is the light: the building is well served with window space, which makes the place feel more open and airy than it already is. Peter Lord's office is at the eastern end of the building and, of an afternoon, he can often step outside it, turn right and find himself walking towards the setting sun: 'I'm regularly stopped in my tracks by how lovely it looks when the sun's streaming in.'

* * *

The truth is, most companies would not go to such lengths to create a workspace so carefully tailored to enhance their employees' work experience; but doing so meshes with Peter and David's philosophy.

Both men have their own particular soft spot for different features of the building, so while David is enraptured by that staircase, Peter takes delight in a small wildlife garden, tucked away behind the back of the building, away from the harbourside: 'Originally it was an old petrol station, a crummy, unloved and polluted piece of land. And now it's a garden. Commercially, no doubt, it's insane, because we could probably have got forty one-bedroom apartments in there and made a fortune. But I kind of love the wildlife garden and take a lively interest in the success of the pond and the hedgerow! It's not exactly a Site of Special Scientific Interest – not yet – just a few birds, and frogs and newts in the pond. But when I look out of the window and I see

252

a couple of blackbirds jumping around on the grass, scoffing worms, it makes me very happy. During the summer months you'll often find people basking out there, holding meetings, reading scripts, writing and even drawing (if they're still using old-fashioned pen and paper). Oh, and catching some rays, I suppose. It's pleasant, it's humane and it works.'

There's very little about the building that hasn't been discussed and finally signed off by Aardman's co-founders – though they were more exacting in their requests about some features than others.

'The stairway, certainly; we wanted a say there,' Peter recalls, 'what it says about the history and culture of the area. I think what David Mellor did was to effectively pull out of us our culture – our philosophy, the way we operate – and find a way to reflect that in the building. He got it pretty well right, actually. There were lots of conversations with heads of departments. '"How do you work? How would you *like* to work? What would be a better way of working here? How do you get this cross-fertilisation between departments?" Because that's really what the building is designed to do. Ideally, you'd have had it in a huge open-plan set-up, but even so, there's a lot of cross-working between departments in a way there wasn't, certainly, when we were geographically separated. It was "out of sight, out of mind". You tend to forget other people when they're not around.'

There was also the dilemma of how to make the people who work at Aztec West feel they were part of the Aardman company ethos.

'The two studios operate quite differently,' Peter says. 'At 80,000 sqft, Aztec West is a huge space where everybody works on a single project (usually a feature film). Whereas at 'Headquarters' – Gas Ferry Road – we work on multiple projects the whole time. There might be twenty or thirty projects – hugely varied – being developed by small teams in different departments. Somehow we've had to pull all that together as a company, to make it feel cohesive and prevent people slipping into a 'silo' mentality. There's a lot of people from Aztec West who don't come here very often, and vice versa, so we have to work hard to bring them together. We have a creative away-day, which is a bit of a round-up of the past year and also the place where the latest creative projects are shared. People are always astonished to discover what their colleagues are up to. Let's face it, *I'm* sometimes astonished. But we do our best to get everyone there, including the Aztec gang, many of whom are freelance. We treat it as a normal working day with the added attraction of beer at the end of it. The important part is that everyone is equally involved and treated the same.'

Their approach appears to have worked well, though David believes it has happened 'almost by accident, or default or something. I guess it's a fairly relaxed management style. And we always bring in highly motivated people, so they're going to get on with it anyway. We really don't want people who aren't pulling their weight.'

* * *

One of the factors that helps Aardman's aspirations for the building is that Bristol is not a large city with far-flung borders. 'Most people here live within fifteen or twenty minutes of the building,' David notes, 'whether they're driving, walking or cycling. I well remember when I was growing up in Walton-on-Thames, my dad used to drive to the BBC at Shepherd's Bush [in west London] most days, and that drive got worse and worse. I always thought, if I can possibly avoid that hour-and-a-half drive at the start and end of each day, I'd do my best. I think if you know you can get home in ten minutes, you're much happier to work till, say, 7 p.m. Whereas if you're in London and you do that, you may not be back home before a quarter to nine. You're more relaxed, and you can't do that commuting in London. On the Tube at rush hour? That's no way to live. During the post-production period for *Early Man*, I stayed in London in a nice little hotel, just about two minutes from Warwick Avenue Tube station, only four stops to Soho, where we were based. But getting there for 9 a.m. on the Tube was absolute purgatory. It was so dreadfully overcrowded. Looking back, I should have taken a fold-up bike to London with me and cycled. If you can avoid all that as a lifestyle choice, that would be good.'

He believes that such factors explain the recent westward drift in population from London to Bristol: 'It's another way of living here.'

David lives in the Montpelier area of Bristol and cycles to work every day. He's by no means alone: 'The bike shed at Aardman has between thirty-five and forty bikes in it most days. And I like cycling here in the morning, along the

255

docks. You even see cormorants sometimes. It's a nice way
to start a day.'

David and Peter agree that if you make a place pleasant to
work in, employees will be happier – and they'll work harder.
And that includes the availability of good food nearby.

'Oddly, before we came here there was nothing, it was
like the Gobi Desert,' David recalls. 'Yes, the SS *GB* was in
place, but nothing else around, no infrastructure, no cafés.
There was literally nowhere to eat nearby, which is one
reason we have a canteen. It's important. The food's good,
reasonably priced and it's a social meeting place. And one
of its attractions, we realised, was that, for employees, this
was going to be their main meal of the day. When we moved
the company into the harbourside area in the early 1990s,
there was nothing to eat anywhere. Then one day this lady,
a caterer named Annette Platts, appeared with a basket of
gorgeous sandwiches. Clearly, she spotted a market with us!
We said, "You make really lovely sandwiches. Do you think
you could come and cook for us?" It turned out she was
Cordon Bleu trained! So she accepted the offer and became
our chef in charge of the canteen. Then, a few years later,
she decided to go off and live in South Africa. We told her:
"You can go if you replace yourself with someone as good
as you." She'd been working evenings in a Bristol restaurant
on Whiteladies Road and she pulled the chef, whose name
was Stuart Briggs, out of that place and said: "I've found
the chap." He's now our catering manager and runs the
canteens both here and at Aztec West. Here, lunch is the
big thing. Of course, Stuart's here for breakfast, but unlike

most chefs his evenings are free. He's been with us for over twenty years now.'

* * *

So memorable and striking is the building that it has been the recipient of several awards – two alone from the Royal Institute of British Architects (RIBA), whose Town and Country Workplace and Supreme awards it won. It was also given the Bristol Civic Society Environmental Award.

'I *love* this building,' Peter enthuses. 'It's calm, it's relaxing – and it was designed for people to meet. That was the single most important idea for us, that people from different parts of the studio should bump into each other and interact. There's a generous feeling to the space and the light and, as much as I appreciate the wide-open spaces out there, of course I like it best when it's busy and the desks are packed.' The hum of industry? 'Yes! The more of that the better. The place was designed for a fluctuating workflow, and sometimes a big project comes in and takes up loads of space. I'm all in favour of squeezing in some series projects. Sarah Cox (who joined Aardman in 2017 as executive creative director) has got plenty of plans for those.'

The old banana-ripening warehouse in front of the new building is still used for shooting stop-motion commercials, and though it may not be lovely to look at, the old warehouse has played a crucial part in the Aardman story. Says Peter: 'All of *The Wrong Trousers* and *A Close Shave* were shot down there. Morph is still shot there, and we'll soon be shooting even more episodes. It's a working studio, which means its stocked with filmmaking kit (some of it pretty esoteric). It's shabby and businesslike and ever-changing and we're all happiest when there are two or three different stop-motion projects in there at the same time.'

The new building venture might have seemed like an adventurous leap into the dark when it was first mooted – but it has paid off handsomely. 'It was a statement – and you don't often have the opportunity to put up a building for yourself,' David observes. 'You might decorate a house or a flat, but you rarely get to build one.'

This privilege came at a price: David agrees that £9 million is 'about right. So, with fitting it out, we've spent £10 million on it. But we already had the land, so effectively the land was free. And the big part of it is, there's a legacy here. It's ours. And we're not at the whim of landlords.'

* * *

While preparatory work on the building was continuing, Aardman was still in the business of conjuring up ideas for films and getting them financed and shot. This was especially important in this particular period. Aardman had enjoyed a good reputation in Hollywood, but after the end of the DreamWorks deal, the company needed to come out fighting.

Nick had already declared that after *Chicken Run* and *Were-Rabbit*, he wanted a return to a half-hour Wallace and Gromit film for the BBC. 'I liked the idea of working with a small crew again,' he said. Over the years he had found thirty minutes an ideal length for the sort of Wallace and Gromit stories he wanted to tell. And at least shooting in Bristol kept him away from Hollywood movie folks, who, with the best will in the world, weren't truly on his wavelength. 'For my own sanity,' he says now, 'I wanted to feel more back in the saddle and holding the reins.'

He and Bob Baker joined forces once more and came up with yet another story that could be summarised in a short, paradoxical phrase: if *The Curse of the Were-Rabbit* had been 'a vegetarian horror story', the new film, *A Matter of Loaf and Death*, would be 'a bread-based murder mystery'. Typically for Nick, with his reverence for old movies, the title was also a splendid pun on one of the greatest British films of all time.

Originally, he had wanted to call the film *Trouble at' Mill*, but it was obvious that this very Lancashire phrase would not translate abroad. In the course of mulling over alternatives, Nick found himself in a taxi whose driver asked him the name of his next film. When Nick said, '*A Matter of Loaf and Death*,' the driver laughed, and that helped clinch the matter.

In the new film, Wallace runs a bread delivery service in a town where all the other bakers seem to be getting murdered. Gromit knows enough to be scared – though not his master, who only has eyes for Piella Bakewell.

The film cost £3 million to make – a record for an Aardman half-hour. The ingredients for its success were all there, however, and it easily justified its extravagant budget.

A staggering 14.4 million people in Britain watched it that Christmas Day – more than any other TV programme broadcast in the UK in all of 2008.

Meanwhile, Peter and his colleagues in the features department were trying to come up with new film ideas. They were looking for an American partner and hired a man called Stephen Moore to act as head of features and CEO, with the brief to negotiate another Hollywood deal. But there didn't seem to be a huge demand for Aardman's type of stop-frame films within major Hollywood studios – most of whom by now had their own animation divisions.

The exception appeared to be Sony Pictures, which had taken over the legendary Hollywood studio Columbia in the late 1980s. Its chairman and CEO was Michael Lynton, a British-born, American-educated executive who had headed up book publisher Penguin's London office for a spell. His senior colleague was Amy Pascal, who was chairman of Sony's Motion Pictures Group. They were clever, charming and agreeable, and Peter felt comfortable around them.

Aardman signed with Sony in 2007, and found themselves dealing with its subsidiary Columbia at a time when Peter was nursing a movie idea he eventually decided he wanted to direct himself. It was based on a comic novel, *The Pirates! In an Adventure with Scientists*, by a young English author named Gideon Defoe. David's long-time partner Sue had spotted it in a bookshop and bought it. At home, David read it too, and then took it along to Aardman to show to a development executive named Mike Cooper, who read it in turn. It was sitting on Mike's desk when Peter picked it up.

Peter was entranced by its sly, surreal humour. It was, he thought, mischievous and clever. The hapless pirates in the service of the bumbling, hopeless Pirate Captain didn't have real names; they were simply 'The Pirate with a Scarf', 'The Pirate Who Likes Sunsets and Kittens' – and even 'The Surprisingly Curvaceous Pirate'. Queen Victoria and Charles Darwin were also characters in this odd little story.

Peter pitched it to Michael and Amy, who were in Britain and came to Aztec West to hear Aardman's ideas. He read them a passage from Defoe's book that featured a fight at the Royal Society in London between Charles Darwin and a pirate dressed as the Holy Ghost. 'Not mainstream material,' he admits, 'in fact, frankly bonkers. But fortunately Amy and Michael laughed a lot.' And, lest there was any doubt, he assured them solemnly it would be nothing like the *Pirates of the Caribbean* franchise.

At this same memorable meeting, Nick briefly showed sketches of an idea for a caveman movie he was starting to work on. No one knew it at the time, but this film would finally open under the title *Early Man* eleven years later.

The original plan was that *Pirates!* would be made as a CGI film, but Peter and Aardman staffers supervised some production design to give an idea of how the film might look. When Amy Pascal saw the beautifully presented set of the Pirate Captain's cabin, she was hugely impressed.

'You *have* to make it in stop-motion,' she told Peter. That was a reaction to be wished for, and she got no argument back from him.

The serious business began once again of converting an

idea into a movie. Peter worked with Sarah Smith to invent a new storyline based only very loosely on Gideon Defoe's original book. After interviewing many possible screen-writing partners, they chose Gideon himself to write the screenplay, despite the fact that his credits at the time were very slight. 'It was an unusual choice,' Peter admits, 'but one that paid off. Gideon proved to be hard-working, immensely funny and only very occasionally grumpy.'

The core team was highly experienced and all good friends – most of them long-term members of the Aardman family. Julie Lockhart – who'd originally joined Aardman to produce commercials – was the producer, and Jeff Newitt, who'd directed the short film *Loves Me, Loves Me Not* for Aardman in 1993, became Peter's co-director. Jay Grace was one of a generation of young animators recruited for *Chicken Run*, and he became animation director. Peter describes the whole crew as 'a super talented and experienced team'.

As a matter of style, the designers, story artists and puppet-makers were invited to embrace a dizzying, absurd-ist approach to the material. Historically accurate it was not. Queen Victoria shares the screen not only with seventeenth-century pirates, but also with Napoleon, Jane Austen and the Elephant Man. And the young Charles Darwin, who is famously revered as a great Englishman, is portrayed as a weedy nerd who can't get a girlfriend.

When it came to the pirate ship, an essential part of any pirate movie, production designer Norman Garwood designed an impossible vessel that was made of two com-pletely different ships imperfectly lashed together with ropes and iron bands. Peter remembers its first appearance in the studio. 'When the model ship was first assembled in all its glorious detail, it was clearly a masterpiece. It was so tall that its masts could only just fit in under the studio roof, and it was absolutely irresistible. When things got tough, or when I was losing my way with the story, I'd go to the studio floor and just marvel at this beautiful thing, which felt like the heart of the movie.'

Shortly afterwards, a second movie from Aardman was green-lit by Sony. *Arthur Christmas* – to be made in 3D CGI rather than stop-motion – was rooted in a delightful conceit: Santa manages to get all those billions of Christmas gifts out to children across the world by employing a huge army of tiny elves to deliver them, but what happens if just one little girl in Cornwall is mistakenly overlooked? How can Santa salvage the situation by arranging for her new bicycle to be under her tree on Christmas morning? Santa needs help from his own family, and it's down to his son Arthur and his father, 136-year-old Grandsanta, to save the day between them.

It was a charming idea. The top brass at Sony approved, and the dynamic Sarah Smith, recently appointed as Aardman's head of development, whose task it was to ramp up these new ideas until they were deemed fit for production, enthused about it wildly.

She then went one step further and decided to direct it in Los Angeles herself, having co-written it with Peter Baynham. Sarah had directed and written for TV in Britain before, but this would be her feature-film debut in both capacities.

'It wasn't our plan to have her direct it,' David recalls. 'She had been brought in to lead the features development team, working with writers and directors to get films to the green-light stage. But she had worked closely with Peter Baynham and now wanted to see the whole thing through. Sarah is formidable, a force of nature, so although we could have said no, it was clear she had a real passion for the project and she would have found it difficult to hand over. But directing an animation feature is a huge undertaking, particularly a CGI feature, what with the complexity of the process. Normally, there would be two directors with complementary skills, splitting the workload.'

She had no animation experience, no experience in CGI and would be working in a production environment at Sony Pictures Animation (SPA) in Los Angeles, which would be totally alien to her, without instant access to the Aardman support network. Sony was also concerned, and recommended bringing in a co-director, leaving Sarah to concentrate on story and performance. Barry Cook was chosen to partner her; he had experience as a visual effects supervisor on CGI feature films and was also beginning to direct. On paper it looked like a great match, but within a matter of months Barry had been squeezed out: Sarah wanted to go it alone.

'We talked her through the issues and stressed the size of the task ahead, but she was determined that having a directing partner wouldn't make life easier for her. This was no easy ride for Sarah. The bulk of the crew were American, from Imageworks/SPA, and clearly cultural differences between the way Aardman hoped to make the film and the way SPA were used to making films caused problems. I can imagine she was overwhelmed and stressed by the size of her task. There was much metaphorical screaming and shouting along the way but, to her credit, Sarah got through it and made a really good film.'

Both projects were blessed by Michael Lynton and Amy Pascal, who were very actively involved in the early years of the relationship. As time passed inevitably, they needed to concentrate on Sony's large slate of live-action movies. Peter was grateful that they'd had so much of their attention early on, but saddened by their gradual disappearance from the scene. 'They are both terrific talents who put great faith in us, for which I'm endlessly grateful.'

The two executives who replaced them in working with Aardman were Hannah Minghella, who turned out to be smart and supportive, and Bob Osher, who came from the business end of things and, as David puts it, 'was more about deals and legal matters than creative content. For a while this was tolerable until, a year later, Hannah too was moved on, and we were left with Bob.'

Aardman was in an extraordinarily strong position: not one but two feature films had been green-lit and there was furious creative effort to get them into production. The world of animation was scoured for visual development artists, storyboarders and the like, and many new appointments were made. In a short space of time, they were up and running, harder and faster than ever before. It felt though the studio spacecraft had slingshotted off the DreamWorks relationship into a thrilling new orbit.

16

SHAUN THE SHEEP THE SUPERSTAR

In 2007, the BBC released a DVD package of Aardman's first three Wallace and Gromit half-hour films – *A Grand Day Out*, *The Wrong Trousers* and *A Close Shave*. All of them had proved to be a huge attraction for Britain's Christmastime TV audiences in their years of release.

Intriguingly, *A Close Shave* was billed on the DVD cover with the words 'starring Shaun the Sheep' next to its title. At the time of the film's original release in 1995, this would have seemed puzzling. Wallace and Gromit, as always, seemed to be every inch the film's stars. Shaun, described by his original creator Nick Park as 'an innocent victim, cute and loveable, with his little crop-top hairstyle, big eyes and simple face', was a minor character who only had about seven minutes of screen time.

True, Shaun got to shine in one memorable scene: Gromit had been wrongly imprisoned for sheep-rustling, and Shaun used an angle grinder to cut the bars of his cell, thus freeing him from jail and paving the way to a happy ending. He never had a single line of dialogue, however: Shaun does not – indeed, cannot – speak. The only sound we ever hear from him is a predictable *'baa'*.

Still, something about Shaun caught the public imagination, and Aardman responded by using his image judiciously. Shaun appeared inside its books and greetings cards, and he popped up in a few of the company's commercials too. He clocked up considerable merchandising sales, and a delightful little backpack adorned with Shaun's face was proving a favoured gift for children.

Shaun's popularity, then, was considerable – but it suddenly skyrocketed in an unexpected way. In 1997, Emma Bunton, also known as 'Baby Spice' of the Spice Girls, was photographed wearing a Shaun the Sheep backpack, and the photo was syndicated to news outlets worldwide. At that time, the Spice Girls were at the peak of their extraordinary popularity. Emma Bunton was twenty-one years old and arguably the most popular member of the group with its younger fans, who were of course the prime audience for Shaun the Sheep.

Almost overnight, as Nick recalls, 'the backpacks were sold out. Sales went through the roof.' His theory about the popularity of his little creation was that somehow Shaun managed to be simultaneously cute and cool. His distinctive shape and design also made him very easy to merchandise.

It was Nick who first had the idea of developing Shaun as the star of his own TV series. For a long while he had been developing two series: *Creature Comforts* and another about Shaun, though he kept these thoughts pretty much to himself. Then came the unhappy fallout from *The Tortoise and the Hare*, which resulted in several freelancers being laid off. 'I was in a meeting with our senior management team,' Nick remembers, 'and they were looking for solutions for projects they could get off the ground quickly. Peter knew that I had these ideas and asked me to present them. So I pitched them two broad treatments – one for *Creature Comforts*, one for Shaun. The team went for them both big time, assuming *Creature Comforts* would get off the ground first as it wouldn't be scripted, but relied on recorded conversations, like the original.' Speed was an important factor; these were ideas to keep people employed.

'I was later asked who would be good to direct *Creature Comforts*,' Nick remembers, 'and I mentioned I'd been thinking about Golly.'

This was in 2002, and Golly was still smarting from the abrupt demise of *The Tortoise and the Hare*, which he had started directing for Aardman a couple of years earlier. When it was shut down he was so dispirited he stayed away from work for months.

A call from Carla Shelley, another Aardman veteran who, like Golly, had joined the company back in its Wetherell Place days, brought him back. By this time Carla was an Aardman producer, and she now asked Golly if he would be interested in directing a new series of *Creature Comforts* for ITV. The initial demand was for thirteen episodes, each running at ten minutes (twice the length of the original *Creature Comforts* films).

Golly had always admired the *Creature Comforts* idea and found directing the TV episodes hugely enjoyable. Two of its episodes were BAFTA-nominated in two separate seasons, and one of them won an award from fellow European animators at the Annecy festival. Hearteningly, all this restored his confidence and his faith in his own abilities.

One of Nick's two pitches to senior management had borne fruit promptly, therefore, but while everyone enthused about his idea for a Shaun the Sheep TV series, it fell into what TV and film executives call 'development limbo'.

Golly had always felt Shaun had real potential and could flourish as a leading character: 'After the Baby Spice photos and then the backpacks flying off the shelves, I think we knew we had a potential star on our hands.'

He found himself mulling over potential pathways for Shaun's future career. At this point in its history, Aardman had spent several years devoting much of its time and resources to full-length feature films, spurred on by its partnership with DreamWorks. *Chicken Run* had been a resounding hit for the two entities (even if Aardman received a modest return on the film from Europe, and none at all from the US), and now even Wallace and Gromit seemed to be graduating from thirty-minute TV specials to feature films for cinema audiences; *The Curse of the Were-Rabbit* would be the first.

Among Aardman's top brass, however, there was an uneasy sense that placing all one's bets on Hollywood and success in the feature-film market might prove to be beyond a relatively small British company. Big films, aimed at audiences in the United States as well as in Britain, were complicated and expensive to make, their outcome and profitability notoriously hard to predict.

Aardman now had a broadcast department, headed up by Miles Bullough, who had joined the company in 2003. One of its tasks was to develop popular content outside the sphere of feature films.

A Shaun TV series seemed the best plan, as it turned out.

Some outline ideas were developed, and Golly came in to direct the pilot episode. But the script he was faced with just didn't work for him: 'Shaun was at the top of the tree – he had a bike, a girlfriend and he could use cash machines. It felt as though, story-wise, there weren't many places for him to go. And there wasn't even a reason for him to be a sheep, either. The stories could have applied to humans. So I said I didn't want to continue.' Miles Bullough had his problems with it, too: 'It was being developed as a family show by a pair of external writers. It was funny, but a one-off – expensive to produce and not right for a long-running series.'

Rather than take Golly off the job, Miles said to him: 'Okay, give us your ideas. What do you think it should be?' As it happened, Golly's ideas chimed with Nick's and also those of Miles, who felt it should be episodic and structured like a sitcom. Given the chance of creating a different world for Shaun, Golly eagerly seized it. 'I aged it up,' he recalls, 'thinking in terms of an audience of children who were eight to ten years of age rather than pre-schoolers. And I made the humour what I thought the comedy should be: They're *sheep*. On a farm. In a field. They're not walking around on hind legs all the time. In fact, they're almost like prisoners. I was thinking of *Porridge* [the classic BBC prison-comedy series], maybe with the sheepdog Bitzer as a Mr Barraclough figure, a kindly character torn between having to obey his master (the farmer), yet also wanting to be friends with the "prisoners" (the flock). That made a difference, because it put Shaun at the bottom of the pile. He had his restrictions in terms of what he could and couldn't do – so that could generate stories more easily.' Effectively, it resembled a workplace comedy.

Each episode would be just seven minutes long – ideal for young attention spans – and they could be broadcast on TV in the afternoons. Episodes could be made at Aardman relatively swiftly, without the need for outrageous budgets, and, best of all, since no one in the series ever utters a single comprehensible word, the calculation was that it would attract audiences the world over, irrespective of the language they spoke.

At this time Nick was distracted, developing and shooting *The Curse of the Were-Rabbit*, so was unable to give any of this much attention. 'Golly took the whole project under his wing,' he recalls. 'He developed the new Shaun and his friends, giving him a full makeover. The farmer, Bitzer and Shaun's family were all created by Golly – he gave this world its new life and tone. It needed someone to give it a big steer, and that's exactly what he did. My ideas were somewhat sketchy and rather broad, and I totally appreciate the way he picked up the project and ran with it. From the beginning I felt Golly was the perfect candidate to create and direct the series. He has a cheeky, offbeat humour and he deserves full credit for creating Shaun's world. I never imagined giving away a project like this, but I'm totally in awe of what he's done with it.'

Golly knew from early on the effect Shaun and his pals had on children: 'When we were producing the first series, I took a couple of episodes into my kids' primary school. I showed it to their class completely blind, without any explanations. I just wanted to gauge their reactions. There was a scene in one of the episodes where the farmer goes upstairs to take a bath. Meanwhile, Shaun and the others are trying to drain his hot bath, so they can warm up their sheep dip. So Shaun's in the bathroom, desperately trying to get out, while the farmer's coming up the stairs. And some of the kids actually stood up and shouted: "Come on! Come ON!" I thought, *Well, that's a* really *good reaction*. Given that it was completely fresh to them, I thought, *This has legs*. And by the end of the first series, I was already thinking we should make a full-length Shaun movie. I wanted to tell longer stories with this character.'

He was now given free rein to devise the series he wanted: 'I thought to myself: *I can do the kind of humour that I like*. No one was telling me to tone it down, and it seemed everyone was enjoying it.'

Rethinking Shaun for an older audience proved to be an inspired idea, but it didn't come cheap. 'The series turned out to be cleverer and more sophisticated, true, but also considerably more expensive than we'd first planned,' Peter recalls, 'but I'm happy to say that the studio went with it. We encouraged the team to make the best possible series that they could, and it paid off. That first series was a terrific foundation for all the Shaun work that was to follow.'

The series made its debut on the BBC's CBeebies (CBBC)

channel in 2007. It quickly became a hit with its young view-ers – and their parents. The demand for Shaun and his flock seemed insatiable. The first two series each comprised forty seven-minute episodes, with a further twenty episodes in the third season. The demand never faltered: by 2018, some 150 episodes had been completed and broadcast.

Aardman took the first season of the series to the inter-national film market in Cannes, where it was snapped up immediately. After two years, it had sold to some 170 territo-ries – 'everywhere except Mongolia,' as Miles puts it.

It even proved popular enough to warrant a spin-off series starring Timmy, the littlest lamb in Shaun's flock. His series was called *Timmy Time,* and it broadened the base of Shaun-mania: if *Shaun the Sheep* was aimed at children aged eight to ten, the appeal of *Timmy Time* was to pre-schoolers.

'I always suspected it would sell rather well abroad,' Golly reflects. 'Still, it's been a shock, how far and wide this show has gone. Germany is a particularly strong market for Shaun. Miles Bullough notes that an astonishing 5 million DVDs of the show were sold there.'

It was clear that a full-length feature film of Shaun the Sheep would be a viable proposition, and work started on developing it. Shooting finally began in 2014.

Golly had brought Shaun the Sheep a long way. 'He may originally have been Nick Park's creation,' Peter Lord says, 'but Golly took up the baton, carried on with Shaun and made him the character he is today.'

The *Shaun the Sheep Movie* represented something of a quantum leap, and the decision was made to bring in Mark

Burton to share screenwriting and directing duties with Golly. Burton was already known to Aardman; he had supplied additional dialogue to the *Chicken Run* script, shared writing credits on *The Curse of the Were-Rabbit* and was later a writer on *Early Man*. He also had an enviable track record in writing TV comedy for such shows as *Spitting Image, Have I Got News for You* and *Room 101*. He even had a credit on an animated Hollywood feature film, as one of the writers of DreamWorks' *Madagascar*.

Peter Lord observed at the time: 'Mark has experience no one else [in Aardman] has, of mainstream radio and TV comedy. If you have any sense, you tap into that.'

The groundwork for the feature film was now in place, but events were happening elsewhere in Aardman that would have a profound effect on the movie's destiny.

* * *

The relationship between Sony and Aardman had gone into a gentle decline ever since Michael Lynton and Amy Pascal had moved on into other parts of the Sony hierarchy, and were no longer the point of contact for Aardman.

It didn't help that neither of the films Aardman had made for Sony was a huge success in box-office terms. *Arthur Christmas* had opened in America on November 2011 – on Thanksgiving weekend, but late enough to attract Christmas audiences four or five weeks later. Still, in a marketplace chock-a-block with four other family entertainment films opening that same week (including *The Muppets*), it was hard to compete.

The film had cost $100 million but grossed only $46 million in the States, which was a disappointment. *Arthur Christmas* performed proportionately well in Britain, grossing £20 million, but then the film had a distinctly British air about it. Its global takings added up to $149 million, and though Sony were relatively diplomatic about it, they clearly regarded that figure as bad news.

David Sproxton says, 'A Christmas film has one slot for release, and *Arthur Christmas* ran into a lot of competition in its year of release. Had they delayed its release for a year, it would have had a clear run.'

Peter's film (which had undergone a rather unimaginative title change at Sony's hands and was now known as *The Pirates! Band of Misfits* in the States) also opened weakly in April 2012; it had cost $65 million, and grossed $31 million in America and another $91 million everywhere else.

David observes: 'Sony "turned down the gas" on the film's publicity and advertising spend, as the marketing tracking wasn't strong, so a poor box-office return was predictable. It was no surprise really. For American audiences it had too much "science" and too many British historical characters.'

The figures were a huge disappointment to Peter. 'I know we made two great films, which deserved a much bigger audience; but releasing a film, especially in the States, falls somewhere between a dark art and a lottery. Personally I felt so happy in the world of the *Pirates!*, so comfortable there. I loved the way it looks and feels, the richness, the warmth, the good humour, the absolute daftness of it all. It seemed like a playground to me, and naturally I wanted to share that feeling with the widest possible audience.'

He had particularly enjoyed working with Hugh Grant, who was clearly playing against type as the Pirate Captain – a world away from the roles that made him famous. In *Pirates!*, Hugh's animated character was a barrel-chested swashbuckler with a luxuriant beard – and, as Peter admits, 'in Hugh's career, he has seldom been asked to bellow, roar or scream with terror when he's falling 300 ft into a gigantic spinning propeller'.

As so many Aardman voice actors have discovered, the director often needs multiple takes of a single line to get it absolutely right. Hugh persevered, although was sometimes driven to madness by Peter's directing. 'I now think that was rather naïve of me,' Peter says, 'that I should have trusted his instinct about the Pirate Captain. The quiet, witty Pirate Captain is infinitely funnier and more attractive. But, with a bit of nagging from me, we got the best of both worlds.' All ended well, however, and Hugh was generous with his time in helping to promote the film.

Still, because of the disappointing box-office results, the Sony relationship, which had lasted five years, was clearly moving towards its natural end. Significantly, neither Michael Lynton nor Amy Pascal attended the New York premiere of *Pirates!*.

He went to talk to Bob Osher, the Sony executive who was now their main point of contact. Peter asked him if Sony would be interested in partnering with them on a movie starring Shaun the Sheep. Osher wasn't excited by the idea:

Aardman owned the character of Shaun, the TV series had yet to find a huge audience in the States at that point, and he couldn't see how a story about a flock of sheep on an English farm would do much for Sony's future in animated films. As a result, he politely declined, leaving Aardman free to take the project elsewhere.

Bob Osher could not have suspected it at the time, but he had done Aardman a gigantic favour.

* * *

Sony called time on the Aardman deal before the end of 2012. The studio had learnt a huge amount from their two forays into the Hollywood studio, and Peter and David's instincts were to seek out another partnership, though not necessarily one based in Hollywood. A single funder rather than multiple partners felt more appealing, and they soon joined forces with StudioCanal, a Paris-based film production and distribution company with a huge film library and a significant London office. StudioCanal regarded itself as a European entity making films for the world – a mission statement that sounded a lot more all-encompassing than any Hollywood studio.

StudioCanal announced in April 2013 that it was teaming up with Aardman for the feature-film debut of Shaun the Sheep. It would be a stop-motion film, which suited everyone at Aardman perfectly. There was no real question of it being CGI, as the sets and models were already available. Encouragingly, its press release noted that Shaun and his flock had 'been enthralling TV audiences in over 170 countries'. Finally, it seemed, Aardman had found partners who looked at business opportunities from a global perspective rather than a mainly American one.

There was an even broader significance in the StudioCanal deal, however, which now looked timely. Like all companies, Aardman had been affected by the recession of 2008, the impact of which started to make itself felt just before the new building at Gas Ferry Road opened its doors.

Most noticeably, the recession caused a slowing-down of commercials work for Aardman. They were also investing in the development of new series (especially for children's TV) and found there was suddenly a hole in the accounts.

They already believed and were supported by various advisers that the wise approach was to look again at characters such as Wallace and Gromit, Morph and the animals from *Creature Comforts*. These creations had originated from within Aardman and so constituted part of the company's intellectual property; the obvious srategy was to explore ways to develop them further.

Shaun the Sheep and his chums were also part of Aardman's IP, of course, and the notion of using them in feature movies now looked like an idea whose time had come.

Sean Clarke, the company's head of rights and brand development, was one of its leading advocates of using and reusing tried-and-tested Aardman characters as a rational policy to help survive the recession. He and David were in complete agreement on this point.

'I don't think Peter had thought of bringing Morph back to

life,' David says. 'I'd been pushing him for a while, knowing he had a loyal following.' Now, though, Peter was enthused by the thought that this new approach could lead to his legendary creation somehow making a return.

He also loved Sean Clarke's idea of a Kickstarter campaign to help fund a new Morph series from public money. There had been recent indications that Morph was held in high esteem by the British public; when Tony Hart died in 2009, a 'flash mob' of Morph fans showed up at the Tate Modern on London's South Bank, all of them with their own clay renditions of Morph, to pay tribute. Who knew the little character was still so deeply beloved? Peter found it genuinely touching. It also boded well for the Kickstarter campaign; Aardman was asking for £75,000 from the public, an amount the company would match to fund the making of ten ninety-second films. 'Dave and I were quite dubious,' Peter recalls, 'our attitude was "surely Aardman can't go out with a begging bowl?". But wiser, younger heads in the studio assured us that this was the new, natural way of fundraising. And they were right; the response was astonishing.' The target was reached in just eight thrilling days – in all, the donations came to £110,000. That surplus allowed for the making of five more Morph shorts.

He ended up writing some of the new stories himself, and the shorts were released on Aardman's YouTube channel. Soon after, the BBC bought them, and in 2015 Morph was back on national television.

It was extremely gratifying – and quite an eye-opener: an excellent example of how to repurpose characters that Aardman already owned.

* * *

In Golly's eyes, the second hugely successful TV series had cemented the success of *Shaun the Sheep*, because it was clear to him that the set-up on the farm was not just a workplace but also a family: 'The farmer's the dad, Bitzer is like an elder brother, well-meaning and trying to maintain order,' Golly says now. 'Shaun is the younger brother in the flock, and he's really mischievous. If he sees a red button marked "Do Not Press", he'll always press it.'

Golly and Mark Burton agreed that for any feature-length film starring Shaun the Sheep, he and his flock needed to be taken out of their comfort zone – that is to say, away from the farm. This shift comes when the entire flock ends up in a big, bustling city. Shaun gets fed up with obeying the farmer's endless demands and engineers a way to give them all a day off. He diverts the farmer's attention and lulls him to sleep by getting him to – literally – count sheep as they repeatedly jump fences. The farmer eventually falls asleep in his caravan, but, without his watchful eye, it starts to career down a hill. He arrives in the city below concussed and suffering memory loss.

There follows a dizzying number of urban adventures, some involving a beastly 'animal containment officer' who consigns Bitzer, then Shaun, to a dog pound. At one point the flock have to dress up in human clothes to avoid being caught; in a delightful self-referential gag (and a nod to Baby Spice), little Timmy disguises himself as a backpack.

The *Shaun the Sheep Movie* opened in Britain in February 2015 and was rolled out that same year to much of the rest of the world, including China, where, by coincidence, 2015 was officially the Year of the Sheep. The box-office totals everywhere were hugely encouraging. In US dollars (the currency the film industry employs to register international totals), it took $106 million worldwide. This was certainly a satisfactory sum, as David Sproxton points out, 'given that its production costs were low compared to our other feature films'.

There was also a hidden story buried in those figures. Revenues from the United States (a reasonable but far from spectacular $19 million) were actually exceeded by British takings, which came in above the equivalent of $21 million – an excellent result. And what *that* meant was that the rest of the world accounted for the remainder – a massive $65 million. In other words, the *Shaun the Sheep Movie* was a huge international hit. In this post-Hollywood era, it was reassuring for Aardman to know that, while American audiences were well worth courting, the US box office on its own could not make or break the global fortunes of such a film. And, of course, many of these overseas territories were places where Shaun was hugely popular on TV.

Part of its success, of course, was how easily it 'translated' to audiences the world over. That's easier to achieve when there is no dialogue to confuse viewers (as Rowan Atkinson had famously discovered with the *Mr Bean* films, which were popular in any number of non-English-speaking territories). By the time the final box-office results were in, it was clear how the remarkable worldwide reception of the *Shaun the Sheep Movie* was shaping up. The filmmakers were not totally surprised.

Golly recalls: 'I was contacted by someone in Oman who said there were lots of UK expats over there (it has a big oil industry), and while the locals and the expats apparently get along fine, as movie audiences there's a lot of segregation. If there's an Asian movie being shown, all the locals will go; if it's a British film, all the British expats will go. This person told me that the *Shaun the Sheep Movie* was the first one where you saw a 50/50 split. And apparently they were all laughing in the same places. That was very satisfying to hear, but we'd already found the same thing. We toured a lot with the film to promote it, and we saw audiences in Japan, China – all sorts of places – laughing at the gags and understanding them. People actually laughed in all the right places! It was very gratifying. There's something very universal about it. It's even set on a farm – and pretty well every country has farms of some sort.'

Later that year, on Boxing Day, *Shaun the Sheep: The Farmer's Llamas*, a thirty-minute short set on the farm, attracted 4.8 million viewers – a creditable total. In truth, the three rowdy football-loving llamas (which the myopic farmer had accidentally 'won' in an auction at the county fair and brought back to the farm) stole the show, but the mere mention of Shaun's name in the title was enough to guarantee a sizeable audience.

None of this escaped the attentions of the hierarchy at Aardman. David Sproxton recalls: 'Certainly, in our early days with DreamWorks, everything seemed very America-centric and, over time, US box office for us went from half to one third for our films. *The Curse of the Were-Rabbit* did roughly a third in the US, a third in the UK, and a third in the rest of the world. Now we're with StudioCanal, and they're interesting because their mantra is: "European films for the world", which is a good thing for them to say, being European-based. And of course the Middle East has opened up, China has opened up, Asia has opened up, which wasn't really the case with *Chicken Run*. Jeffrey Katzenberg more or less just did a cash deal in Japan, where I don't think it even recouped. The world has changed. We've often said that our films play in the United States like a Polish film plays here in Britain. They're deemed to be foreign – of a different culture. And with the best will in the world, apart from the Bond franchise, not many British films ever break through in America. Most recently, *Paddington 2* was a huge hit in the UK, and it did okay in the States – but not great. Very few really make an impact. They might do fine on the East Coast and on the West Coast, but the Midwest bit? Forget it. That's a very hard culture to penetrate with our sort of stuff. So, we're realistic about that. It's not that America isn't nice to have, but our bigger market now is Europe and the east, in a sense. And, of course, Shaun has sold massively. We didn't expect it would take off in a such a massive way, but the quality of the episodes and stories have caught people's imagination.'

* * *

Shaun the Sheep may well be a well-liked character in Britain, but that doesn't begin to account for the success of Shaun's TV series and movie internationally. 'I often come across people in the UK who you talk to about Shaun the Sheep, and they *know* of him,' says Sean Clarke, 'but, in fact, the UK is only the fourth biggest market in the world for us. Shaun is easily Aardman's biggest global brand; we're in 170 countries. Don't ask me to name them all, but you'd never know it from this country.'

One reason for this is that the *Shaun the Sheep* episodes have been broadcast in the afternoons on CBBC, where they function almost as a babysitting device for children. Unlike Wallace and Gromit, who grace prime-time slots on main BBC channels and attract huge audiences, Shaun is only now gradually making his mark on Britain's mainstream culture.

Certainly, other countries have taken Shaun-mania to greater extremes. A Swedish company, for example, partnered with Aardman in 2016 to open the first international Shaun the Sheep family attraction, at Skånes Djurpark, the world's largest zoo for Nordic animals, located in the south of Sweden. The attraction, called 'Shaun the Sheep Land', is set in what looks like a large country fair, and visitors can meet Shaun 'in person' and learn about his journey to the zoo. One of the highlights is a tractor ride to help Shaun track down his lost flock of sheep before the farmer wakes and realises they're missing.

It is in Japan, however, where the series was first broadcast on the NHK educational channel, that Shaun-mania can be viewed at its most extreme. There's the Shaun the Sheep

Brunch Café in Tokyo, for example, where you may be served dishes with Shaun's face embedded in the food. This café began life as a pop-up in 2016, celebrating Aardman's fortieth anniversary, but proved so popular it is now a permanent fixture. Then there's Osaka, which boasts a three-storey Shaun the Sheep café with a similar culinary theme; it is so much in demand you need to book ahead. There is also a Shaun playpark in Osaka, and another in the eastern Japanese city of Sendai. A touring exhibition featuring Shaun's world visited major Japanese cities and sold out everywhere; in Tokyo, it attracted 30,000 people over just five days. And we mustn't forget the two Shaun stage shows that are staged in several Asian and Middle Eastern countries: one lasting forty-five minutes that plays in theatres; and a shorter one, some twenty minutes long, aimed at families visiting shopping malls.

As well as Japan, there are similarly extraordinary stories about Shaun fever in countries as diverse as Indonesia, India, China, Egypt, the United Arab Emirates and elsewhere in the Middle East.

'With something that really appeals to kids, they get attached to it and want more of it in all its forms,' Sean Clarke observes. 'It happened with Harry Potter – the books, the films, the exhibitions, the whole thing. Peppa Pig is another example.'

If there's an irony to all this, it's that Shaun – like Wallace and Gromit and, indeed, all of Aardman's creations – feels unmistakably British, yet he clearly bridges a cultural divide in a host of countries worldwide. Sean Clarke acknowledges that this is a curious phenomenon, though entirely a good thing.

'When you consider we have these restaurants, exhibitions in Japan, mini playparks, all these things going on around the world, it's rather remarkable,' he observes. 'What I think we've learnt in creating series and characters is that something can't just be a success here in the UK and then you export it. These days you have to make things for the whole world, and if that doesn't make it as much of a success in your own market, then so be it. Our feeling now is that if something is always a bigger success in the UK than anywhere else, then clearly there are things about it that are maybe too specific to Britain. We are a British production company – and I hope we will always have that British sensibility in terms of humour – but there's no reason we can't get a global audience as long as the characters are appealing.'

Sean describes Shaun the Sheep as 'the Aardman brand with the biggest reach': 'It's probably our only brand that's growing in a 360-degree way,' he admits. Shaun the Sheep merchandise brings in an estimated $50 million a year, and the brand extends to broadcast and digital platforms, games, live events, exhibitions and promotions.

Shaun's world is so compelling to young audiences worldwide that Aardman and the British Council joined forces in 2018 to launch a series on YouTube called *Learning Time with Timmy*, starring the smallest sheep in the flock. It's a delightful idea with a serious purpose. One of the British Council's priorities and areas of expertise is to spread the learning of English to all corners of the world, and over an initial twenty-six five-minute episodes, young viewers aged between two and six can begin to learn the language while enjoying little Timmy's adventures.

The little sheep shows up in a wealth of places in Britain, too. In recent years, Shaun has featured in promotional efforts for VisitEngland tourism and the Rugby World Cup, which was held in England in 2015. Aardman has also launched Shaun the Sheep Land, an interactive exhibition at Land's End in Cornwall. After Shaun in the City, a 2015 art installation that placed artist-decorated Shaun sculptures around London and Bristol, the sculptures were sold at a charity auction and raised over £1.1 million for Wallace and Gromit's Grand Appeal and Wallace and Gromit's Children's Charity, both of which benefit Bristol's Children's Hospital.

For his part, Golly believes that the widespread appeal of the clever, comical little sheep is 'partly because there's no dialogue', plus the 'universal themes' of the stories in each episode.

Still, taking the woolly celebrity from TV to the big screen required extreme care – and a strong focus on character. The *Shaun the Sheep Movie* producer Paul Kewley explains: 'The worry was that the series had been very successful, and the challenge was to get the movie right while being true to what the world already knew of Shaun.'

A sequel, planned to open in 2019, is to be called *Shaun the Sheep Movie: Farmageddon*. That's another quintessentially Aardman pun, but what is the film actually about? 'It's an alien invasion,' Golly says tersely.

Golly's confidence was shaken badly following the demise

of *The Tortoise and Hare*, and he feared his creative juices might be draining away. However, this proved not to be case, and he thrived when he took on the role of creative director for *Shaun the Sheep*. The success of the series, and indeed the franchise as a whole, proved just what a great powerhouse of ideas and inspiration Golly is, and how important he is to Aardman.

17

BRISTOL

One of the most striking features of Aardman as a company over more than forty years has been its warm, continuous relationship with the city of Bristol. Peter and David arrived together in 1976, intent on starting up careers as animators, and stayed put in the city even when their company became successful.

This makes Aardman unusual in the British film and TV world, which tends to be centred in London. Indeed, as we have seen, some of the people they rubbed shoulders with over the years – notably executives in ad agencies – shook their heads in wonderment at the idea that they would want to live 'out' in Bristol, more than 100 miles west of the capital.

Certainly, there was a pragmatic side to their decision; house prices have always been far cheaper than in the capital, as have office overheads. Companies of Aardman's size rarely get to 'buy the building' in places like London. But in Bristol they could do precisely that.

Yet their decision to stay there was a deep-rooted one. David Sproxton and Peter Lord both grew up (as did Nick

Park) in families that believed in the idea of loyalty to one's community, that strived to treat other people respectfully, whether on a personal basis or in the realm of business, and together they embraced the notion of being as helpful and as supportive to their city as they could.

'I think my involvement was also influenced by my studies of cities at university,' says David now, 'trying to understand what makes a city work and a good city to live in. I've always had an interest in transport in cities, and specifically the way bicycles can transform places.' David, a keen, committed cyclist, is a founding member of Cycle Bag, a Bristol-based group that evolved into the national sustainable transport charity Sustrans.

Of the two, it's David who gets more involved in the city and its various endeavours, since he has a more flexible timetable than Peter, who can find himself confined to the studio if a film is in production (though that happens less often these days). He has sat on various boards (including the Bristol Old Vic theatre, of which he was chairman for a few years), liaises with a range of local organisations and attends meetings where his presence can make a difference. He was also part of the original team that made Bristol's Encounters Short Film and Animation Festival come into being more than twenty years ago, which has since gone from strength to strength.

One of their greatest achievements in Bristol, however, has been their unswerving support for the Grand Appeal, a local charity that helps to maintain Bristol Children's Hospital.

Nicola Masters co-founded the appeal in 1995, and met

Peter and David that same year: 'We were initially set up to raise £12 million for the new building of the hospital, so we approached Peter, David and Nick and asked if they could possibly create a new character for us to spearhead our fundraising.'

David recalls: 'They came to us wanting us to design a logo for the hospital, maybe design a new character. But we thought: *How do you come up with an image for a children's hospital? How do you do that?* It's a really difficult brief. But really it was about raising money to put into a new hospital building that the NHS wouldn't provide ... a one-off fundraising thing. So we thought: *Why don't we lend them Wallace and Gromit?* Having to design a new character was always going to be hard. And when we thought about it, we decided Wallace and Gromit might work better with the public than a newly created character. And besides, we really wanted to help. So we lent them Wallace and Gromit for the duration of their fundraising campaign. It was a good time – after *The Wrong Trousers*, around the time of *A Close Shave* – when Wallace and Gromit were really riding high. And it worked incredibly well. The charity really got behind it, it hit the right nerve with the public, and it was relatively easy to design stuff around the two characters for the hospital.'

Nick adds: 'It's hard to create a character with instant appeal that doesn't have any history with the public, so offering Wallace and Gromit, two known characters, helped us all hit the ground running.'

'It was', says Nicola Masters now, 'an incredibly generous gesture.'

It was also a hugely successful one, and Wallace and Gromit's Grand Appeal – as it came to be called – raised the required £12 million between 1995 and 2001.

More remarkably, the link between Aardman and the charity remains intact to this day. Nicola says: 'That was the start of a great partnership which has lasted twenty-three years. The charity has generated £50 million in that time.'

After the initial figure of £12 million for the new building at Bristol Children's Hospital had been reached, Aardman and the appeal turned to different fundraising initiatives and imaginative creative stunts, including a 'Wrong Trousers Day' – a zany departure from the traditional 'dress-down day', for which people paid £1 for the privilege of wearing deeply mismatched or inappropriate trousers in public. 'And we don't have just ordinary cake sales,' adds Nicola. 'We've had "Wallace and Gromit Big Bake" events – and they certainly raise money.'

The event that finally clinched the relationship between Aardman and the Grand Appeal in the minds of Bristolians, however, was the 'charity trail' in 2013, which they called 'Gromit Unleashed'.

It comprised eighty 5 ft sculptures of Gromit, each one individually painted and decorated by artists and celebrities such as Jools Holland, Joanna Lumley and Quentin Blake, which were then placed strategically across Bristol. Visitors to the trails were given a map and were able to stroll around the city and view each one up close.

'It was a simple idea,' Peter says, 'but it had a spectacular effect on the whole city. We were blessed with good weather and, for the weeks it was on, the city was alive with visitors from all over the world, enjoying fresh air and family time. People loved the collecting element and they also seemed to relish a sort of curated exploration of the city. The Gromit I designed, Salty Sea Dog as he was known, was positioned in the city centre and got a great deal of extra attention on a Saturday night. I passed by one night to see three young women – pretty merry – perched on his back, and a fourth one trying to clamber aboard. But Gromit seemed to take the strain pretty well.'

The 'Gromit Unleashed' sculptures adorned Bristol's streets for ten weeks that summer, and when they were sold off at auction, they raised an astonishing £2.3 million for the charity. Nicola Masters says: 'It was absolutely extraordinary. That event took Bristol by storm.' And Nicola has more ideas. 'Alongside these trails, Aardman also allowed us to create and sell figurines of most of the sculptures. That's been a very successful enterprise. Many thousands of people have collected all our miniature figurines and associated merchandise for the trail. We have a retail outlet for this purpose – at Cribbs Causeway, near Bristol, the south-west's flagship shopping centre. The miniature figurines cost between £35 and £50, and the shop is run by the trading subsidiary of the charity: all the profits are donated to the charity, and it helps us to do more and save more lives.'

In 2015, to coincide with the release of the *Shaun the Sheep Movie*, there was another trail, called 'Shaun in the City', with seventy more character sculptures in Bristol and another fifty in London. 'That also went on to raise many millions for the city,' Nicola Masters recalls. 'And both our character trails – in 2013 and 2015 – brought 1.2 million visitors to Bristol. For the first one, it got to the point where every hotel in the city was fully booked, just because of people coming in to see the Gromit trail. We coined a new word that year: "Gromiteering".'

A Bristol-based trail sequel, 'Gromit Unleashed 2', took place during the summer of 2018, with sixty-five sculptures, not only of Gromit, but of Wallace and also Feathers McGraw, the sinister penguin from *The Wrong Trousers*.

'Mary Lowance, our general manager, soon got personally involved with the charity,' David recalls, 'so more by accident than design you become part of the fabric of the city.'

Nick adds that his personal assistant, Angie Last, has also for years been key to the development of the trails alongside the charity: 'She has represented the characters and Aardman with great fervour, to ensure integrity and authenticity.'

David observes that one of the major achievements of the Grand Appeal has been 'to accommodate the families of kids in that hospital': 'It covers the largest geographic patch of any hospital in England, serving the whole south-western peninsula, as well as south Wales, so you might be bringing children up from as far as Penzance – a long way – for some quite traumatic treatment. And, of course, mums and dads want to be close to their kids when they're in hospital. So the Grand Appeal now owns quite a lot of property, converted into family flats for that very purpose, from the funding drive. You don't get any NHS funding for that, but without it, parents might be sleeping on the floor of their children's ward. The fund also helps the hospital with MRI scanners, things like that.'

In 2012, Nick drew a young Gromit for the fund, as he would have looked when he was a pup. 'He did that to allow us to brand a sub-appeal called Cots for Tots,' Nicola explains. 'And in that sub-appeal we raised money for the special-care babies in Bristol. We also run a family accommodation service called Cots for Tots House, which is free of charge to any family whose baby is being treated in the special-care baby unit in Bristol. We have looked after over a thousand families in the past five years. Everyone knows it as the Cots for Tots House, and when all the families come through the house, they see the young Gromit that brands it. And then, in the mid-2000s, we launched the Wallace and Gromit children's charity, another sub-charity that raises money for children's hospices in the UK. We have distributed over £2 million to more than 200 projects throughout the UK – including Scotland and Ireland.'

David was once invited in to BCH by a surgeon to watch a young child having brain surgery to cure epilepsy. 'It was humbling,' he recalls. 'And seeing all that, and the benefits of what we've helped the hospital to do . . . the feelings have been quite profound.'

He is also full of praise for the people of Bristol: 'That figure they quote now – that over the twenty-plus years, the charity has raised around £50 million,' David says, 'it's really quite amazing. The people of Bristol have been incredibly generous. I think one of the things we've realised is that "near enough is good enough". When you have a children's hospital in your locality, you'll want to support it. The emotional power of supporting "our" hospital is incredible. I don't think even Nicola realised until five or six years ago the emotional power parents and residents have.'

Certainly, the link between Aardman and the children's hospital seems to be universally known in Bristol. Sean Clarke has noticed that when he meets someone in the city for the first time and mentions in conversation that he works for Aardman, 'suddenly you get this big smile from them', and that is mostly due to the link between Aardman and the charity trails.

'It's been an extraordinary success,' says Nicola. 'There's some chemistry that exists between the children's hospital, the Grand Appeal and Aardman. So many people have responded to the appeal. They see it centred in Bristol, they understand what Aardman and its creativity has delivered to the city, and the fact it extends to a charitable venture ... People have really taken it to their hearts.'

* * *

Still, it's not only their good works that make Aardman widely respected in Bristol – the city's business community holds them in high esteem too.

James Durie, director of Bristol Chamber of Commerce & Initiative, BusinessWest, says of Aardman: 'I'd say they are top of the tree in terms of an iconic business, a successful business and a go-to business for people to be proud of.

They've stayed here, based in Bristol, and they've had an amazing track record in producing films, TV commercials and all sorts of things that are successful on a global scale. They've been innovative in their progression from Morph to all the stuff they're doing now, and they make people smile, because it's fun characters they create. In fact, I think their characters are often better known than Aardman itself.'

As for the city's business community, he adds: 'They are very much seen as one of the "trees" that the media and creative sector has been able to grow around. There's lots of smaller businesses – because most businesses in that sector do tend to be smaller – and I think they look to Aardman for leadership. But also they may have worked with them in a combination of different ways – and it may be that Aardman sometimes needs the support of local specialists when they gear up for some of their bigger productions, so it's co-dependent, really.'

Durie is also impressed by the fact Aardman has remained in Bristol: 'It's not that usual for a company like theirs to be based in what would be seen as a provincial city, from the viewpoint of people they collaborate with, who may be in America or elsewhere around the world. I know the kind of talent pool that they can draw from is definitely global; they've got the track record to attract people who also get offers to go and work in California and all sorts of other places.'

He agrees that Peter and David have been enthusiastic about 'banging the drum' for Bristol, and are wholly committed to the city and its community: 'That's clear from the charity work they do, the Grand Appeal, and all the work they have done over the years. They're highly effective with their IP and the machine behind it – it's had an amazing effect. They used it to help build a hospital, then raise a huge amount of money to get people interested, and also give them loads of fun with all those trails around the city. It's been amazing. And for them to offer part of what is a very valuable IP ... They offered [those characters] because they want to make a difference. That works well from my perspective.'

He agrees Peter and David aren't exactly typical businessmen: 'I get the sense they wouldn't want to see themselves as too "establishment". They're creative people and they're a bit more edgy, but David especially gets connected to all sorts of things. So he and I have sat on the board of a local enterprise partnership. That involved him giving his time to a public-private partnership which was set up in 2011 to try to focus on the question: "How do we create the environment for the growth of jobs in the area?" He put a considerable amount of time and energy and effort into it. Some people were surprised he was willing to do that, given the business he's trying to run, but that demonstrated the broader commitment he and Peter have to the place. They have been given the freedom of the city and various titles. I think they've been reluctant to go down some of the establishment routes, by becoming members of one organisation or another, but they do more informal things. Certainly, I see David especially out quite often in all sorts of places, putting himself out there, chatting to people. And he's really keen on helping people and making a difference to the city.'

Durie also approves of the flexible way in which Aardman uses its properties on Gas Ferry Road to lend the occasional helping hand to other businesses by subletting office spaces: 'Those buildings they've got down on the harbourside have all sorts of space to provide a home, a first foothold, for smaller businesses. There's a shortage of business space here. They'll be paying a rent, but it all works quite well, and of course people love to be able to say: "I'm based in the Aardman building."'

James Durie notes that his predecessor John Savage worked with Peter and David, 'and at a significant point helped to advise them on committing to getting that piece of land. It's a gorgeous building, and it's part of the regeneration story for the city.'

As he tells it, Aardman's founders sometimes pitch in to give a boost to Bristol's image: 'If we have dignitaries visiting, for instance, they open their doors. When David Cameron was prime minister and visited the city, he specifically said he wanted to go to Aardman. And they agreed.' (A generous gesture, given the slim likelihood that Mr Cameron or his party would receive David's or Peter's vote.)

The Queen has visited Aardman, as has Prince Charles (who asked Nick personally for a visit) and Tony Blair, when he was touring Britain in his first bid to lead a Labour government.

'If we're going overseas,' says James Durie, 'on a trade mission, for instance, taking Gromit and other characters to show them a bit of Bristol is memorable – it's fun and light, and it shows the spirit of the city. Once a visiting high commissioner on an international trade mission asked for a Gromit as a memento of Bristol.'

Something else that impresses him is Aardman's insistence on including Bristol in the pre-release schedule of their new films: 'When they do their film launches, they don't just do one in London. They also do one in a local cinema in Bristol. When they opened *Pirates!*, Hugh Grant and all sorts of people were here.' (When *Early Man* opened in 2018, its lead voice actress Maisie Williams – who is Bristol-born – came to introduce all the local screenings.)

'We're very lucky to have them,' James Durie concludes. 'They support us and we support them. We see them as part of how we continue to grow the place. They employ lots of young, bright people, and they take that really seriously. And they also help people get into the creative industries.'

* * *

There was no hidden agenda behind Peter and David's relocation to Bristol with their partners in 1976. It was both a rational choice and an emotional one. Peter spent his early years in the city, and only has fond memories. 'Both my parents were in the arts; their friends were broadcasters, artists, journalists and actors. They were very involved in the Bristol Old Vic and the family story goes that Peter O'Toole used to visit our house and dandle me on his knee. The idea of Bristol that they passed on to me was of a creative, bohemian city. I always knew this was the place for us.'

As for moving there after university, Peter and David

had sound reasons. For one, it was far less expensive than London, and David's partner Sue was already there as a student at Bristol University. There was also a relatively small but vibrant creative community in the city.

These were all good reasons for moving, but why did they stay? Quite simply, they committed themselves – and the company – to Bristol.

Peter uses the story of Aardman's sometimes tempestuous years as partners of the Hollywood studio DreamWorks to underline the point. In retrospect, he sees the upside of that era: 'The way I see it now is that we learnt loads from those partnerships. And one of the things we certainly learnt was to appreciate what we have – this city and its culture. As well as developing local talent, the feature-film projects more or less forced us to search the world for exceptional people and bring them into the company. It obliged us to be outward-looking. And, by the way, it brought a lot of money in to the city, too. Because that's one element of what we do. It's an export drive. We beaver away here, doing what we do, which is making films. That's our prime focus; but the side-effect is to provide employment for hundreds of people. And, in the process, we magically transport money from Hollywood into the Bristol economy.'

David's attraction to Bristol blossomed for different reasons: 'I've always been interested in how cities develop, why they work or don't, and the whole business of simply living in a city. For example, why is London so massive, and why does everyone flock to it? And I think my folks – what with my dad being a left-wing minister and stuff – that connected

301

to the idea of giving something back. So I was always think-ing: *How can you make this place better? What little bit can you do to make it more convivial?* Those thoughts have always been bubbling away in the background for me.'

David also remembers talking to Joe Dunton, a man who rented out film cameras to the industry. Joe was close to the wealthy, flamboyant Italian-born Dino De Laurentiis, who produced director David Lynch's brilliant but disturbing 1986 film *Blue Velvet*. It was shot in the small North Carolina city of Wilmington, and something about the city appealed to De Laurentiis, who decided to stay on after shooting had ended and do something positive for Wilmington. He ended up being instrumental in getting a new hospital built.

David says: 'He felt there was good you could do to make a place better. And then in Bristol, Peter, Nick and I were enthusiastic about the Grand Appeal. It was one way that a corporate entity could put back something of worth into a city – in this case, a hospital suitable for kids. It occurred to me later: Dino felt there was social good you can do, so what do you *do* with your profits? And what do you do with the influence you have in a certain place for the better? When this whole thing with Bristol Children's Hospital came up, I thought, *Blimey – you can do these things.* Corporates can put something of important social worth back into a city.'

'They still both come and visit the children's hospital,' Nicola Masters reveals. 'They do it very quietly – definitely no press – and they come in, they see what services we are providing, they let us take their pictures, and they don't talk about it. Then, later, you might get a little note from them:

"Thank you for my visit to the children's hospital. I drew this earlier. I thought you might like it for fundraising." And you get this wonderful sketch to sell, fundraise or put into an auction. Little things like that – it's just magic.'

* * *

Aardman, it seems now, crept upon Bristol by stealth. For a while, it was a productive but relatively little-known company outside the businesses of filmmaking and animation.

David remembers: 'It's a curious thing. We'd been here for quite a while, but our profile was raised for the first time when Nick got an Oscar for *Creature Comforts* way back in 1991.'

All of a sudden, he recalls, the conversations about Aardman changed: 'It was: "These guys in a shed up in Clifton – they've got an Oscar! What's going on there?" And that's around the time when Arthur Sheriff came in all those years ago. He did a lot of great PR work for us. Sometimes it's more by accident than osmosis that you become established and recognised. I often say there's more than just Aardman in Bristol – a lot of young talented people: designers, model-makers, animators. It's a quirkier side of employment than in most other companies, but we're the easy ones to quote. One company ends up dominating – and the Academy Awards gave us more recognition and publicity.'

Still, Peter and David continue to find Bristol a more or less ideal city for them to get on with their business and live in. 'It's a good place,' David muses. 'You find yourself in a city that seems to work and isn't too big. It's quite well connected: us, the universities, the BBC, whatever it is. The Watershed [the city's film, arts and media centre] has what they call a First Friday every month. There's a room, a crate of wine, an informal meeting of people in the media-creative sector. You can tootle along there and as [Watershed MD] Dick Penny has pointed out, most people there are within twenty minutes' travel time. You can meet two vice-chancellors, folks who design computer chips for phones, a bundle of very high-powered people who want to do stuff together. I've thought: *This'd be hard to do in London. You wouldn't get someone to travel across the city for more than an hour to attend.* But the Watershed will have someone there from Airbus, from a university, the BBC, all just turning up for an hour. You can do it here in Bristol, because we're all quite close. It means you're part of the place where you're working. You live there too. The place we work in is the place we live in. It's that whole life/work thing. All those rough work spaces we started out in – Victorian sheds, even the banana warehouse – they've all gone, or they've been converted into high-priced flats or smart, glossy offices. So there's a need somehow to replace all that, so you can live and work close by. The alternative is that at 5 p.m. the place is a desert. In London and New York, they've been getting rid of things that gave a place its social cohesion, and the social consequences of that are quite profound. London has changed dramatically since the 1950s. You can have the same kind of job here, have a nicer lifestyle – and the place works.'

18

CELEBRITIES ON SET

One of the most remarkable aspects of any Aardman film is the quality of its voice casts. It's an indisputable fact that several of Britain's most famous and distinguished actors will go out of their way to land a character role. It doesn't seem to matter that they're never visible as themselves on screen, or that the character voices they use are so different from their own that they're almost unidentifiable.

Early Man was a perfect example. Its lead character, Dug, a teenage boy in a Stone Age tribe, was voiced by Eddie Redmayne, who had won an Oscar for his role as Stephen Hawking in *The Theory of Everything* only three years previously. Also in the cast was Tom Hiddleston, one of Britain's leading international stars – a versatile actor who had played Loki in the *Thor* movies as well as the urbane Jonathan Pine in *The Night Manager*, the award-winning BBC adaptation of John le Carré's novel. In *Early Man*, Hiddleston played Lord Nooth, an arrogant, Bronze Age nobleman with an exaggerated French accent. If you didn't know, you'd never guess it was him.

The third leading actor, Maisie Williams, was younger than the other two, but while barely out of her teens had become globally known for her portrayal of Arya Stark of Winterfell in the hugely successful TV series *Game of Thrones*. In *Early Man*, she played Goona, an athletic young girl who, to the astonishment of everyone in Dug's tribe, turns out to be a very gifted footballer.

All three leading actors happily embraced their first-time experience of voicing characters for Aardman. Maisie recalls that she was given a warm welcome from the crew from the first day she walked through the doors of Aztec West: 'They had an "introduction day" for Goona – a sort of "Welcome Maisie" day for me. That day was incredible. Everyone was so kind and helpful. I felt wanted right away.'

She was shown around the intricate sets and was hugely impressed by the Bronze Age city, with everything about it in minute detail: 'I just couldn't believe the length and scale and the craft that had gone into making it.'

Maisie found Nick a supportive director: 'When you're voicing, he's really good at coming into the booth and telling you: "This part you're doing, it's great – keep it up." And then it was amazing getting the chance to be with Eddie in the booth and watch him work. For him to have won an Academy Award and played serious adult characters, and then completely put himself out there and become this child ... it was wonderful to watch and it gave me confidence. I felt: "Well, if you're going to put yourself out there, then I will too."'

Tom Hiddleston, who describes himself as 'a fan of Aardman before I was even an actor', says, 'What I find so astonishing about Nick and about Aardman is the lightness of touch when you see it finished, compared with the industriousness and diligence and rigour it must have taken in crafting these scenes. I voiced Lord Nooth for sixteen months, but Aardman had been making this film for much longer – and Nick had been crafting it, shooting it and manoeuvring these characters around the set. I just find it extraordinary, the hard work that goes into making these scenes, but the end result is something so light and so silly. And I think it's that duality that I love so much – people working so hard for a really good joke. I think that's something to be admired in our world endlessly.'

Eddie Redmayne recalls: 'When I came home and told my family that I was getting to voice an Aardman character, I've never heard such excitement. It was a rare thing where my parents were as excited as my niece and nephew were. Before you start, you've seen a drawing of what the character's going to look like. I saw a little model of what Nick wanted Dug to be – but you kind of find the character with Nick, and he's there in the booth with you. Nick's the kindest man you've ever met. He has the most generous spirit, with this beautiful clear vision of exactly what he wants. But I did some voicing, and sometimes it would just be noises – "Huh?", "Uh", "Ooh", "Bah", you know? Now, I'm a deeply unfunny person, but Nick would come back months later and they've managed to animate Dug making those noises. I laughed out loud. That was genuinely the funniest I've ever been! So even though Dug is kind of the straight guy, Nick somehow manages to make me funny. I'll be ever grateful to him for that.'

Bill Nighy and Timothy Spall, two of Britain's leading veteran actors, have both been in two Aardman films and relished the experience. Nighy played the ancient Grandsanta in *Arthur Christmas* and the rat Whitey in *Flushed Away*, while Spall played the Stone Age tribe chief Bobnar in *Early Man* and Nick, one of two disreputable Cockney spiv rats, in *Chicken Run*.

'It's actually quite liberating that you don't have to interact with the other actors,' Nighy says. 'It can be slightly tricky, but it's good fun. I'm a great enthusiast about Aardman. I love the radical shift they were responsible for in cartoons. They've made them much more sophisticated and attractive, not least because their characters no longer spoke as if they were in a cartoon – or, indeed, as if they were in a film. The writing is clever and colloquial. They've animated to unexpected regional accents, and the writing is of very high quality. People hadn't troubled to do all that before Aardman, not in popular culture. And the jokes are good.'

Nighy admits that it often requires several takes to get a line voiced exactly right: 'And why not? The whole process is painstaking and there is so much work involved in the drawing and the animation, it seems only correct that they should be equally painstaking in terms of the voices and the delivery of the lines. They have a very clear idea of how they want a character to look and sound – and it can be elusive. It's daunting because sometimes, when you're on your twentieth take, you think, *I'm never going to get this*. Of course, often, you've already got it, but you don't know that at the time.'

In *Flushed Away*, Nighy plays Whitey, 'an ex-lab rat who suffers from brain damage, as a result of exposure to hallucinogenic elements during, I think, shampoo trials. I think I may have embellished that, but certainly Whitey was what you'd call "not the full ticket". He was the slow, dim one. I was very happy to be in it. At a stage of my career when I no longer have to audition for roles, I actually auditioned for it.'

What did he try to bring vocally to the role of Grandsanta? 'Well, it's funny, they show you a drawing of a bandy-legged man, 136 years old, with a stick, a bald head and a big mouth, and he comes up to my knee. So it's a mysterious thing; you just gamble on a sound. And then it's quite hard work finding it, and then maintaining it – even though sessions are sometimes months apart. To be an Aardman animator, I'd think you'd have to be slightly bonkers, in terms of obsessiveness. People who animate, it's three years of their lives, or maybe more. And then they're at the mercy of the critics, and the marketplace – just like everyone else. But it's been so much more of an investment than for a normal film, which would take a fraction of that time. So it's a reckless endeavour – you can only take your hat off to it.'

Timothy Spall recalls meeting Peter Lord at a British festival in Nîmes, France, which was showing retrospectives of their films.

'I was doing an interview with a French journalist in this roof garden overlooking Nîmes and I could see Peter in one corner with a model of Morph. He placed Morph on the rail and put him in a pose to get a picture of him with this lovely Roman temple behind him and this vista of Nîmes. He told me, "I like to bring him with me to lots of places and take pictures of him.'"

Spall was rather touched by this: 'I was able to tell Peter what a great thing that was, because I remember that little fellow Morph. He was the beginning, the Messiah really; he started the whole thing! And to see him there, it was such a treat. Then, of course, recently, I've done *Early Man*. You still have to speak and pretend to be a character, but Peter and Nick, of course, always have a huge film in their head, a whole thing they've already made decisions about, thinking about this animated parallel universe. So I went in and Nick had a very strong idea how he wanted it to be. It's a mixture between a creative process and a technical craft. Nick would show me the models – he's very specific, and he's persistent in getting it right, so he asks you to voice it a lot. The experience is quite challenging because you've been asked to come along and create this character – but you have the sense they have it in their minds already. You're giving a voice to this completely different creature, which is odd. But for both of them, the attention to detail is just as strong in terms of what they want you to do as it is in the amazing, seamless craft they display as animators. They create this world that's both recognisable as our world, but also it's their own world. Great animation does that. The other thing they do which makes them so special is that they always pay a lot of homage to British cinema with references to classic British films. They're not stealing; it's imbued with its own originality, but there are always nods of appreciation towards this culture of the silly and bizarre in our comedy.

They're masters of craft and silliness. Basically, it's lumps of clay moving about, but they're so textured in what they do, it creates this world that no one else has ever done. They're both perfectionists. With a voice or a line reading, they never say "no, no, that's wrong", but you know it's not quite right – you get to read what they want. They're benign, persistent perfectionists. It's tough. It's a challenge. You want to get it right for them. There's fundamentally a power of good about them. Obviously, they have paymasters to pay and profits to worry about, but you get this sense that they're doing it for the love of the craft. It's not skewed by commercial pressure, even if that's in their minds. There's a sense of fun which never gets lost in their world. Their technical ability and their expertise has grown, but that lovely quality is still there. It's very rare – there's nothing jaded about it. That doesn't mean it's sentimental, or lacking in satire – which, in fact, it's riddled with – but there's something gloriously unaffected and pure about it.'

In 2015, the BBC celebrated Aardman's fortieth anniversary with a documentary broadcast on Boxing Day. Several actors and animators weighed in on camera to sing Aardman's praises.

David Tennant, who played Charles Darwin in *Pirates!*, said of Aardman: 'There seems to be an oddness about them all, which I heartily approve of. The script was peculiar when you first read it: this is Charles Darwin, but it's not Charles Darwin, then he's in love with a queen who is trying to murder a dodo and is also a ninja ... But when something's as good as their films are, of course you want to be involved.

311

They don't have to beg actors to sign up – actors are begging them.'

It was widely agreed by these actors that animators needed to be single-minded in their work, to put it mildly. Anne Reid, who voiced Wendolene in *A Close Shave*, commented: 'You have to be passionate about it, obsessed by it.'

Martin Freeman, who played 'The Pirate with a Scarf' in *Pirates!*, agreed: 'Half of your life on your knees, moving a little hand ever so slightly . . .'

Hugh Grant, who played the Pirate Captain, added: 'It's like some weird kind of torture, really . . . To make that look realistic at all seems to me impossible. To make it realistic and funny with perfect timing, and get the Plasticine lips moving in sync with the dialogue . . . that seems pure genius.' As Freeman mused: 'Human beings are very expressive; a lump of Plasticine isn't. How do they do that? I don't know.'

Peter Lord was also interviewed on camera and noted: 'Directing actors is a huge privilege and a pleasure, but I have to admit, we are such control freaks in animation. Actors end up doing a lot of takes and sometimes it's frankly embarrassing.'

Freeman recalls: 'You think: *How many more ways do you want me to say "Captain!"*? But it turns out, there *are* more ways. Because I did them.'

Grant concurred: 'Take seventy-two! I did feel like running my cutlass through Peter Lord occasionally.'

'I apologise to any actors who have been driven mad in the process,' Peter added graciously.

It wasn't only actors but also animators who lined up to

sing Aardman's praises for the cameras: Terry Gilliam, John Lasseter, Matt Groening and Brad Bird (of *Ratatouille* and both *Incredibles* films) also joined in. (Groening once paid a witty tribute to Aardman in a *Simpsons* episode in which Bart and Lisa go to the Academy Awards and find, to their delight, that they are seated across the aisle from Nick Park.)

Brad Bird commented: 'I like seeing the different fingerprints and shapings [in Aardman films] and it makes them feel alive to me in a way that frankly CGI does not. And I speak as a guy who does CGI.'

'Everything I was watching seemed to be CGI,' Gilliam recalled, 'and then I saw *Pirates!* and I was just amazed at how beautiful it was. Because it wasn't computer-generated; it was real light hitting real materials.' He added jokingly: 'I think Aardman is hated by all of us – because they're successful and wonderful and brilliant.'

* * *

In January 2018, Nick Park's feature-length film *Early Man* was finally released. It felt as though it had been a long time coming; the last film Nick had directed was a thirty-minute short, the 'bread-based murder mystery' entitled *A Matter of Loaf and Death*, which had been revealed to the world a whole decade previously. As for his last full-length feature, that had been his triumphant Oscar- and BAFTA-winner *The Curse of the Were-Rabbit*, first released in 2005.

For some time, Nick had been toying with the idea of a film set in prehistoric times, and, following his instinct for a story

313

with two apparently contrasting elements, he began to think along the lines of a caveman movie that would also explain the origins of football. Nick had never seen a pre-historic sports movie before – it seemed original.

He had shown some preliminary sketches of his ideas for *Early Man* to Sony's top brass Michael Lynton and Amy Pascal when they visited Bristol to discuss *Pirates!*, and that was as early as 2007.

Nick clung on to the idea and originally decided on the title 'Early Man United'. This of course was a play on words – 'Man United' being shorthand for Manchester United Football Club. He was talked out of this, however, once it became clear that such a title could raise rights issues with the club. As a result, Nick settled for the simpler *Early Man*.

Nick developed the story alongside Mark Burton and considered several ways of telling it, before finally coming up with a workable outline. His hero would be a teenage caveman, aged about fifteen, named Dug, who would have a pet wild boar named Hognob (who, unusually, was voiced by Nick himself). Dug is a member of a Stone Age tribe, which, for centuries, has inhabited a pleasant valley that happens to be close to a forbidding, industrial city inhabited by more sophisticated Bronze Age people.

The Stone Age tribe had seen cave drawings of their ancestors kicking a ball around, but these cavemen – 'lunkheads', as Nick called them – have totally forgotten their heritage and were utterly inept at the game.

The Bronze Age city boasted its own magnificently appointed stadium and a team of suave, athletic players who played football with casual brilliance and ease. The ruler of this place was a vain, money-crazed nobleman called Lord Nooth, who has designs on invading the Stone Age valley.

At the story's climax, the two teams play each other to settle the ownership of the valley. The Stone Age tribe is clearly outclassed, but greatly helped by the presence on their side of a Bronze Age girl named Goona, a brilliant footballer barred from playing in her home city simply because of her gender.

This idea had grown and changed in Nick's and writer Mark Burton's minds for a long time, but the film finally went into production in May 2016. It was conceived on a grand, ambitious scale, with a multi-million-pound budget.

Early Man was the largest production mounted by Aardman in its forty-year history, and it was a marathon shoot; it finally wrapped in the last few weeks of 2017. But, as always, preparatory work had started well before the cameras began rolling.

Nick had jointly directed two feature-length films prior to this one: *Chicken Run* and *The Curse of the Were-Rabbit*, and he had directed shorter films, including the Wallace and Gromit titles for the BBC. But the mammoth *Early Man* marked his debut as sole director on a full-length feature. He was determined to direct it alone, which meant significant changes in the organisation of the production at the Aztec West studios.

Its producer, Carla Shelley (an Aardman veteran who won a BAFTA in 1996 for her part in producing *A Close Shave*, as well as producing *Chicken Run*), explained that the sheer size of *Early Man* meant that Nick would have to concentrate on

315

directing the voice actors, all the while refining his story with three screenwriters – Mark Burton, John O'Farrell and James Higginson – and a lot of time in edit, building the story reel.

The usual animation director's task of 'running the floor' – that is, overseeing and doing the rounds of all the animators creating different scenes – was assigned to two other Aardman stalwarts, Merlin Crossingham and Will Becher.

The statistics surrounding the production of *Early Man* reveal it as an epic project. Some 150 people were directly involved with the film, including, at the height of production, no fewer than thirty-three animators.

Carla describes the work schedule as 'incredibly intense': 'We had up to forty units working simultaneously; it was a bit mad. Normally we cap out at thirty-five, but one day I heard there were forty cameras on the go at once.'

The film required 273 puppets created by twenty-three different model-makers over two and a half years – an average of a dozen each. It took ten weeks to create each individual puppet. There were eighteen models of little Dug alone, and eight puppets for each member of his Stone Age tribe. No fewer than 3,000 interchangeable mouths were crafted for the film's characters by hand, and as for the Stone Age tribe's forest, the art department created sixty trees to populate it – each one taking a week to complete.

This extraordinary pace was maintained in a gigantic work area of around 51,000sqft, which is approximately the size of four Olympic-standard swimming pools.

In technical terms, Carla regards *Early Man* as a step forward for Aardman: 'As elaborate and expensive as other films may have been, this one has been more challenging in some ways. The reason we pulled it off is we've got such an experienced team that have worked with Nick – some of them for twenty-five years. All the model-makers, the directors of photography, they're the ones who managed to pull it off. They really know what they're doing, they know their craft so well. If we hadn't had that shorthand between them and Nick . . .'

And then there was the set, as intricate and ambitious as anything Aardman had previously attempted, in its replication of the prehistoric era. For most visitors, the 'main attraction' was the Bronze Age city, with its forbidding walls. It includes the gigantic football stadium – scaled down to miniature size, while retaining all sorts of architectural detail.

'Nick pitched the story as *"Gladiator* meets *Dodgeball",'* Carla recalls. 'He really wanted that sort of gladiatorial feel to the stadium – and to the whole football element. So there was a lot of effects work, including computer graphics, creating the huge crowd. We couldn't have built that football stadium for real. It would have been bigger than our whole studio! So there were lots of technicalities around solving all of that.'

* * *

During the arduous shoot of *Early Man* in September 2016, Nick married his girlfriend Mags. They tied the knot at a ceremony near Preston, which is where they both grew up.

His plan after *Early Man* opened in January 2018 was to

spend a lot more time with his wife and stepson, Joe. Mags accompanied him abroad on some of the *Early Man* international press tours, taking in Dublin, Paris, Madrid, Los Angeles and San Francisco.

'We needed some time off, really,' Nick mused. 'It's so exhausting, making films, especially feature films. I just want to be at home with her, though we love going away in our VW camper van. In the past, Mags and I worked in weekends away, taking a few days off for the wedding, but never a proper honeymoon. I think she'll be glad not to see me always exhausted. Feature films take a toll on you,' he observed. 'On the other hand, I've got so many ideas it seems too early to think about retiring. I have nothing specific in mind. We'll see how it goes; I don't want to commit yet. I'd quite like to be able to revisit Wallace and Gromit, in some form.'

* * *

Early Man received generally kindly reviews. In America, the *New York Times*'s influential film reviewer A. O. Scott raved about it. In Britain, *The Guardian*'s veteran critic Peter Bradshaw wrote: 'It's impossible not to laugh at the inspired silliness and charm of Park's universe. *Early Man* is a family film that doesn't just provide gags for adults and gags for children. It locates the adult's inner child and the child's inner adult. It's a treat.'

Yet, for all that, and despite its scale and the expertise that went into its making, the box-office results for *Early Man* unhappily fell below expectations.

While holding its own in Britain, it performed poorly in the United States for a number of reasons, but particularly because of the strong crop of massive blockbusters released at a similar time. Three months after opening in most major territories, it had grossed only around $50 million worldwide, whereas previous Aardman feature films had routinely passed the $100 million mark.

The box-office result was a severe disappointment that was keenly felt throughout Aardman – with an enormous degree of sympathy for Nick, who had given his all to the preparation and production of the film for the best part of a decade.

Though its box-office returns were not strong, *Early Man* is a film that is a cause for pride around Aardman. Nick has always maintained that he doesn't do what he does for the money; Aardman creates films that they are proud of – and *Early Man* was definitely one of those films.

19

WHERE DO WE GO FROM HERE?

Early in 2014, Peter and David had both just turned sixty, and found their thoughts turning towards the future. They had founded Aardman as teenage schoolboys more than four decades before, and it remained very much a company of their own making, an expression of their values and desires.

But what would happen when they decided to call it a day, and there was an inevitable handover of power to others? Without being too controlling, could they realistically safeguard the unique identity that they had forged for the company?

For some time, David had become interested in the idea of employee ownership of companies. He had gone to see author David Erdal, speaking in Bristol about his book *Beyond the Corporation: Humanity Working*. 'It set my mind to thinking,' he recalls.

He had also attended regional meetings of the Employee Ownership Association (EOA) to learn more, and in November 2017 he and Peter went to its annual conference

together. Encouraged by a consultant, the two men separately outlined a legacy document – one that would guide all
Aardman employees in terms of the company's philosophy.

'We each wrote a version,' Peter recalls. 'Rather than trying
to produce something polished or formal, I tried to write as
spontaneously as possible – from the heart. The idea was
to capture the unique spirit of the place, which naturally
derives from the odd chemistry of Dave and me.'

'I wanted it to be clear and concise,' David says, adding: 'I
think we may do it as a video.'

There are words and phrases in this document that would
not be found in the mission statements of more conventional
companies: 'fun', 'not produced to a formula' and 'celebrates
great humour' among them.

'Most owners probably wouldn't write that way,' Peter
concedes. 'But the way we are is our strength. It's important,
indeed it's crucial, that work should also be fun. I've always
wanted it to be exciting, thrilling, or at the very least pleasurable for everyone to come to work every day. People at
Aardman are seldom pushed into working harder, faster or
better. Of course it needs to happen sometimes, but generally
they're not pushed because they don't *need* to be. To carry on
the metaphor, we don't push because most people here are
too busy *pulling* us along to achieve more. People at Aardman
give their best and, as a general rule, they're fabulously self-
motivated. Back when there were maybe twenty of us, and
the world was less complicated, we used to phrase it this
way: "The point of the company is to make the best films
we possibly can, have as much fun as we can – and make as

much money as we can, *given the first two conditions."* Since then we've tidied up the language a bit, filed off the rough edges, but, to me, the essence of it remains in our mission statement.'

The legacy document was the prelude to a process about the whole future of Aardman, and how it would operate after Peter and David relinquished their positions.

'Our guide and mentor in preparing it said: "It's for your successors' successors – it lives on past your time,"' Peter recalls. 'I felt very liberated by that.'

'We've been working on the succession issue quite hard for the last two or three years,' says David, 'and we decided to take it down the employee-ownership route. We'll sell our shares to the company itself, so the employees effectively become the owners. The shares are held in trust.'

From the outside, it seems an unconventional path to take; a trade sale would have been the obvious (and more profitable) option. But, as David explains: 'We were concerned that if we did a trade sale to some media conglomerate, Aardman would definitely change. The buyers would take Shaun the Sheep, they might take Wallace and Gromit – but then let the rest go hang. I don't think they'd understand the interactivity between our various departments. I'm not saying employee ownership is the only way you can run the company, but otherwise I think the fear would be that someone would buy it, grab it, effectively asset-strip it – and it would look very different in five or six years' time. It happens all the time. I saw it for myself in the advertising industry in the '90s. The point is our desire to see the company survive and carry on – so it couldn't be a hard-nosed trade sale deal. Very often, buyers think in terms of three to five years, then they "flip" the company and sell it on. So employee ownership is the plan – and we'd hope that broadly the same mixture of activities would carry on. Some of the things we do might be deemed not to add value to the company in the short term – but they could be valuable in the long term.'

Peter has an example: 'We have something we call the Aardman Academy. It's an educational strand, and a great source of pride for the company. We work with schools and colleges on all sorts of training initiatives, but the highlight is a character animation training course, which we run with the National Film and Television School. We realised that, though there are loads of animation courses in this country, there's surprisingly little emphasis on the pure *craft* of it, and I honestly think we teach it as well here as anybody else in the world. We have a small but amazing team, including some top-rank animators. People get three months of intensive hands-on experience, and every day they have detailed feedback from excellent tutors. None of your distance learning – this is total immersion in our studio. We do it because we care about it and love it, and it brings benefits to the whole Aardman community. It's great to have the students around, joining in with studio life and full of youthful energy. If you look at the books, the academy covers its costs perfectly well, but you wouldn't call it a commercial venture. An outsider, who doesn't understand what makes us tick, might well come in and say, "That has nothing to do with the business, it's not making much money; it has to go." That desire to make sure that what we've built up isn't exploited for share-holder gain is the crucial driver in this decision of ours. It seems a wise thing to do. I know we could make a lot more money by selling Aardman on the open market, but we're not too bothered about that.'

Implicit in the legacy document is the hope that all employees feel part of the Aardman culture. 'It's a trusting culture,' David says, 'and that's why employee ownership is probably the best way forward for us – because you are working for yourselves. This goes back to my early Marxist tendencies!' he adds, smiling. 'Why should you be working for someone else who's not even on the premises, some shareholder out in wherever? Those that sweat from their labour should gain from their labour. It's a pretty simple thing, really. I find the idea of distant ownership quite odd.'

'As to succession planning, it's been an important project across the company for years,' adds Peter, 'and just now, the focus of attention is on who will replace Dave and me. Meanwhile, employee ownership is just that: a question of ownership. It's an idealistic, philosophical issue about fairness, about where ownership *ought* to belong. At the same time, it's also a strategic move. It's a way of making sure that the wrong people don't get their hands on the company and muck around with it. We have never, *ever* seriously considered a buyout,' he adds emphatically. 'Jeffrey Katzenberg suggested it once in our very early days with DreamWorks. We said: "We're not interested." He said: "Come back when you are" – and then I remember him saying: "You will be."'

What Katzenberg failed to recognise was how the

company could be so precious to the two men that they wouldn't want to sell it and see it exploited.

'That's exactly what we didn't want,' Peter says. 'Avoiding the predatory takeover was our main motivation. But, quite separately, people talk about how employee-owned companies are more productive and more efficient – stuff like that. I'm happy to believe all that stuff, but, oddly enough, one of the challenges of employee ownership for us is that we already operate in that way. So the things that, for other companies, might seem a huge step forward – like a less hierarchical structure – in this company, it already exists. We already try to run things fairly; we already try to be very open in our communication with the workforce; we fundamentally believe that people should be allowed to enjoy their working day; we already give people profit shares. So when we make the change to employee ownership, a key part of our message is: "It's to keep Aardman as it is." Of course that doesn't mean it won't evolve and progress, but we keep the heart of the company as it is and avoid the extreme dangers of being asset-stripped.'

David observes: 'When we make the change there will be fundamental shifts – namely, a great sharing of information with the staff, who will by then be partners. They'll have a real voice – and, of course, Peter and I will no longer own the company. On a day-to-day basis, an outsider may not see much difference, but internally there's a real shift in the philosophy.'

He recalls a recent conversation with Peter about the word 'owner': 'I've never felt like an owner. It didn't even hit me until someone started talking about it years ago. I thought: *Hang on, we founded it, we've got all these people around us – does that mean we own the company?* I suppose it does – but it's a curious term. I remember we brought in a producer, Sara Mullock, early on, and she was clearly of a like mind. We've always tended to find people who were of like minds – honest players who wanted people to be treated the way you'd wish to be treated yourself. I guess that's what runs through the company: fairness and social justice.'

When Peter and David wrote their legacy document, they directly addressed the issue of the company's vision, purpose, aims and values. 'And there's also an issue of trust,' David adds, 'to be a company who our clients and partners want to come back to time and time again, because they know we're going to do a good job.'

The two men presented their vision for the future in April 2018 on what they called 'a creative review day'. Attendance was mandatory, and 250 Aardman employees met up at Bristol's Marriott Hotel for the day to hear the plans. 'It went down very well,' says David. 'There was a lot of enthusiasm for it and a lot of good feedback. One of the things we were concerned about – especially with our feature-film work – was that a lot of the people here are on freelance contracts, even though they're on regular work and bring a lot of value to us. So we wanted a structure under which they could be rewarded as well. We'd been thinking long and hard about that – it was one of the things that was really important to us.'

The plan was essentially to make the current senior management team the executive board of Aardman. Thus, the executive board (in alphabetical order) would initially comprise Sean Clarke as head of Aardman rights and brand development; Sarah Cox as executive creative director/ intellectual property development; Kerry Lock as finance director; Paula Newport as head of human resources, talent and training; Nick Park; Carla Shelley as head of long-form content; and Heather Wright as head of partner content. Peter (as creative director) and David (as executive chairman) also sit on the senior management team and will continue to do so – at least in the short term.

Intriguingly, the executive board has a 4:2 majority of women. 'Aardman is actually not a particularly male company,' David reflects. 'In fact, it segments into activity quite neatly. Broadly, our producers and organisers tend to be women – as are a lot of our model-makers. We have a really flexible approach to our colleagues, enabling us to embrace all different lifestyles. When you have a lot of different activities in a company, it's interesting how those gender splits manifest themselves. We do have female animators, and we have male producers and production people. We've also taken on more female directors in commercials and partner content. Broadly speaking, though, that's how it works out. Overall, it's about 50/50 in staff levels.'

* * *

Sean Clarke observes that, of the executive board members, he, Kerry Lock, Paula Newport and Heather Wright all joined Aardman within a short space of time, around 1997–98. Sarah

Cox is new to the company, whereas Carla Shelley is the veteran – joining Aardman in the late '80s, when it was still housed at Wetherell Place – and has been a producer or executive producer on most of Aardman's movies and short films.

Sean explains: 'The company will buy out Peter and David, and the shares will be held in trust on behalf of the employees. There'll be a transitional period where they're still on the board to ensure continuity of business, and then they'd join a board of trustees to whom the executive board are accountable. During the transition there would be a new MD appointed and a succession plan agreed to fulfil the role of creative director, eventually fulfilling the present-day responsibilities of Peter and David. I don't think it's a case of replacing their individual roles [directly]. There'll be a transition period where it could be that a number of people from the board take on a broader responsibility for different parts of their day-to-day roles. During the transition there'll probably be bumps along the way. Right now, the company is owned by two people, and ultimately the buck stops with Peter and David. When the buyout takes place, this will change. The company will be run in a more traditional way, with an executive board running it, based on the values and principles established over the past forty years, but to create the best value and return for the employees. As a company we need to get across that we are forward-thinking. The reason we're doing this move to employee ownership is to future-proof Aardman to carry on the independent creative spirit of bringing new things to life in a sustainable and profitable way.'

328

'We don't want to be known just as the creators of Wallace and Gromit. Clearly, Wallace and Gromit has been a defining, hugely important milestone in the past forty years of the studio, but they shouldn't necessarily define our future. We need to develop new properties and nurture new creative talent to build our portfolio of brands, alongside those that exist. There's a sense that still lingers today that we're this quirky British company, determined to carry on with what people think of as this antiquated, labour-intensive process, making stop-motion films as opposed to embracing CGI and other techniques to make movies – even though the development cycle for both techniques is approximately five years. In fact, when you lift the lid on all things Aardman, we are a global company active in new technologies – including VR and AR [virtual reality and augmented reality] – and we are continually assessing the tools available to tell stories to a new generation who thrive on digital content. I don't think we should be defined by our most successful craft of stop-motion. While it's a craft that Nick and Golly are very good at, that doesn't mean new talent can't come through. And the same humour can come through in CGI. There's a lot more that we do besides stop-motion. We should be defined by our values and our ability to tell entertaining stories with funny and warmly appealing characters irrespective of technique. Otherwise we pigeonhole ourselves. You have to keep an eye on Generation Z, who live on digital content. I think it comes down to us having a portfolio of properties we can build on – that allows us to spread our bets and to be a global company. Which we are.'

329

* * *

So, has Aardman finally arrived at the point Peter and David always wanted?

'It's an interesting question,' says David. 'There have been times over our history when we've thought: *We don't want to get bigger than this.* I seem to recall the first time we thought that we only had eight or ten people! And then, at another time, we said to ourselves: "Thirty is big enough." So it changes over time, but the point is, we don't grow for its own sake. Right now, we have 140 to 150 people full-time, superannuated on staff. The vast majority are here on Gas Ferry Road – with about ten or twelve actual employees over at Aztec West. That's as many full-time staff as we've ever had – but it's a comfortable number, and it seems to work out quite well. I think we've reached a steady state. This building is nearly ten years old now, and it's not at capacity, but it's reached a comfortable level where we can do most of what we want to do with the size and space we've got.'

David stresses that he's only talking here about full-time staff, as Aardman also depends to a huge extent on freelancers: 'For instance, in addition to employees at Aztec West, we have a lot of people who are drafted in as and when. A lot of them work for us on an almost continuous basis, but they are contracted. By the end of *Early Man*, we probably had about 300 people on our books. Most of them were freelance – model-makers, say, or animators.' When the film finally wrapped, most of them took a break. But the majority returned when production started for Aardman's two big releases: *Shaun the Sheep Movie: Farmageddon* and the second *Chicken Run* film.

While full-time staffing levels are at their highest ever, David points out that so many Aardman employees are now engaged in projects that would have been unthinkable until recent years. It's an indication of how many varied ways the company has moved to broaden its scope and heighten awareness of its brand worldwide.

There are currently some twenty-five employees, for example, headed up by Sean Clarke, in the rights and brand franchise department, handling all Aardman's overseas sales and merchandise, selling its intellectual property, as well as promoting the company's best-known characters on YouTube.

Aardman now has seventeen successful YouTube channels for its own intellectual properties. They provide content for a global audience, and between them they can boast an astonishing average of 25 million views per month worldwide.

Angry Kid, Shaun the Sheep, Wallace and Gromit and *Creature Comforts* all have a dedicated channel. Hearteningly, so does Morph. When, in 2013, Peter launched the campaign via Kickstarter to bring back his first major animated creation for a new series of adventures, it proved there were still plenty of Morph fans out there; Morph's channel has some 130,000 subscribers.

Aardman is now looking to share its knowledge and experience in this field, offering a new outlet for independent producers to have their content distributed internationally by their team of video-on-demand experts.

A recent addition to its YouTube range is AardBoiled, a channel curated by Aardman that features promising short films from new animators hoping to get their work widely seen and break into the business. Its philosophy is a simple one: if the film is good enough, and resonates with Aardman values in terms of comedy, character and imagination, it will get shown, exactly as its creators envisaged it. Aardman's executive creative director Sarah Cox underlined the point: '[It's] high-quality work without any interference from "development executives" – all the good stuff, without the edges rounded off.'

'In the bad old days,' David adds, 'we'd make fifty-six episodes of something, put it on TV, spend a lot of money on it and hope people liked it. Now we've started AardBoiled, the idea is: can we show off not only other people's work, but test our own stuff, run it up the flagpole, at a low cost? Can you test stuff before you go all-out with it? Now it's more feasible for us than it used to be.'

* * *

Stroll around the various departments within the Gas Ferry Road building and it becomes apparent that there is far more to the modern-day Aardman than its popular image: this little underdog Bristol company, painstakingly turning out hand-crafted feature films along with the occasional half-hour short for TV audiences over Christmas.

Peter observes: 'People still seem to imagine that there are about ten of us, nerdy artisans working in a shed, but there is a wealth of diverse activity under this one roof – proof positive that in business terms Aardman has several strings to its bow these days.

There are some thirty people working in its CGI department, for example, giving the lie to any notion that Aardman is slavishly devoted to only stop-motion films. It also boasts a studio (the old banana warehouse bought in 1991) where commercials are shot – a relatively unsung but hugely profitable source of income for the company. There are offices outside it too, which Aardman rents out to start-up companies, who are effectively their tenants.

A handful of freelance writers (all of whom tend to work from home) work in the features development department, and there are more engaged in non-features development. Sarah Cox is tasked with driving and pushing ideas for series, a couple of which are steadily being advanced.

One of the newest and most intriguing areas of activity is the department of exhibitions run by a small team in Rights, formed once it became clear that touring exhibitions were an effective (and lucrative) means of spreading the word about Aardman worldwide, while entertaining the public at the same time.

Although Aardman had been putting on exhibitions on a small scale since 1992, with one for the Stuttgart Film Festival, it wasn't until 2015, with a major exhibition at a Paris museum called Art Ludique, that mounting them became a commercial proposition. Art Ludique specialises in art from the entertainment industry, especially animation, and, flatteringly, the exhibition, titled 'Aardman: Art That Takes

Shape', followed in distinguished footsteps: Pixar, Marvel and Japan's Studio Ghibli had been among those companies previously given such a showcase by the museum.

The exhibition offered visitors the chance to view some fifty authentic film sets, the flying machine from *Chicken Run* and the enormous pirates' galleon. Wallace, Gromit, Shaun the Sheep and other Aardman favourites were also on display, to be viewed in their usual habitats, as were original drawings of sets and characters from the original shoots.

On visiting Art Ludique, Peter says he found it 'a joyous exhibition'. 'When I first saw it, I was quite stunned and very moved. The first gallery was an overview, a snapshot of where we'd been and what we'd done. Our story was told with films, drawings, models and photographs. Looking at it, I was, well, awestruck. It felt like the first time that I'd truly stepped back to look at the Aardman story from an objective distance. There was a single drawing of Aardman himself, iconic sets and models of Morph and Wallace and Gromit, an Oscar in a glass case, *Sledgehammer* playing in the background. And it was a story of the people, too, crew members, colleagues and friends from the early days, all looking incredibly young in old photographs. My instant reaction was, "Everyone at Aardman must see this!"'

In due course, Peter also had his wish. Everyone working at the studio was invited on a daytrip to Paris to see the wonderful exhibition for themselves. 'We couldn't quite run to putting everyone up as well, so we made it a very long daytrip on Eurostar. "Aardman goes wild in Paris" – enormous fun. I don't think we lost anybody.' The show was a huge success and ran for five months in Paris. The following year it opened in Frankfurt at the German Filmmuseum to comparable acclaim.

The big hit of the tour was in Melbourne, though, where the Australian Centre for the Moving Image hosted it in 2017. It opened in June that year – yet so popular did the show prove that it was extended through to the following January.

David recalls: 'We'd quite forgotten that those early shows of ours, *Take Hart* and *Vision On*, had sold into Australia. So when we were in Melbourne to open the exhibition that summer, all these Morph fans came out of the woodwork.'

Just to underline how international the following for all things Aardman had become, the next port of call for the touring exhibition was Seoul, South Korea. 'The Art of Aardman Animations: Wallace & Gromit & Friends' ran for three months in the city's Dongdaemun Design Plaza: a further indication of the company's ability to stake its claim in far-flung territories.

* * *

'One of the things we talk about is our creative capacity,' David says. 'There are always great ideas floating around, but you need strong creative people – writers, directors – to drive them. And there's a limited supply of those. You have to make decisions about what ideas you're going to pursue, and drop others, as we simply don't have the creative capacity to do all of them justice. So, are we going to double in size in the next few years? Probably not. In the past we have done two features more or less simultaneously – *Pirates!* and *Arthur Christmas*. But I think if we did a CGI feature along-side a stop-frame feature again, we'd probably outsource a fair chunk of that work, while doing the actual creative work here. Otherwise you might set up a huge CGI pipeline with quite a large crew and have to lay them off after the produc-tion if there isn't another CGI film ready to start. If we take people on, we want to keep them fully employed. So, right now, I think we're a comfortable size. Most of what we want to do we can do. But, at the same time, where's the next Shaun the Sheep? Where's the next Wallace and Gromit? They don't fall off trees. At least there's *Chicken Run 2* and *Shaun the Sheep Movie: Farmageddon*, which keeps the wheels spinning.'

Aardman may have a global reach these days, yet it doesn't feel remotely like some faceless multi-national company. 'There's an inevitable Britishness about what we're doing,' shrugs David, 'and that's simply because we're British. I think that's just how it is. But look how we've changed. We have twenty-five people working in our rights and market-ing department. Ten years ago, we weren't running YouTube channels. Well, we are now. We're talking to the likes of Netflix, Amazon, and those sorts of people – while we still have a good relationship with the BBC and our European broadcasters. So that's changing. What *isn't* changing is the need for good-quality stories, characters and entertainment. For instance, I think there's something about a slapstick character, which Shaun is and Morph is: it's the universal language of comedy, which needs no translation. It's ageless. And people love it.'

* * *

On the subject of their retirement, David is clear on the matter: 'I've always said, on the managing side, when I'm out of here, I'm out of here. I don't think it's fair to be hovering around in the background. If you're going to hand over responsibility you need to do it. I think it's only fair to whoever you're handing it over to that, certainly, they can give you a call, give you a shout if there's some problem they want to run past you. But, basically, you have to let them get on with it. Whether I get employed as a consultant or do more cinematography, who knows? I wouldn't rule it out. Get myself back to the craft a bit,' he smiles, before adding: 'A little bit! I'm on a couple of charity boards, and I might throw myself into those a little more. We shall see. And I'd want to be useful, not just hang around.'

Peter is equally clear in his own way: 'If you love what you do, why on earth should you retire? Happily, in the arts, it's quite possible to keep going; people even respect you for it. Like Dave, I don't expect or want to run the company in any sense. I'll leave that to the next generation and be very happy to concern myself only with creative conversations – if that's possible. And, yes, it'd be a real treat to make my own short film again.'

He and David are credited as executive producers on both major Aardman feature movies in production, in advance of their releases in 2019 – *Chicken Run 2* and *Shaun the Sheep Movie: Farmageddon*, Peter is already talking up the outline of *Chicken Run 2* and what the poster might say: 'This time they're breaking in!' 'We always felt the militaristic element of *Chicken Run*, the mission in the story, was so important,' he recalls.

It's not hard to imagine that Peter, a born animator, might find ways to return to his primary passion. He has long made it clear that he feels other animators are 'his tribe' and that he feels huge satisfaction in making his own short films. And it shouldn't be forgotten that Morph, the first animated character he ever created, has staged a significant comeback in recent years.

Still, it's probably rash to make predictions about what will happen next for Peter or David, given that their working lives have been so dazzlingly unpredictable so far. 'When we set out, we didn't particularly have a vision of what our career could look like,' Peter says. 'That old cliché, "beyond their wildest dreams"? It really feels that way to me now. I was brought up to believe that, if you approached life with open eyes and an open mind, then good things would come your way. I still believe it, but I also know that there's nothing automatic about the process – no guarantee of success. If good things *do* come your way – as they have for Dave and me – if things work out, then you should be deeply grateful.'

And, in fairness, how could they have envisaged that the two of them, after meeting up as schoolboys, would start up, develop and flourish with a unique company that has been so extraordinarily successful? One which continues, after more than four decades, to broaden its vision and its boundaries to reach delighted new audiences across the world?

WHERE DO WE GO FROM HERE?

It's certainly been a long, heady journey since the days when, huddled together as teenagers over an old Victorian table, they first began figuring out how to give clay characters the gift of animated life.

ACKNOWLEDGEMENTS

Thank you to Laura Burr, Sean Clarke, James Durie, Rob Goodchild, Danny Heffer, Jess Houston, Amy Kilmister, Angie Last, Kate Lee, Anna Lewis, Mary Lowance, Nicola Masters, Emily Metcalfe, Nick Park, Michael Rose, Arthur Sheriff, Richard Starzak, Tom Vincent and Katy Weitz for helping make this book happen.

INDEX

(PL indicates Peter Lord Jr; NP is Nick Park; DS is David Sproxton)

341

INDEX

INDEX